Frontiers of Globalization

Series Editor
Jan Nederveen Pieterse
Global Studies Department
University of California
Santa Barbara, CA, USA

With the onset of the twenty-first century, key components of the architecture of twentieth-century globalization have been crumbling. American hegemony has weakened politically and economically. Laissez-faire capitalism that shaped neoliberal globalization has proved to be crisis-prone and is giving way to a plurality of ways of organizing and regulating capitalism. With the rise of emerging societies, the driving forces of the world economy are shifting not merely geographically but structurally; industrializing societies, rather than postindustrial consumer societies, are again propelling the world economy. These changes involve major breaks: an era of multipolarity; the affirmation of the plurality of capitalisms; the emergence of new modernities; and the new patterns of East-South and South-South relations, in contrast to the North-South relations. These changes unfold on a global scale and cannot be properly understood on a national, regional or even international basis. Understanding these changes requires interdisciplinary and kaleidoscopic approaches that range from global political economy to cultural transformations. The series welcomes contributions to global studies that are innovative in topic, approach or theoretical framework. Amid the fin-de-regime of the millennium, with globalization in the throes of dramatic change, the series will cater to the growing interest in material on contemporary globalization and its ramifications. Proposals can be submitted by mail to the series editor: Jan Nederveen Pieterse, Mellichamp Professor of Global Studies and Sociology, Global & International Studies Program, University of California, Santa Barbara, CA 93106-7065, USA

Jacqueline S. Ismael • Tareq Y. Ismael
Leslie T. MacDonald

Pax Americana

Unending War on Iraq

Jacqueline S. Ismael
Faculty of Social Work
University of Calgary
Alberta, AB, Canada

Tareq Y. Ismael
Department of Political Science
University of Calgary
Calgary, AB, Canada

Leslie T. MacDonald
Associate Editor
Journal for Contemporary
Iraq & the Arab World
Toronto, ON, Canada

ISSN 2946-3777   ISSN 2946-3785   (electronic)
Frontiers of Globalization
ISBN 978-3-031-61272-5   ISBN 978-3-031-61273-2   (eBook)
https://doi.org/10.1007/978-3-031-61273-2

© The Editor(s) (if applicable) and The Author(s), under exclusive license to Springer Nature Switzerland AG 2024
This work is subject to copyright. All rights are solely and exclusively licensed by the Publisher, whether the whole or part of the material is concerned, specifically the rights of translation, reprinting, reuse of illustrations, recitation, broadcasting, reproduction on microfilms or in any other physical way, and transmission or information storage and retrieval, electronic adaptation, computer software, or by similar or dissimilar methodology now known or hereafter developed.
The use of general descriptive names, registered names, trademarks, service marks, etc. in this publication does not imply, even in the absence of a specific statement, that such names are exempt from the relevant protective laws and regulations and therefore free for general use.
The publisher, the authors and the editors are safe to assume that the advice and information in this book are believed to be true and accurate at the date of publication. Neither the publisher nor the authors or the editors give a warranty, expressed or implied, with respect to the material contained herein or for any errors or omissions that may have been made. The publisher remains neutral with regard to jurisdictional claims in published maps and institutional affiliations.

This Palgrave Macmillan imprint is published by the registered company Springer Nature Switzerland AG.
The registered company address is: Gewerbestrasse 11, 6330 Cham, Switzerland

Paper in this product is recyclable.

و الله ما طلعت شمسٌ ولا غربت   إلا و حبّك مقرون بأنفاسي

ولا خلوتُ إلى قوم أحدّثهـم   إلا و أنت حديثي بين جلاسـي

ولا ذكرتك محزوناً و لا فرِحا   إلا و أنت بقلبي بين وسواسـي

ولا هممت بشرب الماء من عطش   إلا رَأيْتُ خيالًا منك في الكـأس

ولو قدرتُ على الإتيان جئتكم   سعياً على الوجه .. أو مشياً على الرأس

ابرط يـلـتينغّ نإ يّحلا ىتفـايو   فغنّني وأسفا من قلبك القاسي

ما لي وللناس كم يلحونني سفها   ديني لنفسي .. و دين الناس للناس

قصيدة ابو المغيث الحسين بن منصور الحلاج (858–922)

I swear by God, sun riseth not nor setteth,
But in each breath I breathe my love for Thee
Nor go I e'er apart with friends for discourse
But Thou, as I sit with them, art my theme;
Nor dwell my thoughts on Thee, sadly or gladly,
But Thou art in my heart, I murmur Thee.
Nor have I mind to drink of water in thirst,
But I behold Thine image in the cup.
And could I come to Thee, then speed I would
Upon my face, or walking on my head.

Poem by al-Mughith al-Husayn ibn Mansur al-Hallāj (858–922)
Translated by Martin Lings, Sufi Poems *(2004)*

FOREWORD

NARRATING THE LOGIC OF PAX AMERICANA

Recent references to the Iraq War of 2003 in the West tend mostly to come from the political or anti-war left sources seemingly intent on issuing stern reminders that Russia's 2022 attack on Ukraine was foreshadowed in its most objectionable features by the US/UK attack followed by a long controversial occupation of Iraq, while the mainstream tries to erase America's experience from collective memory.

Those invoking Iraq as a precedent relevant to Ukraine offer a justifiable critique of the imperial aspects of American foreign policy that make a mockery of self-righteous appeals to international law and the UN Charter to mobilize international opposition to Russia while building global support for sanctions, arms shipments, and huge donations of economic assistance. Adopting such an ahistorical, abstract, and Eurocentric optic, however useful, comes at a price. Iraq loses its core reality as a country inhabited by people who have endured the trials and tribulations of tyranny, war, foreign intervention, and prolonged occupation. The US refusal to practice what it preaches when dealing with the Global South, especially in the countries of the Middle East, vividly confirmed by its complicity in Israel's genocidal onslaught upon Gaza, remains a significant precedent in relation to the policy debate about Ukraine, but it is far from telling the whole story of the Iraqi ordeal of the past 80 years.

This remarkable book is written by Jacqueline and Tareq Ismael, both highly respected Iraqi specialists who are longtime scholarly commentators on the sorrowful recent history of the country. They present us with a devastating critique of the American role in Iraq during the 20 years since the ill-conceived aggression of 2003, but they do much more. Above all, they convincingly explicate the comprehensive anatomy of victimization that became the fatal destiny of Iraq and its people, climaxing with the aggressive regime-changing war of 2003. The historical contextualization of the war and the refusal to erase from political consciousness its terrible impact on the Iraqi civilian population is what makes this book such a powerful indictment of American foreign policy. The understanding imparted by their analysis goes far deeper than typically superficial assessments based on a simple model of 'attack and occupation.'

Jacqueline Ismael, who sadly died earlier this year, and Tareq, her Iraqi-born writing partner and husband, have long devoted their scholarly lives to narrating the American desecration of Iraq. Additionally, they have together built an ambitious academic infrastructure that has made major contributions to Iraqi studies. These have included the founding of a journal, organizing international conferences, and publishing books. And perhaps most of all, by developing an international community of scholars committed to probing various less-known, yet integral, aspects of the complex Iraqi experience of the last century. This high-quality scholarship should not be confused with the one-dimensional output of Beltway think tanks that offer the US government menus of policy options that are generally pleasing to the Pentagon and mainstream foreign policy venues. In contrast, the Ismael orientation is objective, exhibiting and encouraging others to undertake interdisciplinary styles of inquiry and assessment. This work also valuably merges standard political and economic concerns with serious attention to the social, ethical, religious, and even artistic and philosophical dimensions of Iraq's extraordinary cultural heritage. It is this heritage that has been shattered by Iraq's encounters with America in the course of fragmenting the political and cultural unity of the Iraqi people.

In this necessarily last collaborative book, the Ismaels draw on their superb qualifications to share with us their cumulative knowledge and wisdom about Iraq. This short but profound book manages to consider both the disasters that have befallen Iraq but also the confused and sinister behavior embedded in this pattern of dysfunctional US deployments of hard and soft power over a period of six decades. What results is a highly instructive book that contextualizes US geopolitical tactics and strategies in a manner that sheds light on a host of other contemporary concerning issues around the world. In essence, the Ismaels have managed to interpret the interplay of America's global and regional hegemonic ambitions in ways that yield a deeply informed narrative of the tragic events that have ravaged Iraq and spilled over its borders to cause comparable forms of distress elsewhere in the region. The book brilliantly depicts the interconnections between the fate of Iraq and that of the Middle East as a whole, presenting an illuminating account of why the impacts of the American imperial agenda should not be conceptualized as mere aggression followed by an occupation devoted to benign 'state-building' undertakings supposedly aimed at constitutional governance and developmental dynamism.

With electrifying clarity, the Ismaels show that contemporary tragedy of Iraq should not begin, as in most assessments with a focus on the two wars in 1991 and 2003, their interim of harsh sanctions, and their chaotic aftermaths, but look at the downward spiral of events starting in 1963. The book's illuminating, mostly ignored or suppressed starting point is the 1963 CIA-facilitated coup that replaced the nationalist Qasim government with the dictatorial repressive Ba'athist Party leadership, eventually headed by Saddam Hussein. Tareq Ismael's personal history of living in exile ever since this coup and forever scarred by these events of 60 years that culminated in the roundup and massacre of at least 5000 Iraqi intellectuals and progressive. political activists, lends an aura of authenticity and significance to these barely recollected events.

In a manner the 1963 coup in Iraq recalls the 1953 coup in Iran that overthrew the Mossadegh government with the covert help and encouragement of the CIA, anticipating in several of its particulars the Iraqi undertaking ten years later. In Iran, the Shah was restored to the Peacock Throne, and more importantly, foreign ownership of the Iranian oil industry was restored, with leading American energy corporations the greatly enriched beneficiaries.

The true character of these events in both major oil producing countries was thinly disguised by then fashionable Cold War rationalizations of saving these countries from a Communist takeover by marginalizing and discrediting Soviet/Marxist/socialist influences that purportedly undermined Western strategic interests in the Middle East, as well as threatening these countries with Stalinist futures. Such state propaganda, spread by an ideologically subservient Western media, downplayed the true strategic motivation for these disruptive political events, which was to keep the energy reserves of the region under secure Western control while entrusting their custodianship to the American oil industry. In this process, the disregard for the sovereign self-determination rights of the state and suffering of the peoples that followed was ignored as were the allegations that the outcomes reflected the maneuvers of the CIA rather than the revolt of nationalist forces. Only years later was the instrumental role of the CIA widely confirmed. The original public rationale portrayed the events as internally driven anti-Communist rejections of hysterical or tyrannical leaders.

The book draws appropriate attention to the critical differences between regime-changing interventions in the period between 1950 and 1990, and those taking place after the Soviet implosion in 1991. Earlier efforts to disrupt the politics of self-determination were hidden and covertly carried out, and hence entrusted to the CIA and collaborating national elites in countries targeted for regime change. The only overt exceptions of any consequence during the Cold War occurred in the two wars taking place in the divided countries of Korea and Vietnam where international fault lines were breached by the revisionist behavior of rival nationalist forces seeking restored unification of the states as single nations. Elsewhere, the United States tried to disrupt what it opposed by acting off-stage and relying on compliant national elements to construct the successor states.

After the Cold War the dynamic of intervention in the Middle East became overtly militarist, tied to arms sales and predatory globalization. The US sought to legitimize these overt interventions at the UN by claiming humanitarian and international law justification or counterinsurgency imperatives in the face of alleged terrorist threats. Among the rationalizations put forward in 2003 for violating Iraq's state boundaries were its possession of non-nuclear weapons of mass destruction and a secret program to develop nuclear weapons; Afghanistan after 9/11 as safe haven for international terrorism; humanitarian urgency in Libya concerning the beleaguered population of Benghazi. If UN legitimation was not granted, as was the case with Iraq (and earlier Kosovo, 1999), then the US together with allies proceeded to intervene openly, feeling no need for the secrecy it relied upon during the Cold War. When the UN Security Council refused the American request for authorization to use force in Iraq, George W. Bush angrily suggesting that if the UN decided to withhold approval of US war plans, it would find itself irrelevant. And regrettably, Bush was to some extent right.

This overtness, also enabled prolonged foreign occupations, and in Iraq was an alleged necessity to complete the challenge of liberating the country from its dictatorial past, which required ensuring that the successor state was a stable and secure exemplar of constitutional democracy. The only thing hidden from view in carrying out such state-building plans are the various aspects of economic exploitation, including a forced entry into neoliberal world economy.

This form of state-building by an occupying foreign power is half of the abusive story exposed by this book. The other half has not been previously explicated. What the Ismaels have managed to demonstrate through their focus on the specifics of the American occupation is a set of policies that had the intended effects of doing the opposite of what was claimed for state-building. In actuality, the American occupation destroyed prospects of a stable, competent, and prosperous Iraq, let alone a state protective of human security and public order. The policies and practices systematically pursued destroyed sturdy pillars of governmental stability that existed in Iraq prior to 2003. The occupation purged the armed forces and bureaucracy of its Sunni highly professional staffing during the Ba'athist period, turned a blind eye to the looting of museums and archeological artifacts undermining cultural identity and national consciousness. Such an approach gave ample political space to the assertion of a variety of subnational grievances and embittered rivalries among religious factions and ethnic minorities. As the Ismaels explain state-building turned out in Iraq to be state-ending, such a dismal assessment of the occupation manifested itself through greatly increased ethnic strife, radical micro-politics, rising criminality, gross corruption, persisting chaos, and increasing poverty.

It is for these reasons that 'state-building,' as argued by the authors, is better conceptualized as a process of 'state-ending' or 'state deconstruction.' This is a radical claim that goes far beyond critiques of the conventional understanding state-building as benevolence gone wrong with Afghanistan and Iraq especially in mind. The shocking argument that the Ismaels advance for our consideration is that this outcome was not a failure of occupation policy but a deliberately orchestrated success. The goal of such an approach may seem perverse, but reflects American deep state thinking on the Middle East, as strongly paralleled by Israeli beliefs and practice, that the cornerstone of regional security is not so much a matter of weaponry as it is in the existence of weak, internally divided and preoccupied states.

In an informative chapter on the aspirations of the Kurdish minority further concreteness is added to the exposition of how occupation misshaped Iraq by showing that the US and Israel both promoted Kurdish aspirations in ways that weakened Iraqi sense of national identity, so vital for successful state formation projects.

The geopolitical hypocrisy of the American role in Iraq is given a bipartisan slant that goes back to the Kennedy role in promoting the 1963 coup against Qasim and forward to the efforts of both Bush's to wage war against their former client state, Iraq. We need to remember that in 1980 Saddam's Iraq had been persuaded to attack Iran in what turned out to be a grueling eight-year war, partly extended by US arms sales to both sides. In addition, Saddam was given ambiguous signals a decade later by the US ambassador in Baghdad about launching an attack on subsequent annexation of Kuwait, only to find Iraq subject to international denunciations by the US President, Arab neighbors, and the UN as a legitimizing prelude to a 'shock and awe' attack, and after another twelve years of punitive sanctions that ravaged the civilian population of Iraq, yet another American aggression launched against its former notorious ally who ended up paying with his life.

This mastery of the Iraq narrative by the Ismaels does what most Iraqi commentators do not do. That is, they present dismaying evidence that the wellbeing of the people of Iraq was consistently sacrificed as a suppressed side-effect of this American quest for political and economic dominance in the post-colonial Middle East. The story of Iraq serves as a metaphor for the twenty-first-century US imperial (mis)adventures throughout the entire world. To be sure, the region was especially vulnerable to imperial design, and a result, has vividly exhibited this state-destroying and people-victimizing behavior by the United States. This reflects several factors: oil geopolitics as its supreme strategic priority, Israel's junior hegemonic status as its unconditional domestic priority, and the blowback threats of Islamic radicalism and expansion of Islamic influence in the region after the 9/11 attacks have shaped its security dialogue at least until the Ukraine War. We can be most thankful to have such a book for its insight, knowledge, wisdom, and empathy, and for getting right the complex story of America's role in Iraq.

University of California, Santa Barbara, CA, USA

February 21, 2024   Richard Falk

PREFACE AND ACKNOWLEDGMENTS

The origins of this work can be traced to an evening in Beirut more than 50 years ago, in the first week of July 1970. We had invited the distinguished Iraqi leftist poet Buland al-Haydari (1926–1996) along with the famous Iraqi musician Munir Bashir (1930–1997), to our residence at the time at the American University of Beirut family housing campus. This event was held to celebrate the arrival of two old Iraqi friends, the painter Khalid Al-Jadir (1924–1990) and poet Ḥusayn Mardān (1927–1972) for the first time in Beirut. Buland informed me that we would have a surprise addition to the group, but would not reveal his name in advance. Both Jacqueline and I were preparing for that evening when, at 7 pm, we opened the door to find another dear old friend, the well-known actor and playwright, Yusuf al-Ani (1927–2016).

Later that evening after dinner, the group, led by Buland, started to sing Iraqi folk songs to Munir's accompaniment on the oud. By the time tea was served, naturally, the discussion led to politics and I asked how things were in the fascist Iraq that I had left behind ten years earlier, without a path to return. The room erupted briefly, then silence took over. Yusuf al-Ani initiated the discussion by saying how lucky I was not to be residing in Iraq. He turned to Jacqueline and my two children and said, 'you would not be here with us now had your father been in Iraq at that time'. They began to share their stories of the American-orchestrated February 1963 coup d'état in which tens of thousands of Iraqi intellectuals, considered to be leftists, anti-nationalists, and communist sympathizers, were gathered into sports arenas to be interrogated. They told of their own experiences and how each endured physical torture, a story common to all of those with us that night.

For Yusuf al-Ani, 'the torture was beyond what can be put into words'. He described the actions and methods of his interrogators as sadist; he said they used people's eyes as ashtrays. Jacqueline asked what that meant, and Buland closed his eyes and showed scars of burnt eyelids. Dalal al-Mufti, Buland's wife, added by saying men's experience of the coup d'état was only half of the story. The women in Iraq suffered as much, if not more, with many experiencing sexual assault witnessed by their children. Al-Ani informed us that he had written a play entitled Awailakh ('Woe unto us') and that he would 'leave it with Buland until the time comes for it to be published'. That time came more than 40 years later, in 2013, when al-Ani's close and long-standing friend Dr. Hamdi Touqmachi published the play in Amman.[1]

That evening was a transformative experience for Jacqueline which motivated her to write on the atrocities and human suffering in Iraq. This book is our final attempt to fulfill our promise to uncover and confront that injustice. Jacqueline said to me on several occasions subsequently that the Americans punished Iraqis by, first, installing the Ba'athists and Saddam Hussein, and eventually punished Iraqis again, for having been forced to endure his depredations. That evening also laid the foundation for Jacqueline's other flagship project. She was instrumental in the formation of the International Association of Contemporary Iraqi Studies, which was formed after the American Occupation of Iraq in 2003, and the publication of the International Journal of Contemporary Iraqi Studies in 2007. She devoted her life to giving an academic voice to the human suffering and highlighting it in academic works.

This book was our last project together, in which Jacqueline was deeply involved in every aspect. She carefully thought out each word and approved the final draft before her passing.

Since that time, our original publisher was reluctant to proceed with the manuscript and, during the subsequent review process with Palgrave Macmillan, the strategic position of the American empire with respect to its adversaries weakened, as we had anticipated in the concluding chapter ('Chapter 4: Two Faces of Pax Americana'). Although we were reluctant

---

[1] Ismael, T. 2019. Legacy, Legitimacy and Compromise: Baghdad's Visionary Yusuf Al-Ani and Postcolonial Iraq. *Journal of Contemporary Iraq & the Arab World* 13 (1): 21–39. https://doi.org/10.1386/jciaw.13.1.21_1.

to update the text which Jacqueline had co-authored, we felt compelled nevertheless to relate our conclusions to world events since her passing, as we have now done in the 'Epilogue'. We would like to thank Elizabeth Graber, Senior Editor, Sociology and Anthropology, Palgrave Macmillan, and Jan Nederveen Pieterse, Mellichamp Chair and Distinguished Professor of Global Studies & Sociology, University of California Santa Barbara, and Series Editor, Frontiers of Globalization for Palgrave Macmillan, for going out of their way to welcome us and assist us in moving the manuscript toward publication. Our sincere appreciation is also extended to Professor Salaam Yousif of the English Department at California State University, San Bernardino, for his invaluable contributions in reviewing sections of the manuscript and providing highly beneficial corrections and advice. We also thank the external reviewers for their very helpful, encouraging, and timely advice.

Part of Chap. 1 was originally published as an article in the *Arab Studies Quarterly*, while parts of Chap. 2 were published in our book with Raymond W. Baker and Shereen T. Ismael, Cultural Cleansing in Iraq (Pluto Press 2010). With the permission of both publishers, portions have been enlarged, reworked, edited, and updated for this book. Our gratitude goes to our collaborators in those works, and to the publishers for enabling us to share this with our audience.

A special thanks go to our dear friend of 40 years, Leslie MacDonald, who has stepped in to shoulder this work, first as an editor and eventually as our co-author upon the deterioration of Jacqueline's health. Without his commitment, diligence, and writing skills, this project would not have reached the finish line. Also, we will be remiss if we do not acknowledge the Social Science Humanities and Research Council of Canada (SSHRC) for supporting our research over the past 50 years, including our currently held research project, which has enriched the content and outlook of our work.

The transliteration system utilized in this study predominantly adheres to the format employed by the International Journal of Middle Eastern Studies. Nonetheless, for the names of political figures and places, we have opted to employ common spelling conventions. The transliterations of Arabic, Farsi, Turkish, and Hebrew that are most widely recognized have been adopted, occasionally prioritizing legibility over absolute accuracy. It is worth noting that in Western literature, variations in transliteration or spelling may occur, such as 'Shi'ism' or 'Shi'ites.' For consistency, we have selected one preferred form, though, in the index, both variants will be represented synonymously. The authors' preferred method for articulating their perspectives within academic forums prior to finalizing a book involves the dissemination of articles, presentations, or papers at international conferences. These materials are subsequently updated, revised, and expanded to align with the fundamental thesis of the present work. This process has similarly been applied to this book. The original contributions are duly acknowledged and cited in the footnotes accordingly.

Finally, I take great pleasure in thanking Richard Falk, my mentor and long-time friend of mine and Jacqueline's, for many things, including his very perceptive and appreciative analysis of our book in the 'Foreword.'

Calgary, AB, Canada   Tareq Y. Ismael
February 2024

Praise for *Pax Americana*

"This short but profound book manages to consider both the disasters that have befallen Iraq but also the confused and sinister behavior embedded in this pattern of dysfunctional U.S. deployments of hard and soft power over a period of six decades. What results is a highly instructive book that contextualizes U.S. geopolitical tactics and strategies in a manner that sheds light on a host of other contemporary concerning issues around the world."

—Richard Falk, *Professor of International Law Emeritus, Princeton University*

"… a searing critique of US foreign and military policy in the Middle East since the Gulf War. It demonstrates with brutal clarity the falsity of American narratives about democracy and human rights promotion and surveys the regional instability Washington left behind."

—Juan Cole, *Richard P. Mitchell Collegiate Professor of History, University of Michigan*

"Jacqueline and Tareq Ismael have written a book that is coolly argued but fired up by outrage at the price that Iraqis have had to pay over the years to conform with US views of what the Middle East should look like. By focusing on these two facets of the unequal US-Iraqi relationship, the authors are to be congratulated for their meticulous and moving portrayal of the impact on the citizens of Iraq of American preoccupations that neither understood nor sympathized with the aspirations of Iraqis themselves."

—Charles Tripp, FBA, *Professor Emeritus of Politics with reference to the Middle East and North Africa, SOAS, University of London*

CONTENTS

ABOUT THE AUTHORS

Jacqueline S. Ismael was Professor of Social Work at the University of Calgary, Canada, and co-editor of the *International Journal of Contemporary Iraqi Studies.* She published extensively on Canadian social policy and international social welfare. She also co-authored a number of works with Tareq Y. Ismael, including *The Communist Movement in Syria and Lebanon* (1998), *The Iraqi Predicament: People in the Quagmire of Power Politics* (2004), and *Government and Politics of the Contemporary Middle East: Continuity and Change* (2nd ed., 2015), *Iraq in the Twenty-First Century: Regime Change and the Making of a Failed State* (2015) and *Government and Politics of the Contemporary Middle East: Discontinuity and Turbulence* (3rd ed., 2024), and also with William Haddad: *Barriers to Reconciliation: Case Studies on Iraq and the Palestine–Israel Conflict* (2006).

Tareq Y. Ismael is Professor of Political Science at the University of Calgary, Canada. He also serves as president of the International Centre for Contemporary Middle Eastern Studies and is author/co-author and editor of numerous works on Iraq and the Middle East, including *Iraq: The Human Cost of History* (2003), *The Iraqi Predicament: People in the Quagmire of Power Politics* (2004), *The Rise and Fall of the Communist Party in Iraq* (2008), *Cultural Cleansing: Why Museums Were Looted, Libraries Burned and Academics Murdered* (2010), *The Sudanese Communist Party: Ideology and Party Politics* (2013), *International Relations of the Contemporary Middle East* (2014), *Government and Politics of the Contemporary Middle East: Continuity and Change* (2nd ed.,

2015), *Iraq in the Twenty-First Century: Regime Change and the Making of a Failed State* (2015), and *Government and Politics of the Contemporary Middle East: Discontinuity and Turbulence* (3rd ed., 2024).

Leslie T. MacDonald worked at the Social Sciences and Humanities Research Council of Canada. Since retirement in 2005 he has advised on questions of research design and is Associate Editor of the *Journal for Contemporary Iraq & the Arab World*. He lives in Toronto, Canada.

ABBREVIATIONS

ABM	Anti-ballistic Missile
BRICS	Brazil, Russia, India, South Africa
CIA	Central Intelligence Agency
CPA	Coalition Provisional Authority
CPI	Commission on Public Integrity
DOE	Department of Energy
DIA	Defense Intelligence Agency
DPG	Defense Planning Guidance
DU	depleted uranium
EIA	Energy Information Administration
G7	Policy forums of leaders of US, UK, Germany, Japan, France, Italy and Canada
IDP	internally displaced persons
ICJ	International Court of Justice
IGC	Iraqi Governing Council
IDF	Israeli Defence Forces
INA	Iraqi National Alliance
INC	Iraqi National Congress
IMF	International Monetary Fund
IOCs	international oil companies
IRGC	Islamic Revolutionary Guard Corps
ISCI	Islamic Supreme Council of Iraq
ISIS	Islamic State of Iraq and the Levant
ITIC	International Tax and Investment Center
JAC	Joint Action Committee
KDP	Kurdistan Democratic Party
KLWCC	Kuala Lumpur War Crimes Commission

KLWCT	Kuala Lumpur War Crimes Tribunal
KRG	Kurdistan Regional Government
MAD	mutually assured destruction
MICS	Multiple Indicator Cluster Survey
NATO	North Atlantic Treaty Organization
NGO	non-governmental organization
OHCHR	Office of the United Nations High Commissioner for Human Rights
OIC	Organization for Islamic Cooperation
OPEC	Organization of the Petroleum Exporting Countries
OPCW	Organization for the Prohibition of Chemical Weapons
ORHA	Office of Reconstruction and Human Assistance in Iraq
OSP	Office of Special Plans
PDS	Public Distribution System
PNAC	Project for a New American Century
PLO	Palestinian Liberation Organization
PSA	Production Sharing Agreements
PUK	Patriotic Union of Kurdistan
R2P	Responsibility to Protect
SCIRI	Supreme Council for Islamic Revolution in Iraq
SOFA	Status of Forces Agreement
TAL	Law of Administration for the State of Iraq for the Transitional Period
UAE	United Arab Emirates
UN	United Nations
UNAMI	United Nations Assistance Mission for Iraq
UNDP	United Nations Development Programme
UNESCO	United Nations Educational, Scientific and Cultural Organization
UNICEF	United Nations Children's Fund
UNMOVIC	United Nations Monitoring, Verification and Inspection Commission
UNSC	United Nations Security Council
UNU	United Nations University
US	United States
USAID	United States Agency for International Development
USSR	Union of Socialist Soviet Republics
UK	United Kingdom
WMDs	weapons of mass destruction
WTI	World Tribunal on Iraq

CHAPTER 1

Pax Americana and the Dissolution of Arab States

Robbers of the world, having by their universal plunder exhausted the land, they rifle the deep. If the enemy be rich, they are rapacious; if he be poor, they lust for dominion; neither the east nor the west has been able to satisfy them. Alone among men they covet with equal eagerness poverty and riches. To robbery, slaughter, plunder, they give the lying name of empire; they make a solitude and call it peace. (Tacitus)

THE PLAGUES OF PAX AMERICANA

The bitter denunciation of Roman depredations, articulated by Roman historian Tacitus as coming from an ancient Caledonian chieftain, would not surprise us today if it were to be directed at the US by almost anyone living in the Middle East, Latin America, Africa, South-east Asia, all regions experiencing the consequences of American intervention and coercion. However, geography and history have combined to place the Middle East in general, and Iraq in particular, at the bull's eye of American imperial ambitions, enabling Iraqis especially to confirm the truth of Tacitus' enduring verdict against imperialism. Iraqis have been punished multiple times by successive American administrations in regard to Saddam Hussein, initially because they were an obstacle to his ambitions, then as collateral damage to his service as a proxy for the empire, and finally for their failure to overthrow Saddam when his usefulness to the empire had expired.

Iraqis were punished for the first time, in 1963, under the Kennedy administration, when the American Central Intelligence Agency (CIA) supported the Iraqi Ba'athist party (including Saddam) in a violent military coup against the leftwing nationalist Qasim regime in 1963 (Aburish 1997: 82, 113, 135–143; Cockburn 1997; Farouk and Sluglett 2001; Dawisha 2003; Morris 2003; Matthews, 2011: 641–643; Esposti 2022). With CIA guidance, the junta massacred about 5000 people, particularly communists and leftists (Aburish 1997: 139; Farouk and Sluglett 2001). Ali Salih al-Sa'di, the Secretary General of the Ba'ath Party of Iraq and the new Deputy Prime Minister declared (evoking the arrival of Lenin in Petrograd on a German-controlled train in 1917): 'We came on the CIA train' (Aburish: 140; Mufti 1996: 144; Ismael and Ismael 2021: 15).

The second time came in 1980, when the Carter Administration encouraged their covert asset, Saddam, to invade the Islamic Republic of Iran (Parry 2015), thereby unleashing a war that lasted eight years and killed hundreds of thousands, and which successive American administrations helped to prolong by supporting both sides.

The third punishment was in unleashing of the Gulf War of 1990–1991, when April Glaspie, George H.W. Bush's ambassador to Baghdad, told Saddam that the Americans had 'no opinion' on Iraq's dispute with Kuwait (Dobbs 2002; Mearsheimer and Walt 2009; Parry 2015), but just eight days later, when Iraq marched into Kuwait, Bush promptly condemned the invasion and orchestrated the United Nations (UN) toward crippling sanctions and a bombing campaign which decimated the Iraqi military as well as its economic and social infrastructure.

The fourth punishment was the thirteen years of UN economic sanctions and the so-called no-fly zones in Iraq, which transformed an international conflict with Kuwait and the UN into an American-directed regime-change operation, including a double civil war engaging the Saddam regime against Kurdish and Shia rebellions.

The fifth atrocity was the Bush Jr. administration's 2003 invasion on the pretext of Saddam's allegedly possessing 'weapons of mass destruction', and which he might transfer to 'terrorists'. The invasion and occupation went beyond the regime-change project initiated during the Gulf War to what is described in Chap. 2 as a state-ending project, the destruction of the state and society of Iraq, including campaigns of targeted assassinations reminiscent of the CIA-supported Ba'athist coup of 1963.

The execution of Saddam in 2006 definitively silenced the former American asset, but did not put an end to the successive American plagues which Iraqis endured on his account. While the specific causes of the Islamic State depredations in Iraq and Syria remain controversial, it is widely acknowledged that the occupation at least set the conditions and enabled what became the sixth American plague to descend upon Iraq since 1963.

Calamitous as this half-century of successive assaults was for Iraq, for the ascending Pax Americana on the contrary, it was the staircase of opportunity. The CIA coup of 1963 was a skirmish in the Cold War with the USSR, a see-saw struggle which had been ongoing since the Americans began replacing the British empire in the Middle East in 1945, intensified with the rise to power of Gamal Abdul Nasser in Egypt. Saddam and the Syrian Ba'athists were recruited as covert American assets in the global anti-Communist campaign. Broadly similar American calculations had brought the Shah of Iran to power in a 1953 CIA-supported coup against the leftwing nationalist Mohammad Mossadegh government. The Iranian Islamic revolution of 1979 was an instance of 'blowback' before that CIA-inspired term came into general use, posing an intensified threat to American petroleum interests and regional power (Johnston 2000, 2004). Although no records have come to light regarding Saddam's motives for invading Iran in 1980, it was a moment when the Carter administration was anxious to free the American hostages in its embassy in Teheran before Carter faced possible electoral defeat (Parry 2015). The circumstances might therefore have appeared opportune or compelling, to both Carter and Saddam to exert military pressure on Iran. If such a gamble were contemplated, it didn't work out well for either man.

However, having Iran and Iraq at war for most of the 1980s did work out well for Pax Americana and its Israeli stronghold. The war with Iran, when it finally ended, also became a key factor in fueling Saddam's dispute with Kuwait (one of the financial backers of the Iran war), and then in igniting the Gulf War, which swiftly confirmed the US as the world's sole superpower. From the perspective of Saddam's role as a covert American asset, the consequences of his career represents an excellent return on investment. The Gulf War therefore represents the pivotal event in the rise of Pax Americana, and the destruction heaped on Iraq since 1963 helped at decisive moments to pave the way for its ascent.

The collateral damage accompanying the ascent of Pax Americana extends beyond Iraq. The post-1990 period across the Arab-majority states of the Middle East region have witnessed increasing authoritarianism, declining incomes and material production, leading to declines in socio-economic development, health and the quality of life of a shrinking middle class (Kadri 2016). Human development and health have been further eroded by the mushrooming growth in illicit trade and both public and private corruption, a ruling class that enriches itself through the exploitation of their fellow citizens and the increasing frequency of violent conflict. This has led to larger outward migration from the states affected as well as some 11 million internally displaced people (IDP) in the Middle East and North Africa as of the end of 2018 (IDMC 2019; Rossi et al. 2018) while the number of refugees having fled their home country stands at between 4 and 5 million. These outcomes result from failed leadership and external interventions, primarily driven by the increasing incidence of violent conflict directed at civilian populations over the last three decades. With many scholars critically examining the failure(s) of the 'Arab state' (Kamrava 2018; Hinnebusch 2016; Kadri 2015) the role of interventionist powers is also acknowledged as a driver (Forte 2012; Blumi 2018).

The perspective presented here, focusing on the experience of Iraq since 1990, is how the predominance of the US has driven such spiraling catastrophes. Beginning in 1991, the US adopted a posture of direct action aimed at shaping the region and its politics. Consideration of the impact of these efforts, while accounting for the humanitarian toll and reversal of human development, will be our primary consideration. The period under investigation differs from that prior to 1990, where US engagement with the region over the Cold War (1947–1991) was less direct and less overt, circumscribed more by deterrence, Cold War rivalry as well as the popularity of opposition to engagement with Cold War dichotomies following the idyll of the Bandung precedent. Following the 1991 Gulf War, US power, no longer inhibited by any Cold War peer competitor, and driven more by the logic of its own expansion of coercive economic and political power in the region, which it mobilized into a hub-and-spoke network of formal relationships with the leaders of Arab states (Brownlee 2012).

The regional posture of the US has been identified by different names, from imperialism, through its varied policy orientations and initiatives launched by individual presidential administrations, and more unreservedly characterized as 'empire of chaos' (Amin 1992; Escobar 2014) and 'empire of lies' (Putin, 2022a, b; Zhang 2022) also derivative from the Roman historian, Tacitus. We have adopted in this volume the designation, 'Pax Americana'—coined by some to evoke the supposed peace and prosperity that was to result from US hegemony, and also to remind us that the act of pacification is inherently a coercive one. The term, borrowed from the Pax Romana of Imperial Rome, is also ironically suggestive of the modern critiques of imperialism, as our opening quotation from Tacitus' imaginative account of the Calidonian leader, Calgacus' denunciation of Roman plundering, slaughter and deception, has been taken up by some contemporary critics of American policy. The dynamics of imperialism, encompassing force, deception and chaos, it is now evident, relate more to the unequal power relationships between peoples generally than to specifics of any time and place.

Emerging as a product of the end of the Cold War as well as the expanding global interdependence of the 1990s, alignment with the US by regional states was understood (or at least promoted) to produce increased security as well as greater prosperity, development opportunity and life chances for the region's peoples. Instead, the period has experienced an immense growth in political violence from state and non-state actors, most often directed at vulnerable civilian populations. New forms of remote killing, illiberal approaches, extra-judicial detention, private security forces and even systemic torture have been supported by sophisticated surveillance technologies which have been introduced as state elites act to protect themselves in a manner similar to that of the foreign militaries introduced into the region since 1990. These elites, made wealthy through neoliberal economic policies championed by the US, European allies and international organizations, such as the World Bank and International Monetary Fund, have led to growing poverty, a shrinking middle class as well as ever-increasing disparities between elites and the vast majority of the population (Khouri 2019).

Pax Americana, like its Roman prototype, suggests the peace of the desert, thus retaining an element of irony, in that violence is typically threatened or implied, and represents a bundle of policy proscriptions alongside direct actions, including military interventions. It also serves as a corrective for the propensity of most studies to limit their focus to a given conflict, country or US political administration. The 1990 American intervention against Iraq stands as a turning point, from which we are able to distinguish other commonalities in US policy following 1990. This wider perspective allows the reader to explore the linkages between these new forms of coercion and violence and those deployed across the history of American imperialism and conquest in other parts of the world (Kinzer 2007, 2017). There can be little doubt that the precarity for contemporary citizens of the post-socialist Arab state as well as growing widespread poverty and inequality are substantially the consequence of the choices adopted by elites in the Middle East; but they have also been induced by the actions of regional and international powers that fuel conflict while rewarding compliant elites (Kadri 2015).

Iraqis have suffered immensely at the hands of the US security state since 1990. The growth of American militarism, as both policy and cultural norm, has infused the discourse over Iraq even prior to the events of 9/11. This has led to a callous disregard for Iraqi loss of life as well as the dampening of concern over the loss of development and life opportunities for millions of Iraqis forced to endure deprivation and war in response to actions taken by a regime wholly beyond their ability to change. Like Iraqis, citizens of Arab states increasingly live in a world made by war, with escalating political violence across the region. The devaluation of human life, driven by wars often initiated by outside actors as well as by the authoritarian Arab state's predation, moves beyond the realm of political culture explanatories due to the evident role played in the region by extractive capitalism (Hanieh 2018; Vogler 2017; Mitchell 2013; Muttitt 2012).

US efforts following 1990 increasingly isolated, blockaded and strangled the Iraqi populace, yet, at the same time, further empowered the Ba'ath regime (Gordon 2012; Sassoon 2011; Tripp 2007). Gestures toward a US desire for regime change, initially publicly denied, before emerging as official policy with the 1998 'Iraq Liberation Act', were predicated on elements of the regime or state apparatus decapitating the clique at the top of the regime rather than the empowerment of popular sovereignty. Through much of the English-language scholarship on contemporary Iraq runs an assumption that American policy and actions are benevolently intentioned, ultimately accountable to the public checks of democratic praxis, and hence incomparable to the predations of Ba'athism. By this framing, disastrous outcomes such as that following the 2003 invasion and occupation are identified as 'mistakes', those who advocated for failed policies retain prominent and often lucrative sinecures, and the suffering of Iraqis under sanctions and occupation is rationalized as the exclusive fault of the Ba'athist regime. Additional assumptions include a profound but implicit belief that Americans can read the minds and motivations of their opponents due to the universality of human motivations—especially with regard to material considerations, as well as an ideational commitment to particular notions of 'freedom'—and that 'History' is an American prerogative. This structured optic extends beyond how Americans gauge others, with an assumption that US motives and actions will be perceived as transparent, comprehensible and fair by others. One affectation that arises across many of the memoirs of American military and civilian leaders who occupied Iraq, was the anecdotal experience of decision-makers, such as David Petraeus, asking Iraqis what they desired with regard a given issue. Having the native informant express shock and joy, this being the first time an American had deigned to reach out, appeared in interviews with returning figures and affected a casual understanding of Iraqis, as well as noting the failures of those who preceded them in ruling Iraq (Sky 2016).

American voices such as Walt, Mearsheimer, Bacevich and others have consistently challenged this triumphalism, captured in the words of John Dower: 'the United States, mesmerized with its own military and technological and economic power and convinced of its moral superiority, keeps imagining a much greater mastery of events than it actually has … [c]ocooned in "triumphalism and righteousness," Americans have been unable to see not only the limits of their power but the real consequences of their actions, domestically and internationally' (Dower 2018). Most glaring is the disconnect between US relations across the region and the conflicts engaged, and the military-industrial complex and drive for weapons sales and procurement; long the largest arms exporter globally, over 2014–2018, 52 per cent of US arms exports went to the Middle East (SIPRI 2019; Feinstein 2012; Der Derian 2009).

Finally, as we argue elsewhere (Ismael and Ismael 2015, 2021), the approach to regime change was dramatically altered over the course of Pax Americana. US consideration of non-military means such as diplomacy to bring about change in a targeted state, was superseded in several instances by an overt methodology that has led to considerable humanitarian calamity and the destruction of state institutions in preference to previously more covert efforts to shift government leaders. This lack of patience is even found in the escalation of economic sanctions such as those placed on the Islamic Republic of Iran, a tacit admission that patience no longer exists for the machinations of market forces to coerce such an opponent.

Increasing US deployment of military force, sanctions as blunt instruments, as well as the increasing selection of potential replacement leaders who are largely unknown within the local community they are being selected to govern, lacking credible skills required to govern or the political legitimacy necessary to attract supporters. Many such differentiations, common to partisan policy-makers of both political parties, can be gleaned in comparing American foreign policy praxis prior to 1990 to subsequent practice. Following an examination of the transition that took place surrounding 1990 with Iraq at its center, we will examine the impacts of these new orientations that have been brought on during the period of Pax Americana and conclude with a suggestion that they may increasingly be costing the US its preeminent position in the global order.

THE 1991 GULF WAR INITIATED A NEW ERA

The period following 1990 saw the entrenchment of US hegemony over the contemporary Middle East, especially the region's majority-Arab states of the Gulf. While the region was long a terrain of contest during the Cold War, the Gulf War of 1990–1991 served as the fulcrum of US engagement and policy assertiveness. That war saw a shift from a posture where US military forces stood offshore and even 'over the horizon', to one thereafter where they became directly and often intimately engaged within the politics of Arab states and peoples. This period, at times referred to as 'Pax Americana' by Anglophone scholars and writers to connote a period of peace and prosperity (Simon and Stevenson 2015) has in fact witnessed immense humanitarian calamity and the destruction of several regional states (Daher 2019; Gani 2019; Lackner 2019; Blumi 2018; Ismael and Ismael 2015, 2021; Kuperman 2013; Prashad 2012). Much attention has been drawn to the dramatic changes and humanitarian crises resulting from the conflicts the Middle East region has suffered following the conjoined events of 9/11 and the March 2003 invasion and subsequent occupation of Iraq. Scholars and analysts have debated, not only the pre-war justifications for the 2003 invasion as a response to 9/11, but also the ongoing effects of the dubious claims and the consequences for Iraq and the region following the intervention (Bacevich 2016; Ismael and Ismael 2015, 2021; Sjursen 2015; Bolger 2014; Mansoor 2013). As violence and humanitarian calamity spread, successive conflicts in Libya (Roberts 2011; Prashad 2012; Forte 2012; Kuperman 2013), Syria (Daher 2019; Gani 2019) and Yemen (Blumi 2018; Lackner 2019) established US policy orientations as well as parameters by which decision-makers were arriving at determinations. However, by focusing on either 9/11 or the 2003 Iraq invasion, the discussion surrounding these events is sometimes absent the critical context that comprehending 1990–1991 as a watershed enables.

US relations with the region emerged predominantly from the Second World War, followed thereafter by Cold War clashes with the Soviets that quickly swamped any past competition with European imperialism over natural resources, market access or imperial design. US interventions occurred, most notably in the support for the clandestine overthrow of the elected Iranian government in 1953, with similar covert efforts made to influence affairs in Syria in 1949 and 1957 as well as Iraq in 1963. The deployment of American military forces to Lebanon in 1958 and naval warfare against the Islamic Republic in the 1980s 'tanker war' established precedents for direct military action, especially following espousal of the January 1980 Carter doctrine. In spite of this pedigree, the scope and magnitude of the effort following 1990 dwarfed these previous engagements and needs to be placed within the historical context of the end of the Cold War for the effects to be gauged accurately. Since 1990 the US deployed military forces to a growing number of bases in Kuwait, Saudi Arabia, Bahrain, Qatar and the UAE. US bases have long stood as the modality by which US power is projected around the world (Johnston 2000, 2004), but it is only after 1990 that there is an expansion of basing to the Middle East broadly and the Gulf region specifically—with the notable exception of Israel prior to 1990. These bases have come to play a pivotal role in subsequent conflicts, not only through their capacity to project force, but more so through their framing of US 'interests' as well as increasing solidarity with the regional regimes that hosted them. What's more, the US greatly expanded its economic relationships, through neo-liberal policy prescription, free trade agreements, weapons sales and the expansion of financial services to the region's wealthy.

These changes only came at the end of the Cold War and the seeming defeat of an ideological challenge to American capitalism and liberal democracy, as well as US leaders' subsequent efforts to expand their influence and dominance over the global order (Walt 2019; Mearsheimer 2018; McCoy 2017). Moreover, US global ambitions were boosted by the demonstration effect resulting from the use of US force-of-arms in the 1991 war against Iraq (Dower 2018; Bacevich 2013). The enormity of the global changes that occurred in the wake of the collapse of the Berlin Wall in November 1989 are today all too often normalized as the expected outcome of four decades of superpower contest following the Second World War. What was greeted with astonishment at the time, is today little remarked upon, unlike the repertory focus on 9/11 as the inauguration of US relations with the region. US triumphalism, which emerged following the transition phase of the Soviet dissolution, was bolstered by a renewed faith in free markets that were spread to the former Soviet Union, with a sense that no alternative way of organizing human society rivaled that of liberal capitalism (Fukuyama 1993). Following the September 1990 Treaty on the Final Settlement with Respect to Germany (also known as the Two Plus Four Agreement) that cemented German reunification, Soviet acquiescence to Germany remaining in NATO, expanded nuclear arms and additional weapons treaties between the US and USSR, and then the dissolution of the Soviet Union in December 1991, the US reaction to these events shifted. The reactive posture of the George H.W. Bush administration saw the US President assuage concerns over potential US hegemony at the United Nations:

> You may wonder about America's role in the new world I have described. Let me assure you, the United States has no intention of striving for a Pax Americana. However, we will remain engaged. We will not retreat and pull back into isolationism. We will offer friendship and leadership. And in short, we seek a *pax universalis* built upon shared responsibilities and aspirations. (Bush 1991)

This approach, however, transitioned rapidly to an aggressive posture looking to assert US hegemony through financial leverage over the post-Soviet economies (Lukin 2016), expansion of NATO eastward (Mearsheimer 2014, 2015, 2018; Sachs and Hedges 2023) and an expanded presence in the Middle East.

When Iraq invaded Kuwait in August 1990, rather than deterring US military action in the Gulf in defense of their former friendship treaty allies in Baghdad, Soviet diplomats and leaders worked with the US to characterize the conflict in global media and lubricate the diplomatic response at the United Nations Security Council. The rapid institution of Chapter VII sanctions at the UN, Soviet acquiescence in the formation of a 35-state coalition under US leadership, as well as linkage of the Iraq conflict to that of Palestine, all spoke to the role played by Soviet leaders to shift away from direct opposition to the US (Gorbachev Foundation 1990). This occurred as the Soviet state moved closer to dissolution and former Soviet patrons and allies were forced to reassess their geopolitical and ideological positions. In this context, the Gulf War was seen to establish not only that there was no effective brake on US military action globally, but that US arms had demonstrated a newfound level of lethality through deployment of a new generation of technologies (so-called smart bombs, global positioning, communications technologies that sped US inter-operability between military units, as well as new armored vehicles and aircraft). This assemblage of weaponry and the absence of a peer competitor state to act as a deterrent, augmented US militarism and an aggressive posture biased toward military action (Freier et al. 2017; Bacevich 2013). While scholarly sources and the official record do not entirely align with a specific empirical total, one study notes that from 1945 American armed forces have been deployed abroad 211 times to 67 countries (Immerwahr 2019). Thus, US interventions and use of military force was commonplace, yet the 1990s and 2000s—especially in the Middle East region—saw an escalation of deployments.

With the US focus on the events transforming Europe and the Soviet Union, Iraq's August 1990 invasion of Kuwait provided an opportune occasion by which the US could engage in the Middle East absent Soviet opposition (Bacevich 2016). As events in Eastern Europe further exposed Soviet inability to respond, the US recognized the opportunity to see their intervention as a means to alter the Middle East regional order to their own benefit. By combining opposition to Iraq's aggression against Kuwait within an ad hoc alliance structure that increased institutional if not political relations with Arab states that had been US adversaries, as well as initiating an accompanying 'peace process' bringing Palestinian and Israeli negotiators together, American influence was paramount and increasingly seen as necessary for all state actors in the region.

Finally, the successful execution of the war effort and public launch of high technology weaponry, provided an extraordinary demonstration effect that would weaken any US domestic reticence toward US military action (Haass 2010). Media portrayals of the coming war trumpeted the size of Iraq's military and potential for a Vietnam-like scenario that could result in quagmire (Immerwahr 2019; MacArthur 1994). In the event, the US war against Iraq succeeded in evicting Iraqi military forces from Kuwait, while also devastating much of Iraq's civil infrastructure. The aerial assault was both devastating and sustained, with the national power grid disabled within the first ten minutes and national communications inoperable within the first hours (Immerwahr 2019; Haass 2010). This devastation, accompanied by orchestrated presentations of US military spokespeople, dazzled spectators around the world. US military press conferences set forth graphic portrayals of air strikes, including cockpit video footage of 'smart bombs' hitting precise targets with unwavering accuracy (Beier 2003; Hallion 1997). That less than ten percent of the munitions dropped in 1991 were technically 'smart' was absent from the briefings, as was the devastation this volume of ordinance was bringing to the urban centers of Iraq. Estimates were that the tonnage (88,500) of bombs dropped on Iraq over those 38 days and number of sorties flown, outpaced previous campaigns by orders of magnitude. The bombing of the Amiriyah air raid shelter in Baghdad led to more than 400 civilians killed and the 'highway of death', also dubbed the 'duckshoot', where retreating Iraqi soldiers were killed in spite of no longer representing a threat, both garnered global attention, however, this was largely to come following the end of hostilities (DeGhett 2014; Hersh 2000). The rapid defeat of Iraqi forces, with such devastating effect, was achieved beyond any pre-war expectations. It instilled a confidence in, and fear of, US military action that has largely continued through the period of Pax Americana, while also dividing public opinion between that of the US, which became largely inured to such attacks, and populations of targeted civilians and third party states, who found the devastation excessive.

With the 1991 'Gulf War' US foreign policy was self-declared as being directed toward a 'new world order' that saw near unanimous scholarly and political acknowledgment of the US as the sole superpower, hegemonic across the Middle East region (Nye 2022; Ismael and Ismael 1991). Over the ensuing three decades, across five US presidential administrations, American relations with the Arab states of the Middle East were driven by militarized logics that led to repeated interventions, as well as neoliberal economic frameworks that transformed the region's political economy. Focusing on the periodization and method of intervention into the regional political order, the impacts of those policies over the period under examination will be identified based on an explication of the Iraqi case. We suggest that detailed outcomes and impacts of additional cases, such as those of Syria, Libya and Yemen, where US forces have been engaged need to be undertaken to support more general conclusions. Increasingly, such data is detailed in the reporting of International Organizations, non-governmental organizations and United Nations member agencies, as noted with respect to Iraq at the end of Chap. 2. In the Iraq case, the resulting destruction of the state apparatus and the immense humanitarian catastrophe experienced by the civilian population have removed any pretense either of Arab sovereignty or of American governmental respect for human and social rights for Arab peoples.

From 'Dual Containment' to 'Regime Change'

Following its invasion of Kuwait in August 1990, Iraq came under stringent Chapter VII United Nations Security Council sanctions that effectively blockaded its economy from global markets, making even basic goods needed to sustain human life inaccessible. These measures, initially intended to enforce an Iraqi military withdrawal from Kuwait, were hastily put in place and not expected to outlive the crisis the Iraqi invasion represented. However, in spite of the eventual forced Iraqi withdrawal through the US-led coalition forces military action of January and February of 1991, the sanctions were to remain in place—albeit with some minor amendments adopted to address humanitarian concerns—until the 2003 Iraq war and removal of the Ba'ath regime. The ad hoc nature of their construction and the opaque nature of their implementation and oversight by members of the United Nations Security Council working behind closed doors and without any oversight, saw the sanctions regime devastate Iraqi society, especially its more vulnerable members.

The US was responsible for the economic sanctions and their impacts on Iraqis (Gordon 2012). Their ability to work opaquely through the United Nations bureaucracy allowed American diplomats to choke Iraqi commerce as well as necessary reconstruction following 1990–1991 air war. From the perspective of the Iraqi regime and many outside observers, the United Nations actions were unpredictable and came across as arbitrary and often without explanation in a system that could not be challenged or appealed. The US took advantage of its unique position at the United Nations Security Council to enable the imposition of sanctions and then craft how they would be implemented against Iraq, maximizing their effect to coerce Iraq and initiate regime change (Gordon 2012). By the American accounting, if the Ba'ath regime were not to be removed through direct action, sanctions could serve as a means to constrain the Iraqi state to such an extent that it could not freely carry out functions that could be seen to support a weapons program.

Through its veto in the Security Council, the US was able to shift the nominal purpose of the sanctions from withdrawal from Kuwait to the monitoring and partial disarmament of Iraq's weapons systems. The US was looking to have sanctions removal dependent on the status of Saddam Hussain, as US policy increasingly focused on bringing about regime change in Iraq. While this was at odds with international law and therefore left unspoken, the objective of regime change was understood by most everyone involved at the United Nations (Ross 2017). US policy went beyond a rational concern with security, with the establishment of the sanctions regime allowing the US to block humanitarian goods from reaching Iraq through its manipulation of the '661 committee' (Ross 2016; Gordon 2012). Of particular focus was equipment and other products related to electricity generation and distribution, telecommunications and transportation. These and many other sectors of the Iraqi economy required refurbishment if not reconstruction following coalition aerial bombardment that occurred during the 1991 Iraq air war. Agriculture, health care supplies and necessary food imports met with less resistance, so Iraq went forward under a nearly total blockade, unable to work toward the reconstruction of the damages inflicted by American and coalition aircraft in 1991 until more than a decade later. Water treatment was of particular concern as the system was devastated by the aerial bombardment. The US justified its continued refusal to allow these goods to be imported on grounds that they constituted 'dual use' and could be used in weapon's manufacture. In effect, very few items necessary to sustain human life could not fit this category.

The impact was devastating to the Iraqi population. Criminal behavior was encouraged, as Iraqi state officials took illicit payments from global purchasers of Iraqi crude in an ill-conceived campaign to circumvent United Nations sanctions—or worse, due to personal corruption. The shortage of goods, especially medicines and specialty food goods encouraged illicit 'black' markets and the porousness of Iraq's borders to neighboring states was exploited to establish a flourishing illicit supply of goods for needy Iraqis. Many sold valuables and then any remaining household goods in an effort to secure necessary medicines, foodstuffs as well as educational materials for children. Over the decade they remained in place, sanctions faced increasing popular opposition from across the world due to their negative impact on the civilian population broadly and children in particular. Imposed in an emergency situation, the sanctions regime had not been structured in a manner conducive to long-term implementation. United Nations humanitarian agencies as well as a number of international NGOs increasingly gathered data to support the notion that sanctions were having a devastating toll on the Iraqi people. In spite of such claims, and no matter the bona fides of their sources, the US refused to alter its policy and reduce the leverage they believed sanctions enabled over the Iraqi regime.

Numerous attempts at reforms were foiled by US actions, especially at the 661 committee. The efforts of the US to ensure any and all items added to Iraqi purchase orders, other states' attempts to deliver humanitarian goods, or a so-called green list of items other 661 committee members suggested could stand permanently as a list of goods not requiring committee oversight on a purchase-by-purchase basis, all met with rejection by US diplomats. US actions repeatedly were directed at preventing importation of goods required for reconstruction, as well as humanitarian supplies not directly tied to the most vulnerable. On the whole, it was apparent that the US meant to use sanctions as a blunt instrument to punish the Iraqi people in an effort to see Iraq denied any potential capacity to resuscitate a weapons program. This was further complicated by the US conflation of nuclear weapons with the euphemism 'weapons of mass destruction' or 'WMD'. This term conflated nuclear weapons with biological and chemical weapons in a manner not previously used within nonproliferation efforts. This was due to the immense difference in their production and maintenance procedures, with nuclear materials vastly more difficult to produce and manage. The term allowed for a wider list of goods to be identified as 'dual use' and added to the fears over Iraqi proliferation in spite of the fact that there was little evidence that they possessed capabilities in the nuclear field, while Iraqi scientists had proven capabilities in the chemical and biological areas, including weaponization, during the Iran-Iraq war (Razoux 2015). The biological and chemical weapons that Iraq had deployed against Iran required much lower levels of laboratory and factory production to ensure weapons capability. Moreover, all three presented areas were complicated by the knowledge base and necessity for a great many 'dual use' equipment and supplies for use in the oil industry and its corollary industries such as plastics and fertilizers. One primary example that impacted every Iraqi was the water treatment system, which required considerable equipment as well as chemicals for water purification. Water took on such importance, as left untreated, it could rapidly infect vulnerable members of society. However, even if the chemicals required to purify the water had been made available, it still would have been necessary to acquire the parts and then repair the pipes as they stood in such disrepair following 1991's bombardment and the inability to maintain the urban system for so many years without replacement parts and other required maintenance materials.

The levels of deprivation and humanitarian consequences of sanctions were catastrophic, although the numbers are nonetheless contested, even following the ouster of the Ba'ath regime. Such figures are by necessity always provided with a range of fatalities and impacted individuals although the headline number provided in executive summaries and media accounts garner the most attention. It is difficult to comprehend the apparent zeal of those wishing to debunk statistical estimates through critiques of methodology and allegations of regime interference in data collection. It remains that most all Iraqis suffered ill effects from the sanction's regime and that abnormally high numbers perished or suffered illness they would not otherwise have experienced had sanctions not been in place. The perniciousness of the policy and its implementation—for in spite of mitigation efforts the most vulnerable were always going to be the most directly affected—was never in doubt. Blockade and quarantine of an entire society in the modern era is rightly understood as an act of warfare and Iraqis were collectively punished for the actions of a tyrannical regime that no one saw as amenable to concerns over the humanitarian calamity being experienced by vulnerable Iraqis.

The sanctions regime against Iraq, however, came to be maintained alongside the US policy of dual containment. A cumbersome policy that was meant to blockade both Iraq and Iran under the Clinton administration through the use of US government or 'unilateral' sanctions. Not to be confused with the UN sanctions imposed on Iraq, the policy was meant to isolate both Gulf states. This effort to isolate Iran and maintain pressure on its ruling regime has continued with increasing sophistication. In spite of these efforts, US policy has not circumscribed Iran's ability to develop proxies and allies across the Arab world and beyond. For our purposes here, however, the critical distinction is in the inability of US policy-makers to forestall Iranian expansion of influence westward into Iraq. The 2003 US invasion and occupation of Iraq resulted in considerable Iranian influence and expanded economic opportunities in Iraq, where it has maintained an influential position since the earliest days of the US occupation. That such an eventuality was both predictable and most likely detrimental to the potential of an independent Iraq following regime change was an aspect of the operation not discussed openly by US decision-makers. Since 2003 there have been routine recriminations, especially following the failure of US plans in Iraq, from American academics and policy analysts; but, the empowerment of Iran as a consequence of the 2003 invasion will stand as one of the most consequential outcomes of that war.

THE OCCUPATION OF IRAQ AND THE NEW REGIME

Regime change in Iraq, as carried out through the exercise of Anglo-American force-of-arms, as with the examples of Afghanistan and Libya, entails external powers imposing their political will on weak and vulnerable societies. Where the strong dictate political conditions to the weak, the weak become dependent on the support of the dictating power(s). In the case of Iraq, a society that had been impoverished by a decade of economic sanctions, pummeled by military assault, and hollowed out through the deconstruction of the state, its newly empowered political class relied on external support over indigenous legitimacy. Much like the dictatorship they replaced, they had only minority support from among the Iraqi populace. Beyond their own narrow base within Iraq they looked predominantly, if not solely, to the support of, in the first instance, the Anglo-American occupation apparatus as the levers of state power.

Nevertheless, having spent much of their political careers outside Iraq, they increasingly came to rely on neighboring states and regional non-state actors. Not wishing to see opponents profit in Iraq, these state and transnational movement actors were increasingly compelled to support their Iraqi clients. The Islamic Republic of Iran, Turkey, the states of the Gulf Cooperation Council, as well as jihadist and other non-state political movements all came to engage Iraq and the state-building project initiated by the occupation. This tendency, the dependence of both political authorities and opposition actors on external powers, was reinforced by the nature of the political class that was empowered in post-invasion Iraq. In the process of deconstructing the Iraqi state (most prominently in de-Ba'athification and the disbanding of the national army), occupation authorities created a political vacuum. Aside from Kurdish parties in the north, this void of legitimacy was filled, not by indigenous anti-Saddam forces, but by repatriated diaspora Iraqis or 'carpetbaggers'. In the chaos of post-invasion Iraq, this new political class served as a chimera of sovereign authority, while centrifugal forces of political-sectarianism, corruption, and general chaos went unchecked and threatened the viability of Iraq as a coherent nation-state. The 'carpetbagger' class, in any case, were quite often implicated in the promotion of the political-sectarianism that dominated post-invasion Iraq, seeking to shore up their legitimacy through appeals to sub-national factionalism of dubious coherence. In such disarray, political office in Iraq often became little more than a vehicle for corruption and personal enrichment.

This combination of factors—military assault on a weaker state, the deconstruction/ reconstruction of a postcolonial-nationalist regime into a weak decentralized state, and the empowerment of an expatriate political class—created an environment in Iraq (and subsequently in Libya following the NATO 'intervention' in that country) that led not to comity and political development, but ruination. The reconstructed state was unable to assert credible political/military authority, allowing for the emergence of political-sectarian militias and tribal affiliations—dependent on external support—as the dominant features of the new (dis)order. This political reality, engineered by occupation authorities, has led to a humanitarian disaster for Iraqis, threatened regional disorder, and proved a challenge to the survival of Iraq as a nation. This is a clear abrogation of self-determination. Against this accumulation of social wreckage, very little in the realm of moral accounting has taken place in the congressional and parliamentary halls of power that planned and executed the Iraq war. Iraqis have been left to deal with consequences of great power politics while those who delivered such trauma remain impervious. Nonetheless, the Iraqi people have increasingly organized, often against an unresponsive and corrupt government, and their attempts to overcome such ruinous forces deserve our attention.

Regime change was a deliberate coercive policy pursued by external powers, and not the result of internal dynamics or forces. It is therefore no surprise that the post-2003 state, created through foreign interference, remained dependent on foreign interference in order to function as a repository for corruption. In other words, the state lacked internal legitimacy and viability, and was therefore non-self-sustaining. The role of the carpetbagger class of political elites is both a symptom of and means of the policy of regime change in the toolkit of foreign powers. Carpetbaggers, as repatriated expatriates who returned to the state targeted for regime change owe their role and influence to external allegiance(s). They have no internal power base or constituency and their role and status are non-self-sustaining. Their primary purpose is to grab all they can, while they can, and sending it outside the target country. This directly relates to the culture of corruption that proliferates in the aftermath of regime change. Regime change sets in motion a chain of events that leads to increasing internal violence and corruption, until the state itself dissolves into an isolated enclave of carpetbaggers (i.e., Iraq's 'Green Zone') under siege from warring factions blossoming among the indigenous population (i.e., Iraq's 'Red Zone'). The basic notion that the US brought the 'gift of democracy' to Iraq, leaving Iraq 'to its people and [as] a fully sovereign Iraqi state that could make decisions about its own future' (Obama 2014), is therefore simply unfounded. The system of government that has been imposed upon the people of Iraq is anything but a democracy. Rather, at the outset of the occupation, the US dismantled the institutions of the established political order and in their place gave Iraq a series of laws— Bremer's diktats through the Coalition Provisional Authority (CPA)— designed to open Iraq's borders to foreign money and influence, excise the extant bureaucracy and military, place the agents of the Anglo-American coalition above the law, and enshrine tribal fiefdoms and sectarian divisions that would become the undoing of the Iraqi nation. Although the CPA was dissolved in June 2004, many of its orders served as the foundation for Iraq's new constitution, which was itself drafted through a contentious selection of the new political class of carpetbaggers imported by the coalition.

Within Iraq's newly formulated constitution lies an assortment of pitfalls to the establishment of a democratic system. These include the lack of limits to government power and the lack of an effective division and separation of executive, legislative and judicial powers allowing for the power of each branch of government to be subject to checks and balances by the other branches. This political subversion of the country's administrative and bureaucratic institutions alongside the centralization of power within the PMO has highly distorted Iraqi 'democracy'.

Another major pitfall to democratization on the constitutional pathway to political development established by the new constitution was the lack of popular sovereignty. The political order that emerged in post-war Iraq was not a happenstance or merely the natural product of a sectarian cultural environment, but had the clear markings of design. The CPA orders at the outset of the Anglo-American occupation, the Iraqi constitution that was midwifed by the occupation authorities and the expatriate carpetbaggers supported by external power, and general political sectarian tone of post-invasion politics were the result of policy, not of some inherent Iraqi national character. Rather, the primacy of religious sectarianism was embedded within the Iraqi system through Article 2 of the Iraqi constitution, which established religion as the foundation of the Iraqi state. Political power in Iraq was thereafter exercised by elite sectarian, and highly corrupt, political blocs that have effectively shut out popular input into government policy, charting instead a blatantly sectarian course.

Pax Americana in the Middle East Since 1990

Our Pax Americana conceptual framing is an effort to reorient previous reliance on frameworks using political administrations or military campaign histories as templates in the scholarly production of knowledge. Perspectives focusing on a given four-year administration, or on a single country study, fail to examine what are often regional conflicts of interconnected social change taking place globally. Studies thus constrained decontextualize the examination and discourage the reader from engaging in richer social and economic histories. When examining the US and the decision-making process, such framings also blur the connection between US foreign policy and military interventions with US domestic politics and longer-term structural factors. Similarly, a focus on the George W. Bush administration's policy toward Iraq in comparison with that of Barak Obama can lead to the silencing of Iraqi voices whose experience of American foreign policy toward Iraq is more continuous, with distinctions between particular presidential administrations being less salient than the institutional culture of the US military and its operations while occupying Iraq. Such studies also reify individuals, no matter their authority and centrality to the issues being examined. The role of individual decision-makers can be crucial, but such interposition should lead to analysis of the individual rather than there being an expectation that every policy-maker, general or elected official impacts policy or events. Individuals miss certain complexities of the moment and always have limited knowledge.

Adoption of the Pax Americana heuristic has presented the reader with a challenge to this standard mode and method of presentation for US foreign policy. It suggests that the longstanding US posture toward Iraq evidenced considerable continuity from 1990 across seven administrations and four presidents (George H.W. Bush, Bill Clinton, George W. Bush and Barack Obama). It contextualizes how those administrations operated within an entrenched complex with a modus operandi to procure and sell military weaponry. How the 1991 war cemented the rising valorization of American martial culture initiated under Ronald Reagan with foreign intervention and calls for regime change proliferating across the US political elites. The 1991 war now embodies what may stand as the inauguration of contemporary American militarism and popular support for technological war-fighting technologies. As we approach what may become a declining trend in public support for military adventures following the wars in Iraq and Afghanistan, what has been termed 'micromilitarism' appears to be proliferating to compensate (Todd 2003). Such cultural markers increasingly saturate American popular culture, promoting the celebration of war as the primary organizing principle of society. While American military preponderance remains, the underlying technological and economic conditions which enable hard power, are in relative decline (McCoy 2017; Freier et al. 2017). Whether so-called peer competitors or non-state actors adopting asymmetrical technologies and tactics, the empirical reality of their ability to erode US technological and economic power has led to the renewal of debates over the potential for US decline and acknowledgment of the waning of the 'unipolar moment'. As we note in Chap. 4, the global interdependence of the 1990s that propelled American power has now allowed for others to also gain similar advantages.

Among those who expressly advocated for the wars in Iraq, the predominant refrain has been to note that the 2003 invasion and occupation was a 'mistake'. Often this admission is not further interrogated or explored. Connection with the events of 1990–1991 are left unconsidered. Yet, even for this seeming agreed 'mistake' no one has paid a price for advocating for policies toward the region that led to such a faulty outcome. Advocates for action in 2002 predominantly continue to advocate and call for action leading to the deployment of the US military today, whether with regard Iran, Venezuela or any number of so-called hot spots. The careerism (of military officers and public intellectuals) as well as the American propensity to situate in allied think tanks out-of-office foreign policy experts of the party not holding the executive, leads to the amplification of these think tanks while driving escalatory rhetoric as necessary conditions for differentiating one party from the other in the effort to attract electoral support. Consensus on principles were not always made coherent regarding their implications for the populations affected by US military intervention. There was little or no acknowledgment of the costs or predictable outcomes, nor the likely reactions by other actors holding an interest. There was largely silence concerning links between advocacy for American wars and the apparent interests of the military-industrial complex, and no evidence of accountability or learning. This stands in stark contrast to previous generations of US leaders. Without engaging in hagiography, one can nonetheless find evidence of greater deftness and a lower bar for expectations from the desire for maintaining predominance and hegemony. In his 1948 speech announcing the Marshall Plan, President Harry Truman emphasized fighting poverty, hunger, desperation, and chaos (Kurtz-Phelan 2018). This pragmatism, whereby American leaders recognized the prioritization of a population's basic economic and political needs was absent at each step of the relationship with Iraq. American decision-makers tasked with the occupation routinely became attached to an Iraqi politician, who they also desired to change in some fundamental ways. More than merely picking a side, Iraq represented the US fabricating a side, mobilizing members of the diaspora community that had no legitimacy within the indigenous population or capabilities to manage the state. Corruption and ineffectiveness followed. American support for Iraqi leaders throughout the new state and political order was disassociated from managerial acumen or assessment of outcomes for Iraqis.

As the historian John Coatsworth noted about American efforts in Latin America, many more civilians were killed and maimed by US proxies across that region from 1960 through 1990 than were killed by the communists they were nominally opposing (Dower 2018). US efforts from 1990 in the Middle East increasingly appear to parallel this experience. Those authoritarian regimes, repressive state apparatus' and illiberal non-state proxies supported by the US provision of training, financing, weapons and political protection both openly and covertly in the guise of promoting 'freedom', have instead perpetrated more violations of international humanitarian law, human rights, and the destruction of civil society while thwarting democratic values in an effort to retain their position under the umbrella provided by Pax Americana. The persistence and resilience demonstrated by Iraqis in the face of such abuses, imperial influence and the shredding of public trust and civil relations will, nevertheless, in time, manifest in self-governance. Recording of and accountability for the crimes perpetrated, insistence on adherence to international humanitarian law and efforts to remove barriers to the expression of popular sovereignty are all tasks that need to be taken up.

When the exercise of American power against Iraq and its population are framed in the light of the more than three decades from 1990, one recognizes the role such policies came to play in the humanitarian catastrophe Iraqis have endured. The Iraqi state and civil society have seen decades of social and economic advance rendered asunder under US blockade, war, and occupation. We have described this result as 'de-development': the successor state established under American auspices has failed to re-establish coherent or actionable development for the population, nor provide basic security as Iraqi individuals are laid bare in the face of an onslaught of criminality, corruption and non-state political actors deploying terrorism to effect political change. The hollowing out of state institutions under sanctions and their lack of capacity to deliver for populations or protect national sovereignty is directly related to the policies imposed through the United Nations and US-led coalition from 1990. The devastation of organized civil society and the forced migration of the intellectuals and technocrats required to rebuild the national infrastructure responsive to Iraqis continues to make the Iraqi population vulnerable and unable to access foreign support. In addition, the rise of non-state actors and illicit crime networks continues to undermine state capacity and personal safety.

The Pax Americana framing suggests a desultory US policy driving ill-considered actions that extend beyond Iraq. These suggest the need for further inquiry and research across the various locales that have seen US military deployment since 1990. Pax Americana:

- saw direct military intervention, followed by expansive basing of US military forces across the region (rather than standing so-called over the horizon as was the case prior to 1990);
- tied virtually every regional state into a hub-and-spoke relationship with the US that retarded regional state-to-state efforts for deeper political and economic relations;
- enmeshed the region into a so-called global economy based on neo-liberal economic orthodoxy;
- attempted to isolate the Islamic Republic of Iran and Syria from the region;
- advanced US preponderance over the so-called peace process between Palestinians and Israel;
- infused US diplomacy into state- and sub-region or ethnic minority separatist cleavages (Kurdistan, Western Sahara, South Yemen); and
- extended US military commitment to selected winners in the region (Saudi Arabia, Israel, UAE, etc.).

Nearly three decades later, all these policies and initiatives have proven to be failures. The American presence has been indirectly tied to the rise of extremism broadly, including the al-Qaida network and its successor, ISIS, while seeing the increased pace and scope of direct engagement in military conflict between US forces and varied regional actors. Regional cooperation and integration efforts have been largely non-existent, with the Arab world noted by economists as the least successful economies and markets to trade with even close neighbors. Similarly, with the notable exceptions of petroleum and finance, the development of connections to the global economy have been largely muted in comparison with other regions. Although Iran's influence faces limitations due to historic enmities and cultural differences, it has increased its regional geostrategic power markedly since 1990 through proxies and allies in a number of Arab-majority states and is developing new links beyond the region with the Shanghai Cooperation Organization (SCO) and its members, notably China and Russia. The Palestinians have been further marginalized, while Israeli settlement expansion has only escalated removing any coherent potential for a two-state solution. Regional sub-state actors have seen advances in autonomy within states, including institutionalization as is the case with the Kurdistan Regional Government (KRG) in Iraq, although such movements have suffered setbacks (as discussed in Chap. 3) and have not secured a stable future, whether within their current states or through full-fledged independence. US military bases helped fuel Saudi and Emirati recklessness and abandonment of diplomacy, whether in dealing within the GCC, Yemen, conflicted Arab states such as Syria, or with regard to the Islamic Republic, the American presence has empowered the monarchies to a more direct exercise of power across the region.

China's recent diplomatic initiatives, notably its summit with Arab countries in Riyadh and its brokering of a reconciliation between the Saudis and Iran, poses a challenge to the hitherto hegemonic status of the US (Global Times 2022; Bhadrakumar 2023). Most critically for our purposes, at least four states (Iraq, Libya, Syria and Yemen) have been devastated to a condition where state institutions developed since independence following the Second World War now lack the necessary capacity to support civilian populations. All four states experienced, and Syria and Iraq continue to experience, substantial intervention by US-led military coalitions that often include regional states. Major military action against Iraq and Libya and significant direct action (weapons and material support to local proxies) in Syria and Yemen have altered the region in a manner unseen in modern memory. This experience has destroyed states, ripped the social fabric of communities and brought about a process of de-development that has undermined and reversed the (albeit limited) gains of the region's modern state apparatus.

Iraq has had the great misfortune of being at the bull's-eye of American imperial penetration of the Middle East, having provided both the incentives (an Arab nationalist regime opposing Israeli regional hegemony, the location of one of the largest petroleum reserves, and the increasing dip-lomatic ineptitude and isolation of its leadership), and the legitimate occa-sion (Saddam Hussein's invasion of Kuwait) for the neoconservative-leaning administrations of Bush senior, Clinton and Bush junior, to make a demonstrative example of Iraq, as once were public executions, *'pour encourager les autres'*. Originally promoted as the application of interna-tional law through the United Nations to repel and punish aggression, the application of trade sanctions and the American-led blockade and bomb-ing of Iraqi forces and infrastructure became widely understood as a proj-ect for regime change and consolidation of Pax Americana.

This chapter has identified the American policy and actions surround-ing the Gulf War as the pivotal moment for the emergence of Pax Americana. No sooner had the phrase been uttered in public than it was already generally acknowledged as an unstoppable force.

Chapter 2, 'Iraq Burning', reviews a collection of case studies (Baker et al. 2010) of the immediate social and cultural consequences of the 2003 invasion, which the overall pattern of desolation indicates, was directed at the termination of the Iraqi state, consistent with the neoconservative agenda of ending states which, according to that narrative, supported ter-rorism. Independent confirmation of the successful implementation of this diabolic agenda is furnished in several reports by international and non-governmental organizations.

Chapter 3, 'Kurdistan and the Iraqi State', focuses on the principal ethnic dimension affecting Iraqi politics dating from the period of British domination and tracing its impact in relations with regional powers and with the imperial hegemon. The Kurdish leaders' longstanding practice of using diplomacy with foreign powers in their struggles with successive regimes in Baghdad have eroded their ability to develop mutually benefi-cial alliances within the post-invasion regime, while failure to develop their own political institutions and democratic culture have compromised their legitimacy and power, internally and externally. The story of the Kurds is illustrative of the typical fate of the proxy under Pax Americana.

Chapter 4, 'Two Faces of Pax Americana', places the destruction of Iraq within the logic of the wider Pax Americana project and proposes an interpretation of the elite decision-making leading up to the invasion. Intended by neoconservative policymakers as the threshold to a global imperial era, Iraq continues to be the site of resurgent challenges to American domination of the region, as the forces, policies and practices that heretofore enabled the ascent of Pax Americana now contribute toward its dissolution.

References

Aburish, Said K. 1997. *A Brutal Friendship: The West and The Arab Elite*. Victor Gollancz.

Amin, Samir. 1992. *Empire of Chaos*. New York: Monthly Review Press.

Bacevich, Andrew J. 2013. *The New American Militarism: How Americans Are Seduced by War*. Oxford University Press.

———. 2016. *America's War for the Greater Middle East: A Military History*. Random House.

Baker, Raymond W., Shereen T. Ismael, and Tareq Y. Ismael. 2010. *Cultural Cleansing in Iraq: Why Museums Were Looted, Libraries Burned and Academics Murdered*. Pluto Press.

Beier, J. Marshall. 2003. Discriminating Tastes: "Smart" Bombs, Non-Combatants, and Notions of Legitimacy in Warfare. *Security Dialogue* 34: 4.

Bhadrakumar, M.K. 2023. China Steps Up, a New Era Has Dawned in World Politics. *Indian Punchline*, 11 March, https://www.indianpunchline.com/china-steps-up-a-new-era-has-dawned-in-world-politics/. Accessed 8 April 2023.

Blumi, Isa. 2018. *Destroying Yemen*. University of California Press.

Bolger, Daniel P. 2014. *Why We Lost: A General's Inside Account of the Iraq and Afghanistan Wars*. Mariner Books.

Brownlee, Jason. 2012. *Democracy Prevention: The Politics of the U.S.-Egyptian Alliance*. Cambridge University Press.

Bush, George H.W. 1991. President Bush Annual UN Address, 23 September, 46th session of the UN General Assembly. https://2009-2017.state.gov/p/io/potusunga/207269.htm. Accessed 18 May 2023.

Cockburn, Patrick. 1997. Revealed: How the West Set Saddam on the Bloody Road to Power. *The Independent*, 28 June, https://www.independent.co.uk/news/world/revealed-how-the-west-set-saddam-on-the-bloody-road-to-power-1258618.html. Accessed 14 April 2023.

Daher, Joseph. 2019. *Syria after the Uprisings: The Political Economy of State Resilience*. Haymarket Books.

Dawisha, Adeed. 2003. *Arab Nationalism in the Twentieth Century: From Triumph to Despair*. Princeton University Press. https://epdf.pub/arab-nationalism-in-the-twentieth-century-from-triumph-to-despair.html. Accessed 6 June 2023.

DeGhett, Torie Rose. 2014. The War Photo No One Would Publish. *Atlantic Magazine*, 8 August 2014, https://www.theatlantic.com/international/archive/2014/08/the-war-photo-no-one-would-publish/375762/. Accessed 18 May 2023.

Der Derian, James. 2009. *Virtuous War: Mapping the Military-Industrial-Media-Entertainment-Network*. 2nd ed. Routledge.

Dobbs, Michael. 2002. U.S. Had Key Role in Iraq Buildup. *Washington Post*, 30 December.

Dower, John W. 2018. *The Violent American Century: War and Terror Since World War II*. Haymarket Books.

Escobar, Pepe. 2014. *Empire of Chaos*. Nimble Pluribus.

Esposti, Nicola Degli. 2022. Land Reform and Kurdish Nationalism in Postcolonial Iraq. London School of Economics & Political Science, UK. http://eprints. lse.ac.uk/114977/1/31.2.Degli_Esposti.Copyedited.pdf, and Middle East Critique, 31:2, pp. 147–163, April, https://doi.org/10.1080/19436149.202 2.2055517. Accessed 21 June 2023.

Feinstein, Andrew. 2012. *Shadow World: Inside the Global Arms Trade*. Picador.

Forte, Maximilian C. 2012. *Slouching Towards Sirte: NATO's War on Libya and Africa*. Baraka Books.

Freier, Nathan P., Christopher M. Bado, Christopher J. Bolan Colonel, and Robert S. Hume. 2017. At Our Own Peril: DoD Risk Assessment in a Post-Primacy World. SSI The U.S. Army War College, June, https://ssi.armywarcollege. edu/pubs/display.cfm?pubID=1358.

Fukuyama, Francis. 1993. *The End of History and the Last Man*. Free Press.

Gani, Jasmine. 2019. US Policy Towards the Syrian Conflict Under Obama: Strategic Patience and Miscalculation. In *The War for Syria: Regional and International Dimensions of the Syrian Uprising*, ed. Raymond Hinnebusch and Adham Saouli. Routledge.

Global Times. 2022. Xi's Mideast Trip Ushers in a New Era of Relations between China and Arab Countries: FM. *Global Times-Xinhua*, 11 December, https:// www.globaltimes.cn/page/202212/1281586.shtml.   Accessed   15 December 2022.

Gorbachev Foundation. 1990. Document 14: Gorbachev Memcon with U.S. Secretary of State James Baker, Moscow, September 13, National Security   Archive.   https://nsarchive.gwu.edu/briefing-book/russia-programs/2020-09-09/inside-gorbachev-bush-partnership-first-gulf-war-1990. Accessed 20 July 2023.

Gordon, Joy. 2012. *Invisible War: The United States and the Iraq Sanctions*. Harvard University Press.

Haass, Richard N. 2010. *War of Necessity, War of Choice: A Memoir of Two Iraq Wars*. Simon & Schuster.

Hallion, Richard. 1997. *Storm over Iraq: Air Power and the Gulf War*. Smithsonian Institution.

Hanieh, Adam. 2018. *Money, Markets, and Monarchies: The Gulf Cooperation Council and the Political Economy of the Contemporary Middle East*. Cambridge University Press.

Hersh, Seymour. 2000. Overwhelming Force: What Happened in the Final Days of the Gulf War? *The New Yorker*, 22 May.

Hinnebusch, Raymond A. 2016. Egypt, Syria and the Arab State System in the New World Order. In *The Middle East in the New World Order*, ed. Haifaa A. Jawad, 2nd ed., 162–182. Springer.

IDMC. 2019. *Global Report on Internal Displacement 2019*. The Internal Displacement Monitoring Centre (IDMC). www.internal-displacement.org/global-report/grid2019. Accessed 18 May 2023.

Immerwahr, Daniel. 2019. *How to Hide an Empire: A History of the Greater United States*. Farrar, Straus and Giroux.

Ismael, Tareq Y., and Jacqueline S. Ismael, eds. 1991. *The Gulf War and the New World Order: International Relations of the Middle East*. University Press of Florida.

———. 2015. *Iraq in the Twenty-First Century: Regime Change and the Making of a Failed State*. Routledge.

———. 2021. *Iraq in the Twenty-First Century: Regime Change and the Making of a Failed State*. Routledge.

Johnston, Charles. 2000. *Blowback: The Costs and Consequences of American Empire*. Metropolitan Books.

Johnston, Chalmers. 2004. *The Sorrows of Empire: Militarism, Secrecy, and the End of the Republic*. Metropolitan Books.

Kadri, Ali. 2015. *Arab Development Denied: Dynamics of Accumulation by Wars of Encroachment*. Anthem Press.

———. 2016. *The Unmaking of Arab Socialism*. Anthem Press.

Kamrava, Mehran. 2018. *Inside the Arab State*. Hurst.

Khouri, Rami. 2019. Why We Should Worry About the Arab Region, *Agence Global*, 10 February, https://www.belfercenter.org/publication/why-we-should-worry-about-arab-region. Accessed 9 May 2023.

Kinzer, Stephen. 2007. *Overthrow: America's Century of Regime Change from Hawaii to Iraq*. Times Books.

———. 2017. *The True Flag: Theodore Roosevelt, Mark Twain, and the Birth of American Empire*. Henry Holt and Co.

Kuperman, Alan. 2013. A Model Humanitarian Intervention? Reassessing NATO's Libya Campaign. *International Security* 38 (1, Summer): 105–136.

Kurtz-Phelan, Daniel. 2018. *The China Mission: George Marshall's Unfinished War, 1945–1947*. W. W. Norton & Company.

Lackner, Helen. 2019. *Yemen in Crisis: Road to War*. Verso.

Lukin, Alexander. 2016. Russia in a Post-Bipolar World. *Survival: Global Politics and Strategy* 58 (1, Feb.): 91–112.

MacArthur, John R. 1994. *Second Front: Censorship and Propaganda in the 1991 Gulf War*. University of California Press.

Mansoor, Peter R. 2013. *Surge: My Journey with General David Petraeus and the Remaking of the Iraq War*. Yale University Press.

Matthews, W.C. 2011. The Kennedy Administration, Counterinsurgency, and Iraq's First Ba'thist Regime. *International Journal of Middle East Studies 43* (4): 635–653.

McCoy, Alfred W. 2017. *In the Shadows of the American Century: The Rise and Decline of US Global Power.* Haymarket Books.

Mearsheimer, John J. 2014. Why the Ukraine Crisis Is the West's Fault: The Liberal Delusions That Provoked Putin. *Foreign Affairs* 93: 77–84, September/October, https://www.foreignaffairs.com/articles/russia-fsu/2014-08-18/why-ukraine-crisis-west-s-fault. Accessed 11 January 2024.

———. 2015. UnCommon Core: The Causes and Consequences of the Ukraine Crisis (vid.). University of Chicago, 25 September, https://www.youtube.com/watch?v=JrMiSQAGOS4. Accessed 11 January 2024.

———. 2018. *The Great Delusion: Liberal Dreams and International Realities.* Yale University Press.

Mearsheimer, John J., and Stephen M. Walt. 2009. An Unnecessary War. *Foreign Policy*, 3 November, https://foreignpolicy.com/2009/11/03/an-unnecessary-war-2/. Accessed 1 April 2023.

Mitchell, Timothy. 2013. *Carbon Democracy: Political Power in the Age of Oil.* Verso.

Morris, Roger. 2003. A Tyrant 40 Years in the Making. *New York Times,* 14 March, https://www.nytimes.com/2003/03/14/opinion/a-tyrant-40-years-in-the-making.html. Accessed 19 May 2023.

Muttitt, Greg. 2012. *Fuel on the Fire: Oil and Politics in Occupied Iraq.* The New Press.

Nye, Joseph S., Jr. 2022. What New World Order? *Foreign Affairs*, Spring 1992. https://www.foreignaffairs.com/united-states/what-new-world-order. Accessed 15 December 2022.

Obama, Barack. 2014. 'Remarks by the President in Address to European Youth'. The White House, 26 March, https://obamawhitehouse.archives.gov/the-press-office/2014/03/26/remarks-president-addresseuropean-youth#:~:text= But even in Iraq, America,decisions about its own future. Accessed 21 June 2024.

Parry, Robert. 2015. Saddam's "Green Light". *Consortium News*, 11 May, https://consortiumnews.com/2015/05/11/saddams-green-light/. Accessed 3 April 2023.

Prashad, Vijay. 2012. *Arab Spring, Libyan Winter.* AK Press.

Putin, Vladimar. 2022a. Address by the President of the Russian Federation, 24 February 2022, President of Russia, http://en.kremlin.ru/events/president/news/67843. Accessed 20 February 2024.

———. 2022b. Western "Empire of Lies" Has Resources, But It Cannot Defeat Truth and Justice—Putin. *TASS*, 16 March 2022, https://tass.com/world/1423145. Accessed 4 February 2023.

Razoux, Pierre. 2015. *The Iran-Iraq War.* Translated by Nicholas Elliott. Belknap Press.

Roberts, Hugh. 2011. Who Said Gaddafi Had to Go? *London Review of Books* 33 (22, Nov.): 8–18.

Ross, Carne. 2016. Iraq: The Story of My Evidence. *Personal Blog*, 13 June, https://www.carneross.com/index.php/2016/06/13/iraq-the-story-of-my-evidence/. Accessed 19 May 2023.

———. 2017. *Independent Diplomat: Despatches from an Unaccountable Elite.* C Hurst & Co Publishers.

Rossi, Lorenza, Rochelle Davis, Grace Benton, Sinan Zeyneloglu, and Salma Al-Shami. 2018. Iraqi IDPs Access to Durable Solutions: Results of Two Rounds of a Longitudinal Study. *International Migration* 57 (2, Apr.): 48–64.

Sachs, Jeffrey, and Chris Hedges. 2023. What JFK Tried to Do Before His Assassination (vid.). *The Chris Hedges Report, The Real News Network*, 29 September, https://www.youtube.com/watch?v=Wqm9Yl1gGEY. Accessed 29 January 2024.

Sassoon, Joseph. 2011. *Saddam Hussein's Ba'th Party: Inside an Authoritarian Regime.* Cambridge University Press.

Simon, Steven, and Jonathan Stevensonm. 2015. The End of Pax Americana: Why Washington's Middle East Pullback Makes Sense. *Foreign Affairs,* November–December, https://www.foreignaffairs.com/articles/middle-east/end-pax-americana. Accessed 19 May 2023.

SIPRI. 2019. Global Arms Trade: USA Increases Dominance; Arms Flows to the Middle East Surge. Stockholm International Peace Research Institute, 11 March, https://www.sipri.org/media/press-release/2019/global-arms-trade-usa-increases-dominance-arms-flows-middle-east-surge-says-sipri. Accessed 19 May 2023.

Sjursen, Danny. 2015. *Ghost Riders of Baghdad: Soldiers, Civilians, and the Myth of the Surge.* ForeEdge / University Press of New England.

Sky, Emma. 2016. *The Unraveling: High Hopes and Missed Opportunities in Iraq.* Public Affairs.

Farouk–Sluglett, Marion, and Peter Sluglett. 2001. *Iraq Since 1958: From Revolution to Dictatorship.* I.B. Tauris.

Todd, Emmanuel. 2003. *After the Empire: The Breakdown of the American Order.* Translated by C. Jon Delogu. Columbia University Press.

Tripp, Charles. 2007. *A History of Iraq.* 3rd ed. Cambridge University Press.

Vogler, Gary. 2017. *Iraq and the Politics of Oil: An Insider's Perspective.* University Press of Kansas.

Walt, Stephen M. 2019. *The Hell of Good Intentions: America's Foreign Policy Elite and the Decline of U.S. Primacy.* Picador.

Zhang Zhouxiang. 2022. The "Empire of lies" Is the US. *China Daily*, March 13, http://global.chinadaily.com.cn/a/202203/13/WS622d4de9a310cdd39bc8c3a6.html. Accessed 9 May 2023.

CHAPTER 2

Iraq Burning

ENDING 'STATES THAT SPONSOR TERRORISM'

Addressing Americans on the evening of the devastating attacks of September 11, 2001, President G.W. Bush declared that he would go after the terrorists who had attacked the US and 'make no distinction between the terrorists who committed these acts and those who harbor them' (Bush 2001a). On September 13, Deputy Defense Secretary Paul Wolfowitz declared that a major focus of US foreign policy would be 'ending states that sponsor terrorism' (Kirk 2003). Responding to a reporter's question shortly afterward, Jerome Powell, re-interpreted Wolfowitz' interpretation of the President's statement: 'We're after ending terrorism, and if there are states and regimes, nations that support terrorism, we hope to persuade them that it is in their interests to stop doing that. But I think ending terrorism is where I would like to leave it, and let—let Mr. Wolfowitz speak for himself' (Kirk). Wolfowitz later corrected his 'misstatement' to meaning 'ending terrorism' (Wolfowitz 2001) but as late as November, after the US coalition had invaded Afghanistan under the banner of 'Operation Enduring Freedom', a BBC journalist interviewing Wolfowitz seemed not to be aware of the distinction Wolfowitz had made, and two years after the invasion of Iraq, Wolfowitz' original avowed 'misstatement' still was widely understood as an accurate characterization of the Bush administration's 'mission' and of the 'Bush Doctrine' (Wilhelmsen and Flikke 2005). Taking into account the calamitous consequences of the

J. S. Ismael et al., *Pax Americana*, Frontiers of Globalization, https://doi.org/10.1007/978-3-031-61273-2_2

Bush Doctrine and the Iraq invasion for states and societies in the Middle East, Wolfowitz' correction, while a sign that not all members of the Bush administration were always on the same page (Kirk 2003), remains more a distinction without a difference.

In his speech to a joint session of Congress on September 20, President Bush declared that '[t]he Taliban must act, and act immediately [to] hand over the terrorists, or they will share in their fate', [and] any nation that continues to harbor or support terrorism will be regarded by the United States as a hostile regime' (Bush 2001b). Bush did not specify in his speech which countries aside from Afghanistan were to be targeted, although he had already told Tony Blair, on September 14, that 'he was planning to "hit" Iraq soon'. Blair, "audibly taken aback ..." pressed Bush for evidence of Iraq's connection to the 9/11 attack and to al-Qaida. Of course, there was none, which British intelligence knew' (Riedel 2021; Stein and Dickinson 2006). Four days later, in a White House conversation, with Cheney and Rice present, Bush told Saudi Ambassador Prince Bandar bin Sultan that 'Iraq must be behind this', to which Bandar responded that 'the Saudis had no evidence of any collaboration between Osama bin Laden and Iraq' (Riedel). Bruce Riedel, at the time on the staff of the National Security Council, related that Bander later told him that the Saudis were 'were very worried about where Bush's obsession with Iraq was going. The Saudis were alarmed that attacking Iraq would only benefit Iran and set in motion severe destabilizing repercussions across the region' (Riedel). And on September 28, Bush received Jordan's King Abdullah, who, like Bander, 'pressed the president to take action to restart Israeli-Palestinian peace talks. He argued that the Palestinian conflict was the driving force behind al-Qaida's popularity and legitimacy. But the president was focused on Iraq' (Riedel). Further evidence of Bush's intent: General Wesley Clark (2007) discovered in a visit with former colleagues at the Pentagon around the same time, that Secretary of Defense Rumsfeld had produced a 'hit list of seven countries in five years ... starting with Iraq, and then Syria, Lebanon, Libya, Somalia, Sudan and, finishing off, Iran'. By the end of November, Rumsfeld had ordered planning to begin for an invasion of Iraq (National Security Archive 2001).

President Bush went on to declare in his 2002 State of the Union address (Bush 2002a):

> States like [Iraq, Iran and North Korea] and their terrorist allies, constitute an axis of evil, arming to threaten the peace of the world. By seeking weapons of mass destruction, these regimes pose a grave and growing danger. They

could provide these arms to terrorists, giving them the means to match their hatred. They could attack our allies or attempt to blackmail the United States. In any of these cases, the price of indifference would be catastrophic.

Bush said he would 'not wait on events, while dangers gather. I will not stand by, as peril draws closer and closer. The United States of America will not permit the world's most dangerous regimes to threaten us with the world's most destructive weapons'.

And again, four months later, at the West Point graduation ceremony:

We cannot put our faith in the word of tyrants, who solemnly sign non-proliferation treaties, and then systemically break them. If we wait for threats to fully materialize, we will have waited too long … the war on terror will not be won on the defensive. We must take the battle to the enemy, disrupt his plans, and confront the worst threats before they emerge. (Bush 2002b)

This is an implied doctrine of war justified on the grounds of preemptive self-defense, the definitive public case for which was skillfully made by US Secretary of State, Jerome Powell, in an audio-visual presentation at the United Nations Security Council (USNC) on February 5, 2003, that Iraqi President Saddam Hussein

harbors ambitions for regional domination, hides weapons of mass destruction and provides haven and active support for terrorists, we are not confronting the past, we are confronting the present. And unless we act, we are confronting an even more frightening future. (Powell 2003)

However, Powell's charges were refuted on March 7 by Hans Blix, chairman of UNMOVIC, the UN's weapons inspectors, and Mohamed ElBaradei, director-general of the International Atomic Energy Agency (Lauria 2023). Most UNSC members were not persuaded that the case had been made to go to war and the resolution jointly sponsored by the US, the UK and Spain was withdrawn. Powell later admitted that much of his presentation was inaccurate, and that it was a 'blot' on his reputation (Powell 2005). He, and much of the American commentary, took some consolation in that it was 'faulty' intelligence that had led to what was presented as an honest mistake. However, some American intelligence professionals have been less generous with Powell and his colleagues in the Bush administration:

Veteran Intelligence Professionals for Sanity were able to see what was coming, and warned Bush on the afternoon of Powell's speech to be wary of 'those advisers clearly bent on a war for which we see no compelling reason and from which we believe the unintended consequences are likely to be catastrophic.' VIPS followed up with two more Memos before the March 2003 U.S./UK attack on Iraq (McGovern 2023a).

Former UNSCOM weapons inspector, Scott Ritter, who had persuaded Saddam Hussein to readmit the weapons inspectors to head off a war, agrees that the invasion was not a mistake and that Powell cannot claim to have been fooled by faulty intelligence:

> He knew. He knew about the existence of the C.I.A.'s Iraq Operations Group. He knew of the successive string of covert 'findings' issued by U.S. presidents authorizing the C.I.A. to remove Saddam Hussein from power using lethal force. He knew that the die had been cast for war long before Bush 43 decided to engage the United Nations in the fall of 2002. … Powell knew all of this, and yet he still allowed himself to be used as a front to sell this conflict to the international community, and by extension the American people, using intelligence that was demonstrably false. If, simply by drawing on my experience as an UNSCOM inspector, I knew every word he uttered before the Security Council was a lie the moment he spoke, Powell should have as well, because every aspect of my work as an UNSCOM inspector was known to, and documented by, the C.I.A. … America went to war because it was our policy as a nation, sustained over three successive presidential administrations, to remove Saddam Hussein from power. (Ritter 2023a)

While many would continue to debate whether mistake, lie or crime (*New York Times* 2004; UK 2016; Hughes 2016; Kaleck 2016; Hathaway 2016; Bellinger 2016; Falk 2017; Riedel 2021; Husseini 2023), Powell told a reporter he was 'glad that Saddam's regime was toppled' (Powell 2005). Wolfowitz' initial, if impolitic expression of American policy as 'ending states that sponsor terrorism' (for the moment, let us give the US the benefit of the doubt as to the validity of the charge of, itself, sponsoring terrorism) was closer to the *de facto* policy acted upon, by both Republican and Democratic administrations, including the 2003 invasion without approval of the UNSC (Hedges 2023).

Mainstream social science has yet to come to terms with the full meaning of 'ending states' as a policy objective. Social science in the era of post-World War II decolonization has focused for the most part on the study of state-building and development. The primary axis of contention among development scholars and policy makers has been between one school espousing state-driven development models and a second advocating neo-liberal market approaches. Little has been written by either school on the question of state-destruction and de-development. Such outcomes have generally been seen as the by-products of war and civil-strife, rather than as desirable policy outcomes. Critical scholarship has challenged the adequacy of such dominant views. Critics draw attention to such phenomena as covert regime subversion, targeted assassinations, death squads, and ethnic cleansing. Such phenomena tend to be dismissed by the mainstream as representing criminal excess rather than explicit state policies. However, the preeminent superpower, the US, and its junior partner Israel, have had a hand in such activities for many decades. This important historical record of such activity tends to be reduced to CIA/Mossad excesses and the product of operating in a 'tough neighborhood', plagued by supposed age-old conflicts and religious extremism. In light of Iraq, such dismissals or rationalizations no longer suffice. There are precedents for violence aimed at undermining or destroying states, although it is the magnitude of the destruction in Iraq that makes unavoidable the recognition and analysis of state-ending as a deliberate policy objective.

The consequences in human and cultural terms of the destruction of the Iraqi state have been enormous: notably, the deaths of over 1 million civilians, the degradation of social infrastructure, including electricity, potable water, and sewage systems; the targeted assassination of over 400 academics and professionals and the displacement of approximately 4 million refugees and internally displaced persons (Baker et al. 2010). All of these terrible losses are compounded by unprecedented levels of cultural devastation, attacks on national archives and monuments that represent the historical identity of the Iraqi people. Rampant chaos and violence hamper efforts at reconstruction, leaving the foundations of the Iraqi state in ruin. Western journalists, academics, and political figures have for the most part refused to recognize the loss of life on such a massive scale and the cultural destruction that accompanied it as the fully predictable consequences of American occupation policy. It would seem that the very idea is considered unthinkable, despite the openness with which this objective was pursued.

It is time to think the unthinkable. The American-led assault on Iraq forces us to consider the meaning and consequences of state-destruction as a policy objective. The architects of the Iraq policy never made explicit what deconstructing and reconstructing the Iraqi state would entail; their actions, however, make the meaning clear. From those actions in Iraq, a fairly precise definition of state-ending can now be read. The campaign to destroy the state in Iraq involved first the removal and execution of Saddam Hussein and the capture of Ba'ath Party figures. However, state destruction went beyond regime change. It also entailed the purposeful dismantling of major state institutions and the launching of a prolonged process of political reshaping.

Contemporary Iraq represents a fragmented pastiche of sectarian forces with the formal trappings of liberal democracy and neoliberal economic structures. Students of history will recognize in the occupation of Iraq the time-honored technique of imperial *divide et imperia* (divide and rule), used to fracture and subdue culturally cohesive regions. The regime installed by occupation forces in Iraq reshaped the country along divisive sectarian lines, dissolving the hard-won unity of a long state-building project. The so-called sovereign Iraqi government, the Iraqi Governing Council (IGC), established by the Coalition Provisional Authority (CPA), was founded as a sectarian ruling body, with a system of quotas for ethnic and confessional groupings. This formula decisively established the sectarian parameters of the 'new Iraq'.

In parallel fashion the occupiers have redesigned the former nationalistic and state-centered economy to conform to an extreme neoliberal market model marked by privatization and the opening of the fragile Iraqi market to foreign capital, especially American. Nowhere is this more evident than in the dismantling of Iraq's national industries. The oil sector in particular was opened to the domination of non-Iraqi, predominantly US companies. Iraq's national industries, the backbone of the country's autonomous national project, were auctioned off through a wrenching process of privatization, plagued by corruption. Iraq's central bank was prohibited outright from financing state-owned enterprise. With the collapse of trade tariffs and tax regimes, Iraq's private sector was overwhelmed by foreign competition.

The political and economic reengineering of Iraq under occupation demands critical evaluation. The Iraq invasion, however, brings into view the equally consequential human and cultural dimensions of state destruction as a war aim. State- ending in Iraq was a comprehensive policy. However, its human and cultural dimensions have yet to be as fully documented and analyzed as an integral part of the destruction of the Iraqi state. The horrors of cultural destruction and targeted assassinations in

Iraq are still seen for the most part as a mere consequence of war and social disorder. The mainstream narrative bemoans the loss of world class cultural treasures and views the murders of individuals through the prism of human rights violations as 'collateral damage'.

Such views obscure more than they reveal. Few would question that state-building has an integral cultural and human dimension. So too, does state-destruction. To be remade, a state must be rendered malleable. Obstacles to this goal in Iraq included an impressive intelligentsia committed to a different societal model and the unifying culture they shared. The actions of the occupying forces indicate that they understood that the emergence of the new Iraq would require liberation from the grip of the inherited intelligentsia and culture of a unified Iraq. Iraq under occupation would see both human and cultural erasures that advanced these goals. Thus, state destruction in Iraq entailed more than regime change and more than political and economic restructuring. It also required cultural cleansing, understood in the Iraqi case as the degrading of a unifying culture and the depletion of an intelligentsia tied to the old order (Baker et al.: ch. 2). The occupiers acted accordingly. For this cultural and social dimension of state destruction, however, we do not have the same explicit policy directives as for the project of political and economic remaking. Nor was the process itself as straightforward. The cultural cleansing of Iraq was achieved in large part by inaction. The occupiers fostered and legitimated a climate of lawlessness with the wholly predictable consequence of weakening a unifying culture and eliminating an intelligentsia that had staffed Iraq's public institutions. One would be hard pressed to find an explicit admission of such aims from the architects of Iraqi occupation. Yet, the issues cannot be avoided simply in absence of an explicit policy declaration along these lines. The parallel cases of Bosnia, Palestine, and the 2008 Israeli rampage in Gaza make it imperative to put the cultural and human dimensions of ideologically driven state destruction front and center. Talk of incompetent planning and 'collateral damage' in the context of a global war against terrorism persuades many precisely because the very idea of deliberate cultural destruction and targeted murders on so wide a scale is so unthinkable to the mainstream.

Ironically, the unembarrassed ideological context within which Iraq was invaded makes it easier to challenge effectively the mainstream inclination to disregard cultural destruction as willed policy. State-ending in Iraq was explicitly intended to have an instructive effect. The invasion of Iraq had the larger purpose of demonstrating precisely how unchallengeable and unrestrained the shock and awe of American power would be to all those forces that stood in its way. Massive loss of life and cultural devastation were acceptable, if not actually desired. For the demonstration of the power of the sole superpower the deaths and depredations were in many ways the most chilling markers. At the same time, ideological forces that set and defined these objectives of state- ending in Iraq stepped out of the shadows and took center stage. To be sure, the real motives behind the assault were covered by the useful talk of 'terror' and liberation. However, it was important for the demonstration effect that the assault itself and the havoc it caused be screened as fully as possible. Consequently, there could be no doubt as to what those forces were, no matter the dis- simulations that obscured their purposes. The ideologically driven aim of state-ending derived from a confluence of influences that included American neoconservatism and its imperial ambitions, Israeli expansionism and its drive for regional domination, and Western multinationals and their relentless quest to regain control of Iraqi oil.

Ideological Imperatives for a 'New' Iraq: The Neoconservative Movement

The cultural and social destruction of Iraq was foreshadowed by a decade of ideological statements and policy planning. And with the controversial presidential election of George W. Bush in 2000, and the *casus belli* provided by the 9/11 terrorist attacks, this ideological vision was put in practice, Iraq representing the preeminent test case. The neoconservative policy pursued an objective to 'remake' Iraq in order to demonstrate American global military dominance at its 'unipolar moment'. The grand objective was the commitment that American global superiority, realized with the collapse of the Soviet Union, would never be surrendered.

America had the unmatched and unprecedented power to assure that its dominance would be made a permanent international reality. The strategically important Middle East would be remade in the American image. To that end, the invasion of Iraq would display America's crushing military power to a world reduced to the status of spectators in a spectacle of a state's destruction, marked by massive civilian casualties, cultural devastation, and the pauperization of its people. In the wake of state-ending, the Americans and their British allies would create a massive regional base in the very heart of the Arab Islamic world to guarantee that Western hegemony in this crucial region would be permanent and unchallenge-able. There would of course be permanent military bases. Iraq would be held up as a bastion of the American example and a model for the trans-formation of the entire area. For its substantial contributions to the effort to subdue and destroy the old Iraq, America's most important regional ally, Israel, would be freed of the one Arab power that had supported the Palestinian resistance in a regional context of ever increasing accommoda-tion and defeatism. Finally, Western corporations, with American compa-nies in the lead, would be in a position to dictate the terms of favorable deals with the Iraqi occupation regime to gain Western control of the nation's oil.

Whatever the ultimate measure of their success or failure, these three ideological forces drove the comprehensive policy of state- ending in Iraq. In any event, all of these ideological motivations proved unrealistic in their maximalist aspirations but not before Iraqis died by the hundreds of thou-sands, Iraqi intellectuals were singled out in the hundreds for targeted assassination, Iraqi institutions were looted and destroyed, and Iraq's glo-rious culture, the pride of all Iraqis—and a treasure of world history—was irreparably wounded.

President George W. Bush was surrounded by a neoconservative and hyper-nationalist coterie that strove to establish a link between September 11 and Saddam Hussein's regime, whatever the actual facts of the matter. Secretary of Defense Donald Rumsfeld pushed the case for war with Iraq, even suggesting that the US forgo attacks on al-Qaeda and Afghanistan in favor of toppling Saddam Hussein's regime, which presented the US with better targets and the opportunity for a superior demonstration effect (Susman 2007).

Leading neoconservative intellectuals and policy makers had long advanced the objective of eliminating the Iraq regime as the first step of an even more ambitious project of re-visioning the Middle East as a whole. After President George H.W. Bush had spared the Hussein regime follow-ing the 1991 Gulf War, Paul Wolfowitz, then the Undersecretary of Defense for Policy, along with similarly staunch-minded neoconservatives, argued that the US had missed a vital opportunity to enact sweeping change throughout the Middle East. Wolfowitz and Zalmay Khalilzad responded by elaborating a new vision to achieve long- term US domi-nance in world affairs, starting with securing the Middle East.

This new thinking was articulated in a secret draft document written by Paul Wolfowitz and the later-incarcerated Lewis 'Scooter' Libby, drawn up in 1992 and subsequently leaked to the *Washington Post*. The document, which was re-written by then Defense Secretary Dick Cheney and entitled 'Defense Planning Guidance' (DPG) argued that the primary objective of US post-Cold War strategy should be preventing the emergence of any rival superpowers by safeguarding American hegemony over vital resources (Cheney 1992). Iraq, of course, sat on the second largest pool of oil in the region and the Iraqi regime posed what was judged to be a serious challenge as well as a great opportunity for the sole superpower to act. The imperative of American dominance was tied rhetorically to efforts to 'increase respect for international law, limit international violence, and encourage the spread of democratic forms of government and open economic systems' (Cheney). In practice, it is not international law but American dominance that is to be preserved, just as the concern for democracy and free markets is always tempered by attention to US interests. American dominance, seen as a 'guarantor of international order', was in neoconservative polemics and policy papers, made a moral imperative, making it possible to associate any challenge to American dominance as a challenge to sacrosanct international values. Among the challengers to the 'moral imperative' of US dominance, Iraq figured prominently. Iraq not only supported Palestinian resistance in the occupied territories but also created obstacles to American 'access to vital raw materials, primarily Persian Gulf oil' and was also responsible for '[proliferating] weapons of mass destruction and ballistic missiles', and 'threat[ening] U.S. citizens [with] terrorism' (Cheney).

The draft DPG served as the first major post-Cold War manifesto of the neoconservative bloc that continued to strategize and create think tanks and press outlets to advance the vision of American dominance. Two major initiatives of the neoconservatives were the reinvigoration of the American Enterprise Institute and the founding of the Project for a New American Century (PNAC), both of which included Dick Cheney as an active member. These organizations played an especially influential role in designing a more aggressive posture for America in a post-Cold War world, particularly in the Middle East.

A bold example of this new assertive thinking was seen in a policy paper drafted in 2000 by PNAC entitled *Rebuilding America's Defenses: Strategy, Forces and Resources for a New Century*, endorsed by Paul Wolfowitz, I. Lewis Libby and a cadre of leading neoconservative intellectuals. It reiterated the major themes of the DPG, citing that document as a major foundation for the updated analysis (Donnelly 2000: ii). The PNAC protocol emphatically reiterated the importance of the Persian Gulf as a region of vital importance, with voluminous references to America's 'special interests' in the region (16, 21, 23, 26, 47, 86, 88). Additionally, the document called for an 'enduring' US presence in this region of strategic and commercial interests (16). In this assessment, the character of the Ba'ath regime in Iraq and its actual domestic and foreign policies were largely irrelevant, though they later figured largely in anti-Iraqi propaganda. What mattered was a pro-US presence in its place. 'Indeed, the United States has for decades sought to play a more permanent role in Gulf regional security ... the need for a substantial American force presence in the Gulf transcends the issue of the regime of Saddam Hussein' (26). Shortly before September 11, Donald Rumsfeld had once again articulated this commitment to ending Iraq, arguing that the toppling of the Ba'ath regime and its replacement by a pro-American state, 'would change everything in the region and beyond it. It would demonstrate what U.S. policy is all about' (Suskind 2004a: 85). Iraq remade by force would be the exemplar of American aspirations for the region.

Given the fixation with American domination in the Persian Gulf, Iraq inevitably became a central component and major target of Bush's foreign policy. An important element of that policy entailed a rethinking of the US relationship with Israel and more aggressive support for Israeli expansionism. America would dominate the world, while Israel would exercise unchallenged hegemony in the Middle East. The moment was right, the neoconservatives argued, for Israel to consolidate by force its maximalist claims against Palestinian nationalism. Iraq figured in a large way in these calculations as representing the single most powerful restraint on Israel's rightful ambitions, as neoconservatives understood them. Within this framework, the removal of the Ba'athist state on which Saddam's regime rested was a priority well before the September 11 attacks.

A Clean Break: A New Strategy for Securing the Realm (1996), co-authored by prominent figures of the American neoconservative movement and pro-Israel lobby, illustrates quite clearly how consistently Iraq loomed large in neoconservative thinking about Israel's prospects. This influential position paper identified Iraq as a primary strategic threat to Israel's dominance in the region and the overthrow of Iraq was heralded as an opportunity to alter 'the strategic balance in the Middle East profoundly' (Perle et al. 1996). This neoconservative call for the destruction of Iraq included the fantasy proposal of restoring 'Hashemite' control over Iraq, which was imagined as a lever to pull the country's Shi'ite majority away from Iranian influence. The idea of restoring the pre-revolutionary monarchy had little to no support in Iraq. This ideologically driven misinformation in a document taken so seriously does help explain why US officials were so credulous when told that Iraq's Shi'ites would be pro-American and prepared to turn away from their Iranian co-religionists.

In the light of the well-documented and longstanding emphasis on toppling Iraq by key figures in the Bush administration, there is little doubt that the September 11 attacks were seized upon as the enabling moment to enact a wide-ranging program in the Persian Gulf region. The imperative to invade Iraq and remodel the Middle East were parts of a larger strategic goal that considered a long-term presence in Iraq to be necessary for the extension of 'US values' throughout the rest of the region. A reengineered Iraq would play a critical role as a staging ground to alter the behavior of recalcitrant states across the region. The consistent, underlying objective was the building of an unchallengeable American global hegemony, Israeli regional dominance as an extension of American power, and the assertion of unquestioned control over the enormous energy resources of the Persian Gulf. All of these objectives would contribute to the larger strategic task of blocking the ascent of any other would-be superpower.

THEORY TO PRACTICE: THE MODALITIES OF STATE-ENDING IN IRAQ

The policy of ending states, announced by Wolfowitz, was enacted with a vengeance in Iraq. Under occupation, Iraq has been stripped of its historical national project of state-building and turned into a shell state with little to no control over its national affairs. The modalities of this state-ending policy deserve close attention for what they reveal about the larger question of American–Israeli regional and global ambition and the engineering of chaos and violence to achieve those objectives. As we have seen, part of the difficulty in coming to terms with the dismantling of the Iraqi state has been a mainstream failure to acknowledge that the violence of state destruction in Iraq was deliberate. In fact, such purposive violence of terrible proportions has antecedents in the chronicles of US and Israeli foreign policy. The levels of violence and the forms that violence took are foreshadowed by the American record in confronting challenges to US dominance in the Americas. In parallel fashion, the Israeli pattern of unre-strained, deliberate violence against the occupied Palestinians regularly targeted both state and civil society institutions that expressed in pacific ways the Palestinian aspiration for statehood. Israel openly defended the necessity of not only torture but of kidnapping and targeted assassination to contain the threat of Palestinian nationalism.

It is important to bring just enough of this history into view to facilitate coming to terms with the appalling levels of violence suffered in post-invasion Iraq. American-trained and -supported death squads wrought havoc in Latin and Central America, matched by the fairly routine Israeli targeted assassinations of Palestinian resistance leaders. The Israeli use of the overwhelming force of one of the world's most advanced military machines against Gaza and its captive and essentially defenseless civilian population in 2008 makes it clear that whatever we can learn of state destruction in Iraq will have continuing relevance (Falk 2009). Such understanding, based on careful review of the consequences of state destruction in Iraq, can also assist in breaking through the obscurantist spell cast by the war on terror. The means and methods of state destruc-tion were already part of the superpower's arsenal as well as that of its regional junior partner, though the war on terror rationalized their use with great effectiveness.

DEATH SQUADS AS A FOREIGN POLICY TOOL

For the theorists of state-ending, there is a long and ignoble history on which they can draw of counterinsurgency efforts based on roving 'death squads' to suppress indigenous resistance (Baker et al.: chs. 6, 7, 8). The techniques were developed during the 1960s and 1970s in Iraq, where the victims outnumbered those in the 911 attacks (Aburish 1997: 135–143), Vietnam, Indonesia and various countries in South America. The apex of this policy was in the anti-Communist terrorist campaigns in 1980s Central America, whose emblem was the Nicaraguan 'Contra' forces. Following the Boland Amendment of 1982 and its extension in 1984, formal American funding for the Contra forces was discontinued. This curtail-ment in the end led to surreptitious and unofficial forms of funding. Best known is the infamous Iran-Contra affair, where arms-for-hostage reve-nues were diverted to fund the Contras. Less discussed was the develop-ment of ties between the Contra army and South American drug traffickers as means of financial support. Suspicions of CIA participation in the

Contra–cocaine nexus have been variously investigated, suggesting a shadowy and hard-to-document network (Webb 1999). At minimum, however, the 1988 Kerry Commission (Senate Committee Report on Drugs, Law Enforcement and Foreign Policy chaired by Senator John F. Kerry) revealed that the US State Department had paid $806,000 to known drug fronts in order to provide assistance to the Nicaraguan Contras. Allegations of direct CIA participation in drug dealings are frequent, though they were officially denied by the CIA in a 1997 internal investigation.

Death-squad activity is inherently murky and therefore it will come as no surprise that the rise of death squads in Iraq is shrouded in secrecy. However, available reportage does provide some illumination into this affair. Organized violence in Iraq falls into three broad categories. The first is the general criminality and gangsterism that exploded following the 2003 invasion. The second comprises various forms of anti-occupation violence and originates from the constellation of groups that target occupation forces and the official Iraqi security forces. The third form, with the clearest relevance to death squads, is the violence of organized paramilitary groups involved in sectarian killings and conflict with the resistance, which some reports tie such violence to the Iraqi Interior Ministry (Adriaensens 2010). In a similar way, the Kurdish *Peshmerga* forces, particularly those alleged to have been trained by Israel, are widely believed to be involved in the targeting of elements of the Shia 'insurgency'. Circumstantial evidence points to death-squad activities, though their violent actions reflect the unique Kurdish circumstance and aspirations.

A direct and clear connection can be established between high American officials involved in 'counterinsurgency' projects of Central America and those involved in contemporary Iraq. The most prominent of these figures is James Steele, who in the 1980s 'honed his tactics leading a Special Forces mission in El Salvador during the country's brutal civil war'. That bloody conflict resulted in 70,000 deaths. A UN truth commission found that as many as 85 percent of those deaths were attributable to US-backed forces (Corn 2005). Steele re-emerged in occupied Iraq as an advisor to the Iraqi Interior Ministry, the Iraqi institution most associated with death-squad activity. He also played an advisory role to the Iraqi counter insurgency force, the Special Police Commandos. The Commandos were formed by Falah al-Naqib, interior minister under the interim government of Ayad Allawi. The Commando forces were drawn from 'veterans of [Saddam] Hussein's special forces and the Republican Guard' (Maass 2005). By 2006 the paramilitary forces of the Interior Ministry were

widely believed to be heavily involved in death-squad activity. The Badr
Organization, the armed wing of the Supreme Council of Islamic
Revolution in Iraq, played a lead role (BBC 2006). In July 2005 the 'Wolf
Brigade', a subset of the Interior Ministry Commandos, was implicated in
a series of sectarian killings and, in November 2005, American soldiers
stumbled upon a 'torture chamber' of 170 'half starved and ... seriously
beaten' prisoners, again operated by the Interior Ministry. In any case,
General Petraeus in 2005 'decided the commandos would receive whatever arms, ammunition and supplies they required' (Maass 2005).

The cooptation of indigenous forces into the occupation forces
extended with the Petraeus-led 'military surge' of 2007 onward, where
the so-called Awakening Councils of *al-Anbar*, a network of Sunni-based
tribes, were armed by the American occupation authorities. They formed
a force numbering over 80,000 'Iraqi Security Volunteers' (ISVs). In the
estimation of Chas Freeman, former ambassador to Saudi Arabia, the policy of 'surge' served to

> essentially support a quasi-feudal devolution of authority to armed enclaves,
> which exist at the expense of central government authority ... Those we are
> arming and training are arming and training themselves not to facilitate our
> objectives but to pursue their own objectives vis-à-vis other Iraqis. It means
> that the sectarian and ethnic conflicts that are now suppressed are likely to
> burst out with even greater ferocity in the future. (Rosen 2008)

In this way, a policy ostensibly designed to curb sectarian violence provided grounds for the escalation of future sectarianism. Indeed, according
to research conducted by the University of California, the 'surge' owes
much of its putative success to ethnic violence.

The 'cleansing' of Iraq's formerly mixed neighborhoods reduced available targets and thus the death tolls fell. This measure of success is dubious, to say the least. 'If the surge had truly "worked" we would expect to
see a steady increase in night-light output over time', says Thomas
Gillespie, one of the study co-authors, in a press release. 'Instead, we
found that the night-light signature diminished in only certain neighborhoods, and the pattern appears to be associated with ethno-sectarian violence and neighborhood ethnic cleansing' (Dickinson 2008).

'Of Course It's About Oil'

Of course it had been about oil long before Americans took an interest in Iraq. Once Winston Churchill decided in 1911 to power the Royal Navy with oil, sourced primarily in Persia, instead of coal from South Wales (Yergin 2006) the Middle East became even more vital than it had been for the British Empire. The Suez Canal was considered essential for shortening the sea route to India, but for the Royal Navy to fight a world war, the Canal was even more vital to transport oil from Persia, and subsequently, from Iraq. Second World War historian, Ashley Jackson (2018), asserts that the 'British Empire's defense of Egypt rather misses the point that this was primarily intended to protect what lays beyond it—the oil of Iran and Iraq'. Thus, after Qasim seized power in Baghdad in 1958, the American embassy in Beirut, according to a respected academic podcast (Abdullah 2023) sent messengers who were prominent Iraqis with close ties to Qasim to warn him against taking any steps that could affect the oil supply and western oil companies. The warning was clear that if the business of oil companies were hurt, he would face serious consequences. Recalling the multiple punishments meted out to Iraqis by the Americans which introduced our Chap. 1, the first instance was the CIA assistance to the Ba'ath overthrow of the Qasim regime in 1963. While Qasim's projected land reform undermined regime support among landowners within Iraq, and his dispute with Kuwait angered the British, it was his intention to create a state-owned oil company which united the Americans and British firmly against him (Aburish: 141–3). Of the six plagues of biblical proportions which the Americans visited upon Iraq, which we introduced in Chap. 1, the first (in 1963) was substantially about oil. The fifth plague, the 2003 Anglo-American invasion to finally destroy the Ba'ath regime which they had ushered in forty years earlier, was also about oil.

The thinking behind the invasion of Iraq did not neglect oil, no matter how often the denials of its role as a motivating consideration. In simple and direct terms, General John Abizaid, the former chief of US Central Command, terminated any official pretense that oil was not a factor in the invasion of Iraq. 'Of course it's about oil', he said bluntly, 'we can't really deny that …' (Abizaid 2007). Alan Greenspan, former chair of the US Federal Reserve, likewise, was 'saddened that it is politically inconvenient to acknowledge what everyone knows: The Iraq war [was] largely about oil' (Patterson 2007). Despite the calculated mists that clouded public discussion of the oil factor, there was already a public record of such acknowledgements of the centrality of oil. In 1999 Dick Cheney, then acting CEO of Halliburton, gave a speech at the Institute of Petroleum highlighting his vision of the critical role of oil in general and Middle Eastern oil in particular. He said:

> [B]y 2010 we will need on the order of an additional fifty million barrels a day. So where is the oil going to come from? Governments and the national oil companies are obviously controlling about ninety per cent of the assets. Oil remains fundamentally a government business. While many regions of the world offer great oil opportunities, the Middle East with two thirds of the world's oil and the lowest cost, is still where the prize ultimately lies, even though companies are anxious for greater access there, progress continues to be slow. (Cheney 2004)

Consistent with the neoconservative vision, Cheney as Vice-President advanced the argument that control of Iraqi oil was key to dominance over the incomparable oil reserves of the entire Middle East. Cheney created the National Energy Policy Development Group on January 29, 2001. The group, commonly known as the 'Cheney Energy Task Force' included many of the chief executive officers of the major energy corporations. It produced a National Energy Policy report in May of its first year of activity. In its recommendations, the group urged the US administration to take the initiative in pressing the governments of the Middle Eastern countries to open their economies for foreign investments.

Earlier, in 1993, six giant oil companies, Royal Dutch Shell, British Petroleum, Conoco Phillips, Exxon Mobil, Halliburton and Chevron, sponsored the International Tax and Investment Center (ITIC) which eventually included 110 corporations. Documents obtained through the Freedom of Information Act reveal that in late 1990s Anglo-American representations were made on behalf of oil companies to secure Iraqi oil contracts. ITIC was advised to write a report emphasizing Production Sharing Agreements (PSA) to ensure the success of long-term control over oil. By April 2002 the State Department had already organized 17 working groups, made up of over 200 Iraqi engineers, lawyers, businesspeople, doctors and other non-Iraqi experts, to strategize on post-Saddam Iraq. This initiative came to be known as the Future of Iraq Project. The group on 'Oil and Energy' envisioned a 'demonopolized' (i.e., privatized) Iraqi National Oil Company, where private investors in upstream oil production would have a free hand, calling for '... production sharing agreements (PSA) structured to facilitate participation in Iraq's upstream oil industry of the best international oil and gas companies' (United States Department of State 2003). On May 12, 2003, Gal Luft, co-director of the Institute for the Analysis of Global Security, in an article entitled 'How Much Oil Does Iraq Have?' wrote:

> Over the past several months, news organizations and experts have regularly cited Department of Energy (DOE) Energy Information Administration (EIA) figures claiming that the territory of Iraq contains over 112 billion barrels (bbl) of proven reserves—oil that has been definitively discovered and is expected to be economically producible. In addition, since Iraq is the least explored of the oil-rich countries, there have been numerous claims of huge undiscovered reserves there as well—oil thought to exist, and expected to become economically recoverable—to the tune of hundreds of billions of barrels. The respected Petroleum Economist Magazine estimates that there may be as many as 200 bbl of oil in Iraq; the Federation of American Scientists estimates 215 bbl; a study by the Council on Foreign Relations and the James A. Baker III Institute at Rice University claimed that Iraq has 220 bbl of undiscovered oil; and another study by the Center for Global Energy Studies and Petrolog & Associates offered an even more optimistic estimate of 300 bbl. (Luft 2008)

In December 2002, *Oil and Gas Journal* published a study to the effect that 'Western oil companies estimate that they can produce a barrel of Iraqi oil for less than $US1.50 and possibly as little as $US1, including all exploration, oilfield development and production costs and including a 15 percent return. This production cost is similar to Saudi Arabia and lower than virtually any other country'. Iraqi oil, henceforth, was envisioned as the petrochemical prize of the Persian Gulf, particularly if denationalized and in the hands of American or American-friendly multinational entities. Under occupation, the oil factor imposed itself in an entirely predictable fashion. Iraq's oil industry, which had been the fulcrum of its national development, was slated for repossession by the forces of corporate capitalism. The US attempted to bully through a comprehensive oil law. If passed that law would have granted Western oil conglomerates 25- to 30-year contracts, awarded on a non-competitive basis, for the production of oil. By such arrangements, the bulk of revenues would return to the corporate giants rather than the Iraqi nation, on the model of the 'glory days' of British domination over the oil-producing Gulf region. Iraq's national oil industry, which for decades had served as a unifying source of pride and the lever of Iraq's socioeconomic development, risked falling into the hands of occupying forces. The bulk of Iraqi society stands opposed to any such outcomes. The Iraq Federation of Oil Unions, which represents over half of the industry workers in southern Iraq, consistently opposed the law. The Federation saw it as an imperial grab by multinational corporations that would mean the surrendering of Iraq's national sovereignty. In spite of this opposition, even from the pro-US parliamentarians who nominally govern the country, the push for a multinational oil grab continued.

A first round in the contest ended in June 2008 when the *New York Times* on June 19 reported that 'deals with Iraq are set to bring oil giants back' (Kramer 2008). In its subtitle the Times summed up the outcome of the negotiations by commenting on 'Rare No-bid Contracts, A Foothold for Western Companies Seeking Future Rewards'. It is worth noting that the four companies involved, were precisely those that lost their concessions in 1972. The agreements fell short of the production sharing arrangements that the four oil giants—Exxon Mobil, Royal Dutch Shell, the French company Total, and BP, formerly British Petroleum—initially sought. The companies did not get quite the level of control they sought, although the agreements did provide a foot in the door and an opportunity to reap huge profits from the rise in oil prices. Iraq, indeed, has been remade economically with the transformation of the oil industry, though not completely and not without significant resistance.

Having noted previously in our assessment of the status of the oil sector that

> the Iraqi constitution stipulates in Articles 111 and 112 that the management of and investment in oil fields must be in the best interest of Iraqis, respecting their collective ownership. However, of the contracts approved by the Iraqi Ministry of Oil, none have been ratified by parliament nor verified to be in the 'best interest' of the Iraqi people, making the legality of these contracts dubious. ... The development of Iraqi oil, while certainly profitable, has not necessarily been conducted in a manner respecting the best interest of Iraqis, many of whom live in squalor while corrupt politicians reap the profits. Thus IOCs [international oil companies] who gain contracts not only set the course for development, as the largest source of technically competent and employable skilled labor, but also have an incentive to support the current political order in Iraq. For Iraq, these contracts, in conjunction with the rampant corruption in Iraqi politics ... represent an erosion of public control of the country's economic lifeblood and the

reversal of modern Iraq's development trajectory based on a public oil sector. (Ismael and Ismael 2021: 98)

Historically, the presence of large, easily accessible petroleum deposits in the Gulf countries, and the dependence of European and American economies on this resource, has destined them to imperial predation. However, oil has also been the driver of internal development and the primary resource for nationalist regimes opposed, first to British and then to American domination. The role of petroleum has therefore been a complex and changing one. The increasing independence of the Organization of the Petroleum Exporting Countries (OPEC) from Western countries and its increasing cooperation with Russia increases the tendency for power to shift toward oil exporting states in comparison with the international oil companies. The fact that over half of Iraq's crude exports now goes to China and India, and the preference of the BRICS countries to reduce trade in American dollars, holds out some promise to Iraq that it can win greater economic benefit from its largest industry, provided it can develop the necessary state capacity and reduce corruption. In the interim, it now seems clear that the American ambition to secure greater control over the petroleum sector in the Gulf region has not born fruit.

The Israeli Example: State Destruction and Chaos in Palestine

Israel has a long record of attacking Palestinian government and civil society institutions to prevent the emergence of the infrastructure for a viable Palestinian state and civil society. The modalities of this Israeli pattern became more pronounced with the apogee of Pax Americana allowing the Israelis and their American patrons a comparatively free hand in the Middle East. In late 2008, the Israelis launched an intensive ground and air offensive against Palestinian society, nominally to end the primitive rocket attacks from Gaza, but in reality, to undermine Hamas as an operational entity and to bolster the compliant Fatah movement. In the end, over 1300 Palestinians were killed, at least a third of whom were civilians, versus 13 Israeli fatalities. Physical damage was initially estimated at over $2 billion (Pleming 2009). Moreover, Palestinian unity—already fragile—was further undermined in light of a widespread belief in Fatah collaboration in the Israeli assault. Accusations of this sort, and the round of anti-Fatah recriminations that followed the Israeli assault, while partly Hamas propaganda, contain more than a kernel of truth.

Hamas has faced attacks on two fronts, from IDF/IAF assaults as well as US-backed Fatah forces. A 2008 investigation revealed that the US had funded and backed an armed force under Fatah strongman Mohammad Dahlan. Beginning in late 2006, the US State Department solicited its Arab allies to bolster Fatah by providing military training and armaments. In conjunction with this fundraising, the US drafted a document titled 'An Action Plan for the Palestinian Presidency', otherwise known as 'Plan B', calling for

> Abbas to 'collapse the government' if HAMAS refused to alter its attitude towards Israel ... Security concerns were paramount ... it was essential for Abbas to maintain 'independent control of the security forces' ... [The Plan] called for increasing the 'level and capacity of 15,000 of Fatah's existing security personnel' while adding 4700 troops in seven new highly trained battalions. (Rose 2008)

Ultimately, the particulars of this plot became public knowledge and contributed to the outbreak of a civil war between Hamas and Fatah forces, to the great detriment of the Palestinian people and the project of Palestinian national unity.

The methods of the US in Iraq and the methods of Israel in the Palestinian territories represent similar modalities of 'counterinsurgency': overwhelming violence against civilian populations—keeping them in a state of confusion and paralysis; the suppression of all forms of resistance—military, political, or social; and a policy of divide-and-rule, the cooption of compliant groups in order to sow division and undermine national unity. In the case of Iraq, Shia-dominated 'death squads' appeared to operate with impunity out of the Iraqi Interior Ministry, and thereafter, the US directly coopted the former resistance of the *Anbar* province, creating a heavily armed force that counterbalanced the Shia armed-parties. These conflicting policies did create a temporary state of equilibrium between warring Shia and Sunni armed groupings. However, they also helped create the conditions of future civil war. Israel likewise vacillated in its cooption of Palestinian groups, first the Islamic movements during the 1980s, and later the corrupt Fatah in order to undermine Hamas. The end result in both cases is engineered fracturing of national unity.

The Israeli role with regard to Iraq has deep and complex roots that go beyond the demonstration effect of its own role in the occupied Palestinian territories. It requires further consideration as one of the three major drivers behind the invasion (Mearsheimer and Walt 2006, 2009b). Since the consolidation of the Israeli state, though particularly following Israel's victory in the 1967 war, the US has relied upon the state of Israel as its junior partner *contra* Arab nationalist movements. Israel, to be sure, was not the only regional power to play this role. Saudi Arabia was the crucial Arab ally in sponsoring reactionary Islamic movements to oppose both assertive Arab nationalist regimes and their Soviet allies.

Within occupied Palestine, Israel also looked in the Islamic direction for allies against the secular nationalism represented by the PLO. According to Zeev Sternell, historian at the Hebrew University of Jerusalem, Israel's tilt to the Islamists included authorizing Islamic forces 'to receive money payments from abroad' (Zerouky 2006). The policy worked in the short run and secular- nationalist forces in Palestine were indeed weakened by the rise of Islamic movements. However, the success had its costs. Nurtured by Israel, the Islamic embryo later emerged as Hamas, Israel's contemporary nemesis.

Beyond the sponsorship of Islamic and traditionalist forces to counter Arab nationalism, regional American–Israeli strategy has aimed, when opportunities arise, for the marginalization or even cooptation of nationalist regimes. Under American auspices, Egypt signed the Camp David Accords in 1978, leading to an Egyptian–Israeli peace treaty and normal diplomatic relations. Egypt, having broken the regional taboo against accommodation with Israel, sacrificed its pretensions of regional leadership in confronting the assertive Zionist state. Iraq attempted to pick up that mantle with overt support for the Palestinian resistance. As a result Iraq, previously a tangential participant in Arab–Israel wars, saw itself attacked by Israel in 1981 when the Osirak nuclear facilities were bombed. That attack had as much to do with undercutting Iraq's pro-Palestinian stance as with any nuclear threat to Israel. Both were viewed as challenges to unquestioned Israeli regional hegemony. As a matter of doctrine, Israel asserts a unilateral right to nuclear weaponry within the region, a posture that continues to tease possible strikes against Iran.

As with Egypt, there have been Israeli attempts to co-opt Iraq with the hope of converting it from a rejectionist to accommodationist regime. In 1984, Donald Rumsfeld presented Iraqi Foreign Minister Tariq Aziz with a proposal from Yitzhak Shamir to reopen the trans-Arabian oil pipeline, according to Nigel Ashton (2010) in *Hussein: A Political Life*. Ashton tells us that when the offer was presented by Rumsfeld, 'Aziz turned pale and begged Rumsfeld to take back his message' (Oren 2009). An apparent follow-up was attempted in 1995, where Israel sought improved relations with Iraq as part of an attempt to marginalize Assad's Syria and the growing Iranian presence. This secret diplomacy, undertaken through King Hussein's Jordan, apparently saw Saddam 'not rul[ing] out direct contacts with [Prime Minister Yitzhak] Rabin'. In any event, this secret diplomacy ended with the deterioration of Israeli–Jordanian relations.

The US has found it politically necessary to disavow any level of Israeli–US cooperation in the invasion and occupation of Iraq, making the unlikely claim that Israel took no position on the matter of invading Iraq (Benhorin 2008). Investigative journalism suggests an entirely different and far more plausible picture. In fact, given Israel's deep resentment of Iraq as the erstwhile champion of Arab nationalism and the Palestinian cause, Israel clearly had a stake in weakening or eliminating the Iraqi state. It should come as no surprise, therefore, that the Office of Special Plans, an unofficial intelligence cadre answerable to Vice-President Dick Cheney, 'forged close ties to a parallel, *ad hoc*, intelligence operation inside Ariel Sharon's office in Israel. This channel aimed specifically to bypass the Mossad and provide the Bush administration with more alarmist reports of Saddam's Iraq than the Mossad was prepared to authorize' (Borger 2003).

As Iraq was in the thrall of occupation and domination by Anglo-American forces, available reports suggest anything but Israeli passivity. In late 2003 Seymour Hersh wrote:

> Israeli commandos and intelligence units have been working closely with their American counterparts at the Special Forces training base at Fort Bragg, North Carolina, and in Israel to help them prepare for operations in Iraq. Israeli commandos are expected to serve as ad-hoc advisers—again, in secret—when full-field operations begin. (Hersh 2003b)

Israel took an even more direct role in Iraq in 2003, providing materiel support and training for Kurdish *Peshmerga* forces in order first to 'penetrate, gather intelligence on, and then kill off the leadership of the Shi'ite and Sunni insurgencies in Iraq', and finally to aid in Israeli efforts 'to install sensors and other sensitive devices that primarily target suspected Iranian nuclear facilities' (Hersh 2004b). In the context of intensified sectarian conflict and Arab–Kurdish wrangling over the fate of oil-rich Kirkuk, such actions had a highly incendiary effect.

Israeli involvement in Iraqi national affairs extends to the political and diplomatic. Israel has always drawn attention to the ethno-religious diversity of Iraq and has consistently sought to exploit those differences. Again, the Kurdish connection stands out. Relations between the Zionist movement and the Kurds predate the founding of Israel. As early as the 1930s Ruvin Shiloh, a delegate of the Jewish national agency met with members of the Barzani clan as part of efforts to forge relations with the various Kurdish factions within Iraq. Israel has maintained sporadic ties to the Kurdish factions ever since, with the notable exception of the PKK, given their leftism and vigorous support for the Palestinian cause. These relations allegedly extended as far as Mossad participation in the creation of the *Paristan*—the Kurdish Intelligence Agency—working with Massoud al-Barzani, head of the organization, who

> underwent a concentrated training program in Kurdistan and Israel. According to Obaidullah al-Barzani, son of Mulla Barzani, Israelis were permanently accompanying my father, were always calling Israel by a wireless device and performed espionage acts in Iraq. (Ose 2008)

In 1980 Israel's Prime Minister Menachem Begin acknowledged that his country had been providing the Kurds with military and humanitarian aid for years (Ose).

Israel today continues to make overtures to the Kurds, even though at present diplomatic contacts between Israel and Iraq are limited. During an official visit to Kuwait in 2006 Massoud commented pointedly that, in principle, 'it is not a crime to have relations with Israel'. Noting that such important Arab countries as Egypt and Jordan already had such relations, Massoud announced that 'should Baghdad establish diplomatic relations with Israel, we could open a consulate in Irbil' (Institut Kurde de Paris 2006). Massoud was clearly signaling interest in open accommodation of the Israeli regime with the inevitable consequence of compromise on support for Palestinian nationalism. Similar possibilities were suggested on July 1, 2008, with a brief meeting and public handshake between Jalal Talabani, head of the Patriotic Union of Kurdistan (PUK) and President of Iraq, and then Israeli Defense Minister Ehud Barak. The meeting occurred during the 23rd congress of the Socialist International (of which

Israel's Labour Party and the PUK are members) (Associated Press 2008; Baroud 2008).

The US in Iraq, and Israel in the occupied territories, share the goal of undermining and de-legitimating national-minded resistance movements and independent-minded regimes (Ismael and Ismael 2021: 34). At the same time, they aim to bolster the power of regional clients to the frequent detriment of the societies they claim to represent. These objectives fit into a larger pattern of interests shaped by the American vision of global dominance, the Israeli goals of a greater Israel, and the aspirations of the multinational oil companies to regain more effective control of Middle East oil. The coming together of these powerful ideological forces produced the invasion of Iraq with its objective of state-ending and with all the disastrous consequences that have followed from it, most of all for Iraqis.

CULTURAL CLEANSING THROUGH ENGINEERED CHAOS

With an understanding of the ideologically driven goal of dismantling the Iraqi state, we can now turn to an overview of the cultural and human costs of the policy as they are reflected in the facts on the ground. The magnitude of the destruction and its systematic character cannot possibly be explained as a series of unforeseen, unrelated, and/or tragic mishaps. The authors of a collection of detailed post-invasion case studies (Baker et al.) the killings and destruction flowed from the inherently violent policy objective of remaking rather than reforming Iraq. In these studies, a pattern emerges of available, protective actions not taken, and the failure to investigate and prosecute violations. Even more striking in the record are the documented cases where the occupiers themselves fostered, facilitated, or directly engaged in the calculated destruction of Iraq's culture and the degrading of the intelligentsia who embodied it and protected it. This calculated neglect has left crimes against culture unreported, the dead unnamed, and all the crimes of cultural cleansing uninvestigated. The evidence assembled in these studies makes the case that state-ending in Iraq did entail willful efforts at cultural cleansing. In view of the consistent pattern reported in the case studies, the counter arguments of accidents of chance or poor planning simply do not make reasonable sense of the facts on the ground.

According to Lebanese archeologist Joanne Farchakh, who assisted in the investigation of the stolen historical wealth from Iraq after the invasion, 'Iraq may soon end up with no history' (Fisk 2007a). With the protective shield of the state and the educated elite removed, Iraq's incomparable cultural riches were an easy target. The military onslaught of American-led forces against the Iraqi state and society already weakened by twelve years of economic sanctions coincided with a multi-dimensional pattern of cultural cleansing.

Such cleansing began in the very early days of the invasion, with the wide-scale looting of all of the symbols of Iraqi historical and cultural identity. Museums, archeological sites, palaces, monuments, mosques, libraries and social centers all suffered looting and devastation. They did so under the watchful eyes of the occupation troops. American forces in Baghdad guarded only, and very carefully, the Iraqi Oil Ministry, which securely kept all oil data, as well as the Ministry of the Interior, where the potentially compromising files of Saddam's security apparatus were housed.

On America's watch we now know that thousands of cultural artifacts disappeared during 'Operation Iraqi Freedom'. These objects included, no less than 15,000 invaluable Mesopotamian artifacts from the National Museum in Baghdad, and many others from the 12,000 archeological sites that the occupation forces, unlike even Saddam's despotic regime, left unguarded (Buckley 2007). While the Museum was robbed of its historical collection, the National Library that preserved the continuity and pride of Iraqi history was destroyed by deliberate arson. As Nabil al-Takriti points out (Baker et al.), Iraqi and international cultural specialists knew the exact location of the most important cultural sites and so informed the occupiers. However, once the looting began, occupation authorities took no effective measures to protect them.

Some 4000 historical artifacts have been recovered, at times in inventive ways as when some Shi'ite clerics exhorted women 'not to sleep with their husbands if looted objects were not returned' (Jenkins 2007). However, many treasures were smuggled out of Iraq and auctioned abroad. These thefts often occurred with the help of foreigners who arrived with the occupation forces, like journalist and Middle East expert, Joseph Braude (Gugliotta 2005) who was arrested at New York JFK International Airport with ancient Mesopotamian antiquities. Braude was sentenced to six months of house arrest and two years of probation. Priceless artifacts may have also been auctioned off on the Internet as forewarned by a professor of anthropology at Arizona State University (Smith 2003). According to one estimate, by an archeologist, Francis Deblauwe, on the number of stolen artifacts, some 8500 objects remained missing, in addition to 4000 artifacts said to be recovered abroad but had not by that time returned to Iraq (Smith 2006). More recently, following American Department of Justice charges against an American museum for purchasing artifacts of doubtful provenance, about 17,000 artifacts were returned to Iraq in a single operation (Arraf 2021). While the return of artifacts is a positive development for Iraq, these events underscore the immense scale of the looting, and the impossibility of ever knowing its true extent: thefts which go undiscovered necessarily evade measurement.

During the Iran–Iraq war that raged for eight years neither side deliberately targeted the archeological sites or the cultural resources of the other. There is no comparison between the impact of that war on Iraq's cultural treasures and the subsequent American-led invasion and the terrible destruction that followed. American failure to protect the Iraq's cultural treasures, notwithstanding later professional and governmental cooperation in identifying and returning looted artifacts, directly contravened the Geneva Convention stipulation that an occupation army should use all means within its power to guard the cultural heritage of the defeated state (Jenkins 2007). As a result, 'legions of antiquities looters' emerged, and established mass- smuggling networks of armed cars, trucks, planes and boats to ship Iraq's plundered historical patrimony to the US, Europe and the Gulf region (Fisk 2007a; Baker et al.).

The attitude of the US-led forces to this pillage was, at best, indifference. In 2003 Defense Secretary Donald Rumsfeld sneered at reports of widespread looting, glibly commenting that 'stuff happens' during war, while dismissing the looting as the understandable targeting of the hated symbols of the ousted regime (Loughlin 2003). Answering journalists' questions about the destructive chaos with disdain, Rumsfeld responded that

> very often the pictures are pictures of people going into the symbols of the regime, into the palaces, into the boats and into the Baath Party headquarters and into the places that have been part of that repression .... And while no one condones looting, on the other hand one can understand the pent-up feelings that may result from decades of repression and people who've had members of their family killed by that regime, for them to be taking their feelings out on that regime. (Baker et al.)

Representing the looting, arson and destruction of Iraq's heritage as 'understandable' and almost 'natural' and unavoidable under the 'circumstances', as Rumsfeld does, contradicts the fact that

> For several months before the start of the Iraq war, scholars of the ancient history of Iraq repeatedly spoke to various arms of the US government about this risk. Individual archeologists as well as representatives of the Archaeological Institute of America met with members of the State Department, the Defense Department and the Pentagon. We provided comprehensive lists of archeological sites and museums throughout Iraq, including their map coordinates. We put up a website providing this same information. All of us said the top priority was the immediate placement of security guards at all museums and archeological sites. US government officials claimed that they were gravely concerned about the protection of cultural heritage, yet they chose not to follow our advice ... and the US troops abused [archeological] sites themselves. (Bahrani 2003)

In 2006 the American-sponsored Iraqi government, despite reports of a budget surplus in 2006 and a problem with unspent funds, cut the budget of the Antiquities Department. Its small task force was deprived of the necessary funds to pay for patrol-car fuel. This cut meant, for example, that the Antiquities Task Force sat in its offices attempting to fight looting that was taking place dozens of miles away at 800 archeological sites in the province of Dhi Qar (Fisk 2007b). When outraged Iraqis, desperate to prod the Americans to action, told US forces that the Saddam regime had made looting of the heritage a capital offense, the occupation force declared irrelevantly that 'we weren't going to fly helicopters over the sites and start shooting people' (Gugliotta 2005). The demand was not that the Americans adopt Saddam's methods but rather that they assume responsibility as international law required for protecting Iraq's incomparable treasures. Consistently, such exhortations fell on deaf ears.

In the summer of 2004 world outrage over the pillaging of Iraq's cultural treasures seriously affected the international image of the Bush administration. At that point, USAID finally arranged a program, headed by Professor Elizabeth Stone, from Stony Brook University, to furnish Iraqi graduate students in archeological studies with state of the art equipment. The aim was also to train Iraqi specialists in the most recent methods of the field from which they had been isolated when for the last two decades Iraq under Saddam was cut off from the rest of the world by the Anglo-American imposed sanctions. Several Iraqi students went to study in the US. However, one year later, the program was suddenly stopped (Deblauwe 2005). While the US could afford to spend $US 1 billion per day on its military machine in Iraq, the administration declined to spare few millions to enhance the training of Iraqi archeological students and teachers who could help repair the Iraqi cultural patrimony.

The failure of the US to carry out its responsibilities under international law to take positive and protective actions was compounded by egregious direct actions taken that severely damaged the Iraqi cultural heritage. Following the invasion in March 2003, the US-led forces transformed at least seven historical sites into bases or camps for the military. These desecrated sites included Ur, one of the most ancient cities in the world, which is said to be the birthplace of Abraham, father of the three great monotheistic religions. The brickwork of the Temple Ziggurat at the site of Ur, which Iraqis had preserved and maintained with national pride, were damaged under the weight of American military equipment and the callous treatment of military forces. When Abbas al-Hussaini, then head of the Iraqi Board of Antiquities and Heritage attempted to inspect the site of Ur in early 2007, the US military refused him access (Baker et al.: ch 4). Such was also been the fate of Babylon where a US military camp has irreparably damaged the ancient city. Such ancient sites are not Sunni, Shi'ite, Yazidi or Christian, nor are they Turkoman, Kurdish or Arab— these historical sites are the Mesopotamian historical patrimony of all Iraqis (Baker et al.: 29).

Such massive cultural destruction has a devastating impact on two distinct levels. The first pertains to all humanity because of Iraq's unique provenance of artifacts and monuments that record in a well-documented, material way an unmatched sense of the continuity of human civilizations in this unique site. The second level is crucial to the Iraqi people and their distinctive historical identity, shaped by the way they understand their own history. Memory in all its forms, personal, cognitive, and social, provides the imaginative infrastructure of identity, whether of the individual or group, national or sub-national. Memory evokes emotionally charged images as well as desires, which link one's past to the future through the present interpreted in light of recollection. However, memory is mortal in two senses: first it dies with the body; second, it changes through forgetfulness. Hence, memory, particularly people's or social memory, needs to be preserved actively to supply the continuity of social meaning from the past to the future. The preservation of memory is the function of museums and historical monuments. Museums are the storehouses of historical relics that nurture social memories, that is to say the imaginative recollection of past events. Monuments are the eyewitnesses to historical events. In all these ways, the Baghdad Museum was memory-objectified, not only of the Mesopotamian cradle of civilization but also for the Iraqi people. By selecting what to keep, display, and remember, the Baghdad Museum enacted the permanence and continuity of a culture and a nation since time immemorial, to which archeological sites and monuments bear witness. The objects and artifacts were staged to trigger 'memories in, and for multiple, diverse collectives', and 'the memories become components of identity' (Crane 2000: 3). Without a framework of collective memory, there is no mode of articulation for individual memory. Individual memory requires the context of group identity which is inseparable from the history and cultural artifacts that the Baghdad Museum, the Central Library in Baghdad and the monument sites once preserved. However questions of intent on the part of the occupiers are eventually resolved, the actual consequences of policies pursued in post- invasion Iraq, as Nabil al-Takriti argues (Baker et al.: ch. 5) can fairly be characterized as the destruction of cultural memory.

This desecration of the past and undermining of contemporary social gains is now giving way in occupied Iraq to the destruction of a meaningful future. Iraq is being handed over to the disintegrative forces of sectarianism and regionalism. Iraqis, stripped of their shared heritage and living today in the ruins of contemporary social institutions that sustained a coherent and unified society, are now bombarded by the forces of civil war, social and religious atavism, and widespread criminality. Iraqi nationalism that had emerged through a prolonged process of state-building and social interaction is now routinely disparaged. Dominant narratives now falsely claim that sectarianism and ethnic chauvinism have always been the basis of Iraqi society, recycling yet again the persistent and destructive myth of age-old conflicts with no resolution and for which the conquerors bear no responsibility.

Concomitant with the ruination of so many of Iraq's historical treasures has been the rampant destruction of Iraq's social and cultural institutions. Iraq's education system, once vaunted as the most advanced in the region, has suffered a patterned process of degradation and dismantling. Under the occupation, according to a report by the United Nations University (UNU) International Leadership Institute in Jordan:

The devastation of the Iraqi system of higher education has been overlooked amid other cataclysmic war results but represents an important consequence of the conflicts, economic sanctions, and ongoing turmoil in Iraq .... The Iraqi Academy of Sciences, founded in 1948 to promote the Arabic language and heritage, saw its digital and traditional library partially looted during the war and it alone needs almost one million dollars in infrastructure repairs to re-establish itself as a leading research centre. (Hassan 2005; Baker et al.)

According to Jairam Reddy, director of the UNU, 'some 84 percent of Iraq's institutions of higher education have been burnt, looted, or destroyed. Some 2000 laboratories need to be re-equipped and 30,000 computers need to be procured and installed nationwide' (Hasan).

Immediately after the occupation of Iraq, the American authorities also imposed a new curriculum that removed any criticism of the US policy in the Middle East, as well as any reference to either the 1991 war or to Israeli policy in the occupied territories. An estimated $US 62 billion was awarded to Creative Associates Int. and $US 1.8 billion to Bechtel by USAID in April 2003 to re-build Iraq's infrastructure, including schools and higher education institutions. However, these efforts have been plagued by shoddy construction, signaled by the frequent flooding of schools with sewage, by inadequate infrastructure, and the failure to replace outdated equipment and teaching materials. The rapidly deteriorating conditions and a complete failure to establish a functioning education system has produced a spiraling dropout rate of almost 50 percent (Hasan). Iraqi academic institutions, once leaders among universities and research centers in the rest of the Arab world, were instrumental in creating a strong Iraqi national identity after years of foreign colonization. The virtual collapse of Iraq's educational infrastructure has gutted the vehicle that had served to cement a unifying history in the public mind. Massive out-migration in the wake of the foreign invasion has undermined national coherence in even more direct and devastating ways. Between January and October 2007, the war in Iraq displaced nearly 1 million Iraqis to Syria, in addition to the nearly 450,000 that had fled Iraq in 2006. The refugees come disproportionally from the educated middle class, who embodied this hard-won sense of national coherence. The literacy of refugee children is falling precipitously, which bodes ill for the next generation. Iraqi young women and girls are being forced by the destitution of their families into survival sex and organized prostitution (Cole 2007; Baker et al.).

From the outset, something more ominous than displacement by the chaos of war was at work in Iraq. The cultural elite of a nation is being killed in what Max Fuller and Dirk Adriaesens (Baker et al: ch. 7) concluded had all the earmarks of a systematic campaign of targeted assassinations. While their work focuses on academics, they emphasize that the decimation of professorial ranks took place in the context of a generalized assault on Iraq's professional middle class, including doctors, lawyers, judges as well as political and religious leaders. The killings of over 400 university professors took place at the hands of professional and able killers as the means and timing of the murders makes clear. By 2006, some 2500 faculty members had been killed, kidnapped, or intimidated into leaving the country or face assassination. There has been no systematic investigation of this phenomenon by the occupation authorities, and Dirk Adriaesens reported four years later, not a single arrest had been announced in regard to this terrorization of the intellectuals (Baker et al.: ch. 6). The inclination to treat this systematic assault on Iraqi professionals as somehow inconsequential is consistent with the occupation powers' more general role in the decapitation of Iraqi society. That aspect of post-invasion Iraq is best exemplified by the Bremer de-Ba'athification policy that had the effect of removing professional leadership cadres in the political, economic, and military spheres. It is less often remembered that this bureaucratic purging extended to the educational and cultural spheres with alarming consequences. As Dahr Jamail reports (Baker et al.: ch. 4) the end result of the purge of Ba'athists has been the almost complete and quite clearly deliberate destruction of Iraq's human capital. With a parallel argument, Philip Marfleet (Baker et al.: ch. 9) examined the patterns of emigration from Iraq and concluded that they were indicators of a purposive assault on the institutions and ideological resources of Iraq as a national society. This loss of intellectual capital deprived Iraq of the professional cadres that reconstruction would have required.

It is simply not true that the war planners could not have gauged the scale of responsibilities that occupation would entail or the resources that would be required to maintain order and protect human and cultural resources. Military sources had made it abundantly clear that the troop levels committed to maintaining responsible governance in post-invasion Iraq were completely inadequate. US General Eric Shinseki was most explicit and precise in detailing the responsibilities the occupiers would assume by the invasion. What attracted most attention in Shinseki's remarks to congressional committees was his firm judgment that troop

2 IRAQ BURNING 63

levels provided for post-invasion Iraq could not possibly fulfill the role they were assigned. 'Beware a 12-division strategy for a 10-division Army', Shinseki cautioned with memorable succinctness. In comments to US Senator Carl Levin in February 2003 Shinseki said clearly that 'something on the order of several hundred thousand soldiers' would be needed as an occupation force. Shinseki provided a prescient warning that ethnic tension might well spill over into civil war and that the task of providing basic security and services for the Iraqi people should not be underestimated. Less than 48 hours later, Shinseki's 38 years of military experience and two purple hearts were ridiculed by Wolfowitz, himself lacking any military background at all. The Deputy Defense Secretary pronounced that Shinseki's figures to be 'wildly off the mark'. Shinseki was removed and his career sidelined until his appointment by President Barack Obama to the honorable, but low-profile, post of Secretary of Veterans Affairs (Thompson 2008).

Nor can it be said that the policy makers had no more reasonable and humane alternatives to the disastrous course taken. It is too often forgotten now that Paul Bremer was not the first American pro-consul. Nor were the destructive policies he pursued the first to have been put on the table. There were alternatives to the engineered chaos, structural dismantling, and cultural cleansing over which Bremer presided. In early April 2003, the Pentagon appointed retired general Jay Garner as Head of the Office of Reconstruction and Human Assistance in Iraq (ORHA). He arrived in Baghdad on April 20, 2003, and drafted his 'Unified Mission Plan' that aimed to minimize American intrusions. The basic foundation of his plan rested on a firm commitment to create and maintain a secure and stable environment of law and order from day one. Garner set the immediate goal of enabling provisions to reach the 60 percent of Iraqis who vitally depended on the Oil-for-Food Program. More generally, the Garner plan provided, among other things, that oil would remain in Iraqi hands, lower rank police officers would remain on paid, active duty, and the major bureaucratic, technocratic and judiciary institutions would be kept in place to carry out basic government functions (Frontline n.d.; Baker et al. 2010; Alpher 2017). In short, Garner proposed to use state institutions and Iraqi oil wealth to provide security for the people. He too was removed.

Paul Bremer arrived in Iraq in early May to replace Garner. Bremer quite deliberately rejected and reversed Garner's stabilizing orientation. On May 10, 2003, Bremer drafted a memorandum to dissolve eleven key state institutions, including the National Assembly, as well as their

affiliated offices, all military organizations, and the major military industries. With explicit blessings from the Pentagon (PBS 2006) the dissolution of these critical state structures was achieved by his first two orders
issued on May 16 and May 23. Order number one provided for de-
Ba'athification, which meant the removal of all Ba'ath Party members, and
not just the top leadership figures, from their positions. In practice, this
order meant that the majority of the Iraqi workforce was laid off without
pay. In Saddam's Iraq, the state was the primary employer, and one had to
join the ruling Ba'ath Party to be eligible for positions. Membership in the
party had less to do with ideological commitment or support for Saddam
than with the necessity of earning a living. For the regime, the party was
above all an instrument of absolute control. Bremer's de-Ba'athification
stripped the professions, industry, and social projects of experienced and
skilled personnel. Many institutions simply collapsed while others limped
along with greatly diminished competence. Bremer's order number two
disbanded the army and its civil affiliates, also without pay. In both cases,
pensioners as well were deprived of their income. What is clear in terms of
stated intent and observable outcomes is that Bremer's policies quite con-
sciously decapitated the country's governing elite and dismantled the
major state institutions. Bremer's raft of 97 edicts in total disemboweled
the middle class that cemented Iraqi society, and thrust some 15,500
researchers, scientists, teachers and professors into unemployment. The
order to disband the army created approximately 500,000 jobless people,
many of them with military experience.

Predictably, a huge human pool of angry, pauperized Iraqis turned to
the rising insurgency for redress. The occupation forces dampened down
the emerging resistance with indiscriminate collective punishment that
took on the character of yet another 'shock and awe' that overwhelmed
Iraqis and left them helpless and desperate. With the protective shield of
the state removed, criminal elements of all descriptions moved to prey on
the defenseless and disorientated population. The Iraqi people and their
extraordinary cultural heritage were left unprotected and vulnerable. This
policy of state-ending led to the fully predictable and willful cultural
cleansing of Iraq (Spectacles 2024).

In the 2010 study on the *Cultural Cleansing in Iraq* (Baker et al.) the
cultural destruction and targeted assassinations that took place in post-
invasion Iraq, the authors carefully weighed the record of conscious
choices made that created precipitating conditions of chaos and lawlessness, of inaction in the face of attacks on cultural monuments and

intellectuals when action was possible, and of documented direct actions by the occupying powers that had dire human and cultural consequences. In many cases this work first required simple and straightforward documentation of cultural artifacts destroyed, archeological sites damaged, and intellectuals murdered. The occupying powers and the post-invasion governments they installed consistently showed no interest at all in keeping such records. They showed even less inclination toward investigating the crimes and to bring the perpetrators to justice. This seemingly calculated disinterest, documented in that collective volume, is revealing.

The case studies (Baker et al.) also note those occasions when official spokespersons or agents gave overt expression to the pervasive inclination of the occupiers to view chaos and lawlessness as 'creative' in the sense of providing opportunities to wipe the slate clean, to create new beginnings, or start over from scratch. This permissive attitude to destruction was rationalized by the vision of a new Iraq that would arise under American and British tutelage from the ruins of the old Iraq. Looting became 'privatization' by direct, mass means in such an ideological framework. The destruction of cultural monuments was taken to represent constructive cleansing that prepared the ground for renewed building. There was even a silver lining to the demise of the old intelligentsia whose disappearance opened opportunities for a new generation of Iraqis with the 'right' values and social commitments.

In the context of engineered chaos, the wanton degradation of Iraq's once vaunted educational and health systems represented an opportunity to begin again, unencumbered by the attachments to the old order that had generated those social services. As a result, the occupying authorities, as Nabil al-Takriti documents (Baker et al: ch. 5) displayed a remarkably cavalier attitude to this deliberate destruction of Iraq's public infrastructure and its reserves of educated human resources. In the wake of sweeping privatization measures, Peter McPherson, senior economic advisor to proconsul Paul Bremer, characterized the dismantling of the public sector as 'shrinkage' (Klein 2007: 406). John Agresto, then director of higher education reconstruction for the occupation, described the devastation of Iraq's schools and universities as an 'opportunity for a clean start' (Klein: 407).

To make the case for cultural cleansing we cannot point to one single directive or policy statement, like Bremer's de-Ba'athification order for dismantling state structures or the new laws to remake the economy. For the cultural cleansing dimension of state- ending what we have instead is the painstaking accumulation of documented incident after incident. They add up to a clear pattern that shows how conditions of chaos resulted from actions taken or not taken. The case studies (Baker et al.) document how those conditions and the lawlessness they enabled were welcomed and rationalized by the occupiers as being in the interest of the Iraq yet to be created. Chaos, once created, released violent forces and impulses. Once released, those forces could not be directed and purposeful, and therefore destructive behaviors became more and more erratic. The creativity in chaos is revealed to reside not so much in purposive destruction but rather in the removal of all obstacles—political, economic, cultural, and human— to ending the Iraqi state and beginning anew.

Successive Iraqi states and regimes, whatever their shortcomings and at times terrible limitations, had nevertheless held together a layered and culturally rich nation. Iraq, as Mokhtar Lamani explains (Baker et al.: ch. 10) was an incredibly complex but fragile mosaic. It was formed not only of the three major ethnic and sectarian groupings on which the occupation forces concentrated but also of numerous minority communities. In conditions of engineered chaos, that intricate fabric that had persisted for thousands of years in embracing astonishing diversity was rent and perhaps destroyed forever. The major ethno-religious groups were deliberately separated out. With the bonds of national unity weakened, they were played one against the other. The small and vulnerable minorities were more often than not simply swallowed up in the turmoil.

To refashion Iraq into the neoliberal model for the Middle East it was first necessary to destroy in these ways Iraqi national identity and those social forces and cultural productions that expressed it. The occupiers acted in ways that clearly signaled that weakening of collective identity and the decimation of an intelligentsia with ties and mentalities linked to the old Iraq was not a loss at all. Rather, in the eyes of the occupiers it was an opportunity. It helped enormously that those placed in charge of Iraq's fate had little or no experience or knowledge of the country. Ignorance of the past and of the layered complexity of contemporary Iraqi society made it easy to look forward to turning the page. Iraq, after all, was viewed as a 'terrorist state' and, somehow this small and battered country with its glorious cultural heritage was transformed into an existential threat to the West and to civilization itself. In such a climate, Iraq's culture was ravaged and its intellectual class decimated.

The findings of the case studies (Baker et al.) reveal a pattern of cultural cleansing, etched in the facts on the ground of museums looted, libraries burned, and the most prominent and productive intellectuals systematically eliminated. The occupiers showed no inclination at all to protect those cultural and human resources and they failed to do so, in violation of international and humanitarian law. Worse, at critical moments they contributed in substantial ways to the destruction, as for example, by the stationing of occupation troops in the midst of some of the nation's most important archeological sites, thereby doing them great damage, as Abbas al-Hussainy documents (Baker et al: ch. 4). These outcomes were not tragic, unintended consequences. The culture that was ravaged, as Zainab Bahrani explains (Baker et al.: ch. 3) was an Iraqi cultural patrimony in the first instance, destroyed in an occupied country on the watch of the occupiers, the US and Britain. The intellectuals who were murdered and whose killings have not been investigated to this day represented some of the most productive and creative of the Iraqi intelligentsia who were educated, trained, and employed by the Iraqi state, as Dirk Adriaensens, Max Fuller and Dahr Jamail document (Baker et al.: chs. 6, 7, 8). They were the human embodiment of the Iraqi state and thus targets for termination. They were killed not primarily for sectarian reasons, though such incidents did occur, but simply because they were the best of Iraqi brains, as a careful review of the statistical evidence makes clear. These cultural erasures and eliminations testify to a concerted effort to shatter Iraqi collective memory as an essential condition for state-ending. These devastating outcomes represent the consequences, both direct and indirect, of an ideological, totalizing vision. That vision of state-ending required the dismantling not just of the pre-existing political and economic structures. It demanded as well the destruction of the cultural and human reserves of the Iraqi state, all in the interest of an imagined remaking.

The war planners asserted that the violence of shock and awe was a gift to Iraqis. The putative aim was to end dictatorship and open the way to the dismantling of the tyrannical state that had terrorized the people of Iraq. From the beginning, critics have debunked these explanations and argued forcefully that the invasion aimed for domination. It is important to note, however, that all sides in that debate took for granted that the aim of the invasion was the violent remaking of the Iraqi state, whether for liberation or for domination. In the US and Britain, a self-referential debate focused on these issues of the motivations of American and British policy makers for the remaking of Iraq. Did the invasion aim to remake Iraq in order to bring freedom to Iraq and the Middle East beyond, as the neoconservatives would claim, or was the aim imperial domination, as the critics charge? Regrettably, with attention riveted on the ideological rationale for the invasion, the depredations suffered by Iraqis recede into the background, no matter which position is taken. What emerges out of this insular debate are questions of Anglo-American motives rather than a consideration of the actual consequences for Iraqi culture and humanity. Eyes glaze over when figures on Iraqi civilian casualties are debated. When the museums in Baghdad were looted and libraries burned, the world did pay attention, but not for long. The pillage in Baghdad was only the tip of the iceberg. Abbas al-Hussainy surveyed the richness of the Iraqi cultural legacy (Baker et al.: ch. 4) noting that there are some 12,000 registered archeological treasures within Iraq's borders. Tragically, as he concludes, no other nation in modern terms has ever suffered destruction of its cultural legacy comparable to what Iraq endured under occupation. But the occupiers and their publics at home found it hard to focus on the fate of Iraqi culture. As Zainab Bahrani explains (Baker et al.: ch. 3) the really catastrophic cultural devastation took place in the five years following the initial destruction in Baghdad. It eventually engulfed the whole country, though these prolonged acts of pillage have met with a remarkable silence and culpable inaction. Had there been any inclination to do so, there was ample time to put protective measures in place. This course of action was simply not taken and very few even noticed.

Across the board, Iraq's unprotected cultural and social institutions were wantonly looted and in many cases irreparably damaged or destroyed. In these ways contemporary Iraq has been stripped both of its impressive historic past as well as its more recent social attainments. Iraq's modern institutions, in particular its once vaunted health and education infrastructure funded by the national oil industry, were degraded by initial bombardment and subsequent civil disorder. Dahr Jamail documents (Baker et al.: ch. 8) the devastating consequences, pointing out that many medical and educational facilities in Iraq were barely operating with skeletal staffing and little supplies. Hard-won social gains, among the most advanced of Arab states, were then further undermined by the haphazard privatization and reform schemes of Iraq's imperial- appointed rulers. Iraq's human resources, notably its educated and technocratic classes were seriously depleted, either by flight, forced exile, or assassination (Baker et al.: chs 6, 7, 8) a careful evaluation of the evidence pointing toward responsibility for this outcome on the shoulders of the occupiers.

Those human and cultural outcomes on the ground in Iraq do matter, in the first instance for Iraqis and their prospects for the future. They also matter for American and British citizens who want to understand how and why power was exercised in their name and what responsibility they bear for its outcomes. Whatever the motive, a totalitarian and inherently violent aim of state-ending was deliberately pursued, with particularly devastating cultural and human consequences. Ending and remaking are inherently violent processes. Nation- building, as Glenn Perry points out (Baker et al.: ch. 2) implies a prior process of nation- destroying that we are inclined to overlook, even in the context of Western history. Cultural identity is everywhere a component of state power and empires have always known that to weaken the collective identity of a people is to make them available for occupation, colonization, and oblivion. The destruction of archives and historical monuments, so wanton in Iraq, has always been part of the wars of empires, as Zainab Bahrani explains (Baker et al.: ch. 3). Everywhere in the modern world there is a strong and complex linkage between the intelligentsia and the state. Philip Marfleet explains (Baker et al.: ch. 9) that attenuating or breaking that connection and clearing out the old intelligentsia facilitates the pathway to a new Iraqi state of imperial design. One would have to ignore these implications of a totalizing war objective in order to entertain the facile notion that the terrible destruction that has taken place in Iraq could be the product of chance and lack of foresight.

PLANNED CHAOS IN IRAQ AND SYRIA

The appalling destruction of Iraq is more comprehensible when understood as one stepping stone in a series of targets of the neoconservative strategy of making the Middle-East 'safe' for American domination, supported by Israeli regional hegemony. These targets were the Arab nationalist states that most energetically opposed the Zionist project in Palestine and which had struggled to wring control over their petroleum resources from American and European corporations. The September 11, 2001 attack on the World Trade Centre and the Pentagon became the 'Pearl Harbor' opportunity that politically enabled this strategy, formally launched by President G.W. Bush in his 2002 State of the Union Address as 'The War on Terror', to destroy 'the axis of evil', in which he included Iran, Iraq, and North Korea. However, Bush's threats were not limited to the alleged perpetrators, but to the Arab nationalists generally and to the entire world: 'Either you are with us, or you are with the terrorists.' Former NATO Commander General Wesley Clark (2007) recalled the list of targeted states approved around the time of 9/11 by Defense Secretary Rumsfeld to begin 'with Iraq, and then Syria, Lebanon, Libya, Somalia, Sudan and, finishing off, Iran.'

Three of the targeted countries on Rumsfeld's list, Syria, Lebanon and Iran, would be well within American striking distance from bases in Iraq. In November 2007, the US administration and the dependent regime in Iraq signed a 'Declaration of Principles', establishing an open-ended US military involvement in Iraq, and thus, the Persian Gulf. Key Bush administration officials, notably Vice-President Dick Cheney and Deputy Defense Secretary Paul Wolfowitz, had from the outset aimed at permanent military bases in Iraq. However, the Iraqis proved far more resistant to these infringements on national sovereignty than anticipated. It took another year before Iraq and the US agreed on a Status of Forces Agreement (SOFA) that committed all US combat forces would withdraw and from all Iraqi territory by the end of 2011. Bush's Democratic successor, Barack Obama, not a supporter of Bush's invasion of Iraq, and mindful of the erosion of American public support for American forces in remaining in the Middle East, showed no reluctance in taking advantage of the opportunity to announce the withdrawal of American forces. Optimists could have been forgiven for believing that the neoconservative era of American military intervention in the Middle East was finally winding down.

However, the eruption of mass anti-government demonstrations, first in Tunisia in January 2011, then in Egypt later that month, followed by Bahrain, Libya and Yemen by February, and in southern Syria in March, quickly turned the tide. Each disturbance appears to have been linked to local conditions and grievances, giving rise to protesting crowds in the streets, followed by violent confrontations involving state authorities and protestors, the latter sometimes unarmed, sometimes armed. Western media and Qatar-based al Jazeera and western governments were almost universally sympathetic to the anti-government protestors, part of the phenomenon which they called 'the Arab Spring', evocative of the 'Prague Spring' label for the Czechoslovak revolt against the USSR in 1968. The case of Libya was met immediately with outrage and resolution from western countries: acting on unconfirmed British and French media reports of Libyan government using aircraft to bomb protesters, France, the UK and the US commandeered the UN Security Council (amid abstentions from Russia and China) to suspend the Libyan government credentials at the UN headquarters in New York and to pass a Security Council resolution enabling a NATO coalition to mount an armed 'Responsibility to Protect' ('R2P') operation to take control over Libyan airspace and bomb Libyan government forces (Forte 2012). In October, Muammar Gaddafi's fleeing convoy was attacked by NATO aircraft, and he was captured, apparently tortured and murdered by anti-government fighters. On hearing this news, US Secretary of State, Hillary Clinton (2011) triumphantly laughed while riffing on Julius Caesar's *'veni, vidi, vici'* , 'We came, we saw, he died.'

As with former American Vice-President Dick Cheney's famous aphorism, 'stuff happens', no sooner had American forces departed from Iraq, then the events of the Arab Spring conspired somehow to invite them back in, initially by way of Libya, then in a third NATO coalition, 'Operation Inherent Resolve', in declared opposition to the Wahhabist insurgents (publicized labels morphing repeatedly, chameleon-style, from the time of the American invasion, including 'ISIS', or the 'Islamic State') devastating Iraq and Syria. With the NATO victory in Libya, Wahhabist militants, armed by the NATO coalition, were infiltrated through Turkey and Jordan to Syria, as happened also with weapons from the conflict, to attack the Shi'ite enemies of the US and the Saudis (Hersh 2007, 2014; Moon of Alabama 2013g; Cockburn 2014). A US government consultant had told Seymour Hersh (2007):

> Bandar and other Saudis have assured the White House that 'they will keep a very close eye' on the religious fundamentalists. Their message to us was 'We've created this movement, and we can control it.' It's not that we don't want the Salafis to throw bombs; it's who they throw them at—Hezbollah, Moqtada al-Sadr, Iran, and at the Syrians, if they continue to work with Hezbollah and Iran.

Under the banner, 'Assad must go', the coalition of the willing assembled as 'The Friends of Syria', including Saudi Arabia, Qatar and other Sunni Arab states and NATO states, to supply militants and weapons to feed a growing US-Iran proxy war, masquerading as a Syrian civil war (Abouzeid 2012; Moon of Alabama 2013b, 2013c, 2013f; Hersh 2014; Cockburn 2014, 2015; Nahigyan 2014; Gerstein 2014; Hoff 2012; Chossudovsky 2023). Although the neoconservative G.W. Bush administration had been replaced by an outwardly more progressive Obama administration, the tactic of exploiting sectarian divisions to weaken and destroy potential enemy states continued. US Secretary of State John

Kerry 'warned [Iraqi] Prime Minister Maliki to stop flights from Iran over Iraq to Syria', that the Americans were 'watching what Iraq was doing' and 'wondering how it is a partner' (Moon of Alabama 2013a).

As the Syrian government offensive against the Islamic insurgents gained ground, media reports of chemical weapons use by government forces provoked a statement by Obama that 'We have been very clear to the Assad regime, but also to other players on the ground, that a red line for us is we start seeing a whole bunch of chemical weapons moving around or being utilized. That would change my calculus. That would change my equation' (Obama 2012; Goldberg 2016). Whatever Obama may have intended, his statement was understood by anti- Assad forces as a commitment to invade in support of the opposition if it could be demonstrated that Assad had indeed resorted to chemical weapons. As the need is father to the invention, occasions to test Obama's 'red line' duly arose, with the opposition forces and western media substantially united in accusations against the Syrian government, countered by far fewer dissenting views from the Syrian, Russian and Iranian governments and some alternative media and experts (Lloyd and Postol 2014; Moon of Alabama 2013d, 2013e, 2013f, 2013g, 2013h; Hersh 2014; Cockburn 2014; Nahigyan 2014; Ritter 2017).

However, Obama was spared the fate of being another American president to destroy a country over charges of weapons of mass destruction: in this case, by a UK House of Commons vote against participation, and by a timely offer by Russian President Putin to persuade Syria to destroy its chemical weapons under international supervision. Allegations of chemical weapons atrocities continued to appear in news coverage of the Syrian war, leading to US, French and British airstrikes in announced retaliation for the alleged use of chemical weapons by the Syrian government (OPCW 2017; Falk 2018) while a minority of dissenting opinions pointed toward staged provocations and manipulation of the OPCW investigation procedures to falsely implicate the Syrian government (Postol 2017; Falk 2018; Syria Propaganda Media 2019; Institute for Public Accuracy 2019; Peries 2019; Maté 2019).

The prospects for the Assad government's survival improved with the arrival in September 2015 of Russian air support for the Syrian Arab Army, as well as training and logistical assistance in a sustained offensive against Islamic fighters in Idlib and Aleppo provinces, and against Islamic State militants in the center of the country and toward the west bank of the Euphrates. Meanwhile, the US coalition's Operation Inherent Resolve, based in Iraq, led Iraqi forces ostensibly against the Islamic State from the east. Also fighting the Islamic State were Shia militias, organizationally linked to the Iraqi armed forces, but which American sources claimed were controlled by Iran. A proxy war between the poles of Iran and the US (Hoff 2012) began to reveal further polarities: US vs Russia, Saudi Arabia vs Iran, Turkey vs Syria, Turkey vs the Kurdish militias, Qatar vs Syria, and even more dyads. While the US was claiming to fight the Islamic State, Syrian armed forces managed to get in the way of American bombing runs, with a substantial force protecting the largely government-held city of Deir Ezzor suffering about a hundred killed in an American 'targeting error' (Porter 2016; Moon of Alabama 2017c; Fisk 2016). The Islamic State militants nearby quickly took advantage of the American attack, captured the Syrian position and reinforced their offensive against Deir Ezzor. There were other misunderstandings, although the Russian and American air forces generally followed 'deconfliction' arrangements to reduce the chances of a direct Russia-US conflict. In the American-led siege of Mosul, it required a protest from Iran to close a planned escape route for ISIS fighters to head west out of Mosul toward Syria (Fisk 2016). Later, in the final assault on Raqqa, ISIS forces and their dependents were permitted to escape toward the southeast along the Euphrates River (Sommerville and Dalati 2017; Camu and Louet 2017) into territory near Deir Ezzor, contested by the Islamic State and the Syrian government forces (Evans and Coskun 2017; Moon of Alabama 2017c). Syrian, Russian, Hizbollah (The Cradle 2023) and Iranian sources claimed on several occasions that the Americans were facilitating Islamic State attacks on Syrian forces and their allies, that ISIS was acting in effect as if it were a proxy for the Americans. Years later, retired Indian diplomat M.K. Bhadrakumar noted that, in Central Asia, they are 'wary of the West's dalliance with extremist groups. The widely held belief in Central Asia is that the Islamic State is an American creation' (Bhadrakumar 2023c, 2023e).

To view the Islamic State as an American proxy is not to imply that the American strategy was for ISIS to overthrow the governments of the targeted countries. The Americans, like the Saudis, Qataris and Israelis, saw the Islamic radicals as their instruments, not their allies. Better to have them wreak destruction abroad then nearer to home, and where better than in countries governed by their enemies? One might say they had revised the classic motto of inter-state strategy to: 'The enemy of my enemy is my tool'. After Obama's 2011 exit from Iraq, the Islamic State opportunely posed the threat that became the invitation for the Americans and their coalition to return in force to resume their participation in the destruction of Iraq, and to extend that devastation to Syria. American tactics were similar in both countries: massive aerial and artillery bombardment of cities and infrastructure with commensurate civilian casualties (McNerney et al. 2022), sometimes with the Islamic fighters themselves escaping, arguably, on occasion with tacit American consent, the better to fight the Syrian forces on another day. If one could be sufficiently perverse as to imagine a battle plan designed to cause prolonged and maximum damage to a population, it would be similar to the actions of the Americans and their allies in Iraq and Syria (Frontline 1990; The Cradle 2023; Mortada 2023). Recalling that the G.W. Bush administration's intentions in 2007 had been to retain permanent bases in Iraq, it is indeed the case that American forces remain there (as of February 2024), and also in Syria, in defiance of the protests of the Syrian government, and as convenient 'red lines', to justify future interventions against pro-Iranian militias seeking to expel Pax Americana from the region. Whether the result of the short-sightedness of American occupiers (Thompson 2015), or a sophisticated 'divide and rule' strategy, the Islamic State has been the gift that keeps on giving.

THE SOCIAL CONSEQUENCES OF STATE-ENDING IN IRAQ

In the wake of three decades of inter-state and civil conflict, the additional damage to Iraq society ensuing from the Islamic State and its struggle with the American-led Operation Inherent Resolve was profound (Spectacles 2024). Previously in this chapter, we presented the work of a collective of researchers (Baker et al. 2010) documenting the destruction of Iraq in a wide range of social and cultural areas. As we have seen, from those authors' perspective, the magnitude of the devastation was tantamount to the effective destruction—the ending—of the Iraqi state. It is reasonable to conjecture that those authors could not have imagined how things could possibly deteriorate from that point. However, several survey and analytical reports published since 2014 by international and non-governmental organizations would testify to the contrary.

At the most general level, the report published by the World Bank, 'Losing the Gains of the Past: The Welfare and Distributional Impacts of the Twin Crises in Iraq 2014' (Krishnan and Olivieri 2016), based on an economic simulation from 2012 household survey data, estimates that the GDP of Iraq dropped by 14 percent as a consequence of the ISIS depredations and the concurrent drop in the international price of oil. Income declines in the regions affected by ISIS were much higher, by almost half. Unsurprisingly, Iraq has suffered 'an almost complete erosion of the welfare gains of the past, with poverty falling back to 2007 levels and a 20 percent increase in the number of the poor'.

The remaining reports trace a consistent pattern across the full range of social activity. The United Nations (2015) '2016 Humanitarian Needs Overview' asserts that '[o]ver 10 million people need some form of humanitarian assistance', while 'the Government's social protection floor, including support for front-line health care, emergency shelter, education, and water and sanitation, is contracting'. Meanwhile, the World Food Program (Stephen 2016) estimated that the national poverty 'head count' following the conflict in 2014 was 22.5 percent, and 41.2 percent in areas directly affected by the conflict. Iraq's Public Distribution System (PDS), established by the Iraqi government in 1990 'offering blanket distribution of staple food items to the population in addition to humanitarian assistance', was 'affected' by the '[s]ocio-economic events' related to the ISIS conflict. It had, nevertheless, become the mainstay for cereals for 'almost one third of resident families and 40 percent of IDP [internally displaced persons] families'. The report noted that '53.2 percent of residents and 65.5 percent of IDPs—were vulnerable to food insecurity', higher in rural areas and among IDP groups, portions of whom exhibited symptoms of malnutrition and wasting.

Insecurity extended beyond nutritional needs and preceded the conflict with the Islamic State. Between December 2012 and April 2013, Human Rights Watch (2014) interviewed '27 women and 7 girls, Sunni and Shia; their families and lawyers; medical service providers in women's prisons; civil society representatives; foreign embassy and United Nations staff in Baghdad; Justice, Interior, Defense, and Human Rights ministry officials, and two deputy prime ministers … [and also] reviewed court documents, lawyers' case files, and government decisions and reports'. That report alleged that the Iraqi law enforcement authorities arbitrarily detained, threatened, assaulted (including sexually) women and girls, sometimes in order to extract information on male family members. UNICEF's 2015 report 'Education Under Fire: how conflict in the Middle East is depriving children of their schooling' combined statistical and anecdotal information to document the effect of insecurity caused by conflict to restrict educational opportunities for children in Iraq, Syria, Lebanon, Palestine, Yemen, Sudan and Libya. Some of the causes of this insecurity, including the forced displacement of populations, destruction of homes and collective punishment, is documented in Amnesty International's 2016 report, 'Banished and Dispossessed: Forced Displacement and Deliberate Destruction in Northern Iraq'. Amnesty's finding are reinforced in the 'Report on the Protection of Civilians in the Armed Conflict in Iraq, 1 May–31 October 2015' jointly authored by the United Nations Assistance Mission for Iraq (UNAMI) and the Office of the United Nations High Commissioner for Human Rights (OHCHR), in which it is reported '[f]rom 1 January 2014 through to the end of October 2015 … at least 55,047 civilian casualties [resulted from] the non-international [sic] armed conflict in Iraq: 18,802 killed and 36,245 wounded'. The report documents violations committed by ISIS and other armed groups, including killings of civilians, including community and religious leaders, former Iraqi armed forces members, police, and those associated with them, abductions, deliberate targeting of civilians and civilian infrastructure, use of chemical weapons, attacks on ethnic and religious minority communities, on women and children, gender-based violence, including sexual violence, forced recruitment and use of children, and the denial of other fundamental rights and freedoms. In addition, pro-government forces were alleged to have committed a wide range of offences, including restrictions on freedom of movement, police raids and arbitrary arrests, forced evictions, unlawful killings, abductions, and airstrikes on and shelling of civilians (UNAMI/OHCHR 2015). A related finding was documented in a World Bank (2019) report on 'Child Labour in Iraq', which revealed that '[c]hildren in Iraq engage in the worst forms of child labor, including in forced begging and in commercial sexual exploitation, each sometimes as a result of human trafficking'.

The UNICEF supported (2019) survey of about 35,000 Iraqi households undertaken in 2018 collected data on a wide range of aspects concerning the situation of women and children. The survey included questions on a wide range of factors that go together to affect the environment in which women give birth to and support children. Included are questions on the dates of births and deaths of all children, enabling under-five child mortality rates to be calculated from information collected in the birth histories of the women's questionnaires (UNICEF 2019: 66). That report derives a rate of 26 per thousand live births for Iraq as a whole, with higher rates in rural areas, somewhat lower than the figure of 30 given in UNICEF's 2018 report. This compares to 17 for Jordan, 15 for Iran, 8 for Kuwait, 8 for Lebanon, and 5 for Europe (UNICEF 2019; World Bank n.d.).

These reports each focus on specific phenomena with their associated indicators, often expressed in specialized, sometimes technocratic jargon. As we observed from the (Baker et al.) case studies, however, a consistent pattern emerges: a series of violent disruptions of state and community infrastructure has shattered people's lives, and generalized insecurity has replaced whatever sense of civic and national culture that may have existed previously. Understood in the full context of Iraqi experience since the US exercised power in the region, the phenomena that these different reports document are the collective consequence of an American project to terminate the Iraqi state.

REFERENCES

Abdullah, Hamid. 2023. Tilk al-Ayam (Arabic), 15 June, (vid.) https://www.youtube.com/watch?v=r-d-xbnoyG4. Accessed 2 July 2023.

Abizaid, John. 2007. Gen. Abizaid on Iraq War: "Of Course It's About Oil". *Democracy Now*, 16 October, https://www.democracynow.org/2007/10/16/headlines/gen_abizaid_on_iraq_war_of_course_its_about_oil. Accessed 29 April 2023.

Abouzeid, Rania. 2012. Meet the Islamist Militants Fighting Alongside Syria's Rebels. *Time*, 26 July, https://world.time.com/2012/07/26/time-exclusive-meet-the-islamist-militants-fighting-alongside-syrias-rebels/. Accessed 9 March 2023.

Aburish, Said K. 1997. *A Brutal Friendship: The West and The Arab Elite*. Victor Gollancz.

Adriaensens, Dirk. 2010.'Ending States that Sponsor Terrorism: Dismantling the Iraqi State, Destroying an Entire Country, Destroying Iraqi culture, erasing collective memory. *Global Research*, 5 November, https://www.globalresearch.ca/ending-states-that-sponsor-terrorism-dismantling-the-iraqi-state-destroying-an-entire-country/21781. Accessed 16 March 2023.

Alpher, David. 2017. *Past Is Prologue: Abroad in Syria with the Ghosts of Iraq*. United States Department of the Army, Peacekeeping and Stability Operations Institute (PKSOI), January, https://apps.dtic.mil/sti/trecms/pdf/AD1058528.pdf. Accessed 1 March 2023.

Amnesty International. 2016. *Banished and Dispossessed: Forced Displacement and Deliberate Destruction in Northern Iraq*. Amnesty International. https://www.amnesty.org/en/documents/mde14/3229/2016/en/. Accessed 3 May 2023.

Arraf, Jane. 2021. Iraq Reclaims 17,000 Looted Artifacts, Its Biggest-Ever Repatriation. *New York Times*, 3 August, https://www.nytimes.com/2021/08/03/world/middleeast/iraq-looted-artifacts-return.html. Accessed 18 May 2023.

Ashton, Nigel. 2010. *Hussein: A Political Life*. Yale University Press.
Associated Press. 2008. Historic Handshake: Barak Meets Iraq's President in Athens. *Haaretz*, 1 July, 2008, https://www.haaretz.com/2008-07-01/ty-article/historic-handshake-barak-meets-iraqs-president-in-athens/0000017f-f110-df98-a5ff-f3bdde660000. Accessed 29 April 2023.
Bahrani, Zainab. 2003. Looting and Conquest. *The Nation*, 14 May, http://www.thenation.com/doc/20030526/bahrani. Accessed December 2008.
Baker, Raymond W., Shereen T. Ismael, and Tareq Y. Ismael. 2010. *Cultural Cleansing in Iraq: Why Museums Were Looted, Libraries Burned and Academics Murdered*. Pluto Press.
Baroud, Ramzy. 2008. The Not-so-Historic Barak-Talabani Handshake. *Counterpunch*, 11 July, http://www.counterpunch.org/baroud07112008.html. Accessed 15 March 2009.
BBC News. 2006. Iraq 'Death Squad Caught in Act, 16 February, http://news.bbc.co.uk/2/hi/middle_east/4719252.stm. Accessed March 2009.
Bellinger, John. 2016. The Chilcot Inquiry and the Legal Basis for the Iraq War. *Lawfare*, 11 July, https://www.lawfareblog.com/chilcot-inquiry-and-legal-basis-iraq-war. Accessed 24 March.
Benhorin, Yitzhak. 2008. Doug Feith: Israel Didn'T Push for Iraq War. *Ynet*, 13 May, https://www.ynetnews.com/articles/0,7340,L-3542925,00.html. Accessed 18 May 2023.
Bhadrakumar, M.K. 2023c. Foreign Devils on the Road to Afghanistan. *Indian Punchline*, 12 March, https://www.indianpunchline.com/foreign-devils-on-the-road-to-afghanistan/. Accessed 12 March 2023.
———. 2023e. US Is Stirring Up the Syrian Cauldron. *Indian Punchline*, 26 March, https://www.indianpunchline.com/us-is-stirring-up-the-syrian-cauldron/. Accessed 3 March 2023.
Borger, Julian. 2003. The Spies Who Pushed for War. *Guardian*, 17 July, http://www.guardian.co.uk/world/2003/jul/17/iraq.usa. Accessed March 2009.
Buckley, Cara. 2007. Rare Look Inside Baghdad Museum. *New York Times*, 12 December, https://www.nytimes.com/2007/12/12/world/middleeast/12iraq.html. Accessed 29 April 2023.
Bush, George W. 2001a. Statement by the President in His Address to the Nation. *The White House*, 11 September, https://georgewbush-whitehouse.archives.gov/news/releases/2001/09/20010911-16.html. Accessed 4 April 2023.
———. 2001b. Address to a Joint Session of Congress and the American People, 20 September, https://georgewbush-whitehouse.archives.gov/news/releases/2001/09/20010920-8.html. Accessed 3 April 2023.
———. 2002a. State of the Union Address, 20 January, National Security Archive. https://nsarchive.gwu.edu/document/28048-document-08-george-w-bush-state-union-address-january-20-2002. Accessed 21 March 2023.

———. 2002b. President Bush Delivers Graduation Speech at West Point United States Military Academy, West Point, New York. *The White House*, 1 June, https://georgewbush-whitehouse.archives.gov/news/releases/2002/06/20020601-3.html. Accessed 22 March 2023.

Camu, Cyril, and Louet, Sophie. 2017. French Military Says Coalition Opposed IS Withdrawal from Raqqa, 16 November, https://www.reuters.com/article/us-mideast-crisis-syria-france/french-military-says-coalition-opposed-is-withdrawal-from-raqqa-idUSKBN1DG1VP. Accessed 16 March 2023.

Cheney, Dick. 1992. Defense Planning Guidance. *National Archives*. https://www.archives.gov/files/declassification/iscap/pdf/2008-003-doc14.pdf. Accessed 2 May 2023.

———. 2004. *Full Text of Dick Cheney's Speech at the Institute of Petroleum Autumn Lunch 1999*. London Institute of Petroleum, 8 June, http://www.energybulletin.net/559.html. Accessed December 2008.

Chossudovsky, Michel. 2023. Twelve Years Ago: The US-NATO-Israel Sponsored Al Qaeda Insurgency in Syria. Who Was Behind The 2011 "Protest Movement"? *Global Research*, 17 March 2023, https://www.globalresearch.ca/syria-who-is-behind-the-protest-movement-fabricating-a-pretext-for-a-us-nato-humanitarian-intervention/24591. Accessed 8 May 2023.

Clark, Wesley. 2007. Gen. Wesley Clark Weighs Presidential Bid: "I Think About It Every Day. *Democracy Now*, 2 March, https://www.democracynow.org/2007/3/2/gen_wesley_clark_weighs_presidential_bid. Accessed 13 March 2023.

Clinton, Hillary. 2011. Hillary Clinton Laughing About Muammar Gaddafi's Death. *YouTube Video*. https://www.youtube.com/watch?v=7voBEfcHfJg. Accessed 1 May 2023.

Cockburn, Patrick. 2014. MI6, the CIA and Turkey's Rogue Game in Syria: World View: New Claims Say Ankara Worked with the US and Britain to Smuggle Gaddafi's Guns to Rebel Groups. *The Independent*, 13 April, https://www.independent.co.uk/voices/comment/mi6-the-cia-and-turkey-s-rogue-game-in-syria-9256551.html. Accessed 18 March 2023.

———. 2015. *The Rise of Islamic State: ISIS and the New Sunni Revolution*. Verso.

Cole, Juan. 2007. Informed Comment, 20 December, http://www.juancole.com. Accessed December 2008.

Corn, David. 2005. From Iran-Contra to Iraq. *The Nation*, 6 May, https://www.thenation.com/article/archive/iran-contra-iraq/. Accessed 29 April 2023.

Crane, Susan A., ed. 2000. *Museums and Memory*. Stanford University Press.

Deblauwe, Francis. 2005. Mesopotamian Ruins and American Scholars, August, http://www.bibleinterp.com/articles/Deblauwe_ Mesopotamian_Scholars.htm. Accessed December 2008.

Dickinson, Elizabeth. 2008. Study: Surge of Violence Led to Peace in Iraq. *Foreign Policy: Passport*, 19 September, https://foreignpolicy.com/2008/09/19/study-surge-of-violence-led-to-peace-in-iraq/. Accessed 29 April 2023.

Donnelly, Thomas. 2000. *Rebuilding America's Defenses: Strategy, Forces and Resources for a New Century*. Washington: Project for a New American Century, 1 September, https://archive.org/details/RebuildingAmericasDefenses. Accessed 28 February 2023.

Evans, Dominic, and Orhan Coskun. 2017. Defector Says Thousands of Islamic State Fighters Left Raqqa in Secret Deal. *Reuters*, 7 December, https://www.reuters.com/article/us-mideast-crisis-syria-defector-idUSKBN1E12AP. Accessed 15 March 2023.

Falk, Richard. 2009. Israeli War Crimes. *Le Monde diplomatique*, March. https://mondediplo.com/2009/03/03warcrimes. Accessed 30 April 2023.

———. 2017. What the Chilcot Report Teaches Us. *International Journal of Contemporary Iraqi Studies* 11 (1): 13–22, March, https://intellectdiscover.com/content/journals/10.1386/ijcis.11.1-2.13_1. Accessed 24 March 2023.

———. 2018. The West, Led By the US, Has Shown as Much Contempt for International Law as Assad in the Conflict. *Middle East Eye*, 13 June, https://www.middleeasteye.net/opinion/hypocrisy-wests-syria-policy. Accessed 2 April 2023.

Fisk, Robert. 2007a. It Is the Death of History. *The Independent*, 17 September, http://www.independent.co.uk/opinion/commentators/fisk/robert-fisk-it-is-the-death-of-history-402571.html. Accessed March 2008.

———. 2007b. Another Crime of Occupation Iraq: Cultural Heritage Looted, Pillaged. *The Independent*, 17 September 2007, http://www. alternet.org/waroniraq/62810/. Accessed December 2008.

———. 2016. After Mosul Falls, ISIS Will Flee to Syria. Then What? *Consortium News*, 18 October, https://www.counterpunch.org/2016/10/18/after-mosul-falls-isis-will-flee-to-syria-then-what/. Accessed 18 May 2023.

Forte, Maximilian C. 2012. *Slouching Towards Sirte: NATO's War on Libya and Africa*. Baraka Books.

Frontline. 1990. The Arming of Iraq. 11 September, https://www.pbs.org/wgbh/pages/frontline/shows/longroad/etc/arming.html. Accessed 12 June 2023.

Gerstein, Josh. 2014. Biden Sorry for ISIL Funding Remarks That Echoed Obama. *Politico*, 6 October, https://www.politico.com/blogs/under-the-radar/2014/10/biden-sorry-for-isil-funding-remarks-that-echoed-obama-196622. Accessed 20 May 2023.

Goldberg, Geoffrey. 2016. The Obama Doctrine. *The Atlantic*, April, https://www.theatlantic.com/magazine/archive/2016/04/the-obama-doctrine/471525/. Accessed 15 March 2023.

Gugliotta, Guy. 2005. Looted Iraqi Relics Slow to Resurface; Some Famous Pieces Unlikely to Re-appear. *Washington Post*, 8 November, http://www.washingtonpost.com/wp-dyn/content/article/2005/11/07/AR2005110701479.html. Accessed December 2008.

Hassan, Ghali. 2005. The Destruction of Iraq's Educational System Under US Occupation, 11 May, http://www.globalresearch.ca/articles/HAS505B.html. Accessed December 2008.

Hathaway, Oona A. 2016. What the Chilcot Report Teaches Us About National Security Lawyering. *Just Security*, 11 July, https://www.justsecurity. org/31946/chilcot-report-teaches-national-security-lawyering/. Accessed 18 May 2023.

Hedges, Chris. 2023. The Lords of Chaos. *Consortium News*, 20 March, https:// consortiumnews.com/2023/03/20/iraq-20-years-chris-hedges-the-lords-of-chaos/. Accessed 22 March 2023.

Hersh, Seymour M. 2003b. Moving Targets. *The New Yorker*, 15 December, http://www.newyorker.com/archive/2003/12/15/031215fa_fact. Accessed March 2009.

———. 2004b. Plan B. *The New Yorker*, June 28, http://www.newyorker.com/ archive/2004/06/28/040628fa_fact. Accessed March 2009.

———. 2007. The Redirection: Is the Administration's New Policy Benefitting Our Enemies in the War on Terrorism? *The New Yorker*, 25 February, https:// www.newyorker.com/magazine/2007/03/05/the-redirection. Accessed 9 March 2023.

———. 2014. The Red Line and the Rat Line. *London Review of Books*, April.

Hoff, Brad. 2012. Defense Intelligence Agency Document: West Will Facilitate Rise of Islamic State "In Order to Isolate the Syrian Regime", Levant Report. https://levantreport.com/2015/05/19/2012-defense-intelligence-agency-document-west-will-facilitate-rise-of-islamic-state-in-order-to-isolate-the-syrian-regime/. Accessed 15 March 2023.

Hughes, David. 2016. Chilcot Report: John Prescott Says Iraq War Was Illegal. *The Independent*, 9 July, https://www.independent.co.uk/news/uk/politics/ chilcot-report-john-prescott-says-tony-blair-led-uk-into-illegal-war-in-iraq-a7129106.html. Accessed 24 March 2023.

Human Rights Watch. 2014. "No-One is Safe": The Abuse of Women in Iraq's Criminal Justice System. *Human Rights Watch*, February, https://www.hrw. org/report/2014/02/06/no-one-safe/abuse-women-iraqs-criminal-justice-system. Accessed 4 May 2023.

Husseini, Sam. 2023. The Lies, and Lies About the Lies, About the Invasion. *Consortium News*, March 20, https://consortiumnews.com/2023/03/20/ iraq-20-years-sam-husseini-the-lies-and-lies-about-the-lies-about-the-invasion/. Accessed 22 March 2023.

Institut Kurde de Paris. 2006. Iraqi Kurdistan Unifies its Administration with a Single Government. Institut Kurde de Paris 254, May, p. 2, http://www.institutkurde.org/en/publications/bulletins/254.html. Accessed March 2009.

Institute for Public Accuracy. 2019. *Postol: Newly Revealed Documents Show Syrian Chemical "Attacks Were Staged"*. Institute for Public Accuracy, 21 May 2019, https://accuracy.org/release/postol-newly-revealed-documents-show-syrian-chemical-attacks-were-staged. Accessed 18 March 2023.

Ismael, Tareq Y., and Jacqueline S. Ismael. 2021. *Iraq in the Twenty-First Century: Regime Change and the Making of a Failed State*. Routledge.

Jackson, Ashley. 2018. *Persian Gulf Command: A History of the Second World War in Iran and Iraq*. Yale University Press.

Jenkins, Simon. 2007. In Iraq's Four-Year Looting Frenzy, the Allies Have Become the Vandals. *Guardian*, 8 June, http://www. guardian.co.uk/Iraq/Story/0,2098273,00.html. Accessed December 2008.

Kaleck, Wolfgang. 2016. *The Iraq Invasion Is a Crime*. European Centre for Constitutional and Human Rights. https://www.ecchr.eu/en/publication/the-iraq-invasion-is-a-crime/. Accessed 24 March 2023.

Kirk, Michael. 2003. The War Behind Closed Doors: Excerpts from 1992 Draft "Defense Planning Guidance". *PBS: Frontline*, https://www.pbs.org/wgbh/pages/frontline/shows/iraq/etc/script.html. Accessed 3 April 2023.

Klein, Naomi. 2007. *The Shock Doctrine*. Alfred A. Knopf Canada.

Kramer, Andrew E. 2008. Deals With Iraq Are Set to Bring Oil Giants Back. *New York Times*, 19 June, https://www.nytimes.com/2008/06/19/world/middleeast/19iraq.html. Accessed 29 April 2023.

Krishnan, Nandini, and Sergio Olivieri. 2016. Losing the Gains of the Past: The Welfare and Distributional Impacts of the Twin Crises in Iraq 2014. Policy Research Working Paper; No. WPS 7567. Washington, DC: World Bank Group. https://documents1.worldbank.org/curated/en/217401467995379476/pdf/WPS7567.pdf. Accessed 29 March 2023.

Lauria, Joe. 2023. Covering the "Vial Display". *Consortium News*, 19 March, https://consortiumnews.com/2023/03/19/iraq-20-years-joe-lauria-one-resignation-may-have-stopped-the-disastrous-invasion/. Accessed 22 March 2023.

Lloyd, Richard, and Theodore A. Postol. 2014. Possible Implications of Faulty US Technical Intelligence in the Damascus Nerve Agent Attack of August 21, 2013. MIT, Science, Technology, and Global Security Working Group, 14 January, https://s3.amazonaws.com/s3.documentcloud.org/documents/1006045/possible-implications-of-bad-intelligence.pdf. Accessed 18 March 2023.

Loughlin, Sean. 2003. Rumsfeldw on Looting in Iraq: "Stuff Happens". *CNN*, 12 April, https://www.cnn.com/2003/US/04/11/sprj.irq.pentagon/. Accessed 4 April 2023.

Maass, Pater. 2005. The Way of the Commandos. *New York Times*, 1 May. https://www.nytimes.com/2005/05/01/magazine/the-way-of-the-commandos.html. Accessed 29 April 2023.

Maté, Aaron. 2019. Top Scientist Slams OPCW Leadership for Repressing Dissenting Report on Syria Gas Attack. *The Greyzone*, 18 June, https://thegrayzone.com/2019/06/18/theodore-postol-opcw-syria-gas-attack-douma/. Accessed 18 March 2023.

McGovern, Ray. 2023a. Iraq 20 Years: The Uses and Abuses of National Intelligence Estimates. *Consortium News*, 19 March, https://consortiumnews.com/2023/03/19/iraq-20-years-ray-mcgovern-the-uses-and-abuses-of-national-intelligence-estimates/. Accessed 20 March 2023.

McNerney, Michael J., Gabrielle Tarini, Nate Rosenblatt, Karen M. Sudkamp, Pauline Moore, Benjamin J. Sacks Grise, and Larry Lewis. 2022. *Understanding Civilian Harm in Raqqa and Its Implications for Future Conflicts*. Rand Corporation. https://www.rand.org/content/dam/rand/pubs/research_reports/RRA700/RRA753-1/RAND_RRA753-1.pdf. Accessed 16 March 2023.

Mearsheimer, John J. and Stephen M. Walt. 2006. The Israel Lobby. *London Review of Books*, 23 March, https://www.lrb.co.uk/the-paper/v28/n06/john-mearsheimer/the-israel-lobby. Accessed 17 January 2024.

Mearsheimer, John J., and Stephen M. Walt. 2009b. *The Israel Lobby and U.S. Foreign Policy*. Macmillan.

Moon of Alabama. 2013a. More Disarray in the Syrian Opposition, 24 March, https://www.moonofalabama.org/2013/03/index.html. Accessed 10 March 2023.

———. 2013b. Syria: NYT Starts Telling the Truth About Syria, 28 April, https://www.moonofalabama.org/2013/04/index.html. Accessed 10 March 2023.

———. 2013c. Syria: News Roundup, 17 May, https://www.moonofalabama.org/2013/05/index.html. Accessed 10 March 2023.

———. 2013d. What We DO Know About Chemical Weapons in Syria, 14 June, https://www.moonofalabama.org/2013/06/index.html. Accessed 9 March 2023.

———. 2013e. Syria: Another False Flag "Chemical Weapon" Attack, 21 August, https://www.moonofalabama.org/2013/08/index.html. Accessed 9 March 2023.

———. 2013f. A Short History of the War on Syria—2006–2014, 14 September, https://www.moonofalabama.org/2013/09/index.html. Accessed 9 March 2023.

———. 2013g. Syria: NYT, HRW Wrong to Claim Chemical Attack Origin, 22 September, https://www.moonofalabama.org/2013/09/index.html. Accessed 9 March 2023.

———. 2013h. The "de-Americanized" World' and 'NYT's OPCW "He Said, She Said" Reporting Misses Major Judgement, 15 October, https://www.moonofalabama.org/2013/11/index.html. Accessed 9 March 2023.

————. 2017c. How The U.S. Enabled ISIS to Take Deir Ezzor, 17 January, https://www.moonofalabama.org/2017/01/index.html. Accessed 9 March 2023.

Mortada, Radwan. 2023. Iraq's ex-PM Adil Abdul-Mahdi: "The US Doesn't Defeat Terror, It Only Tries to Balance It". *The Cradle*, 9 June, https://the-cradle.co/article-view/25706/iraqs-ex-pm-adil-abdul-mahdi-the-us-doesnt-defeat-terror-it-only-tries-to-balance-it. Accessed 11 June 2023.

Nahigyan, Pierce. 2014. Seymour Hersh Links Turkey to Benghazi, Syria and Sarin. *Foreign Policy*, 6 May, https://www.foreignpolicyjournal.com/2014/05/06/seymour-hersh-links-turkey-to-benghazi-syria-and-sarin/. Accessed 18 March 2023.

National Security Archive. 2001. The Iraq War—Part I: The U.S. Prepares for Conflict, 2001, 21 September, https://nsarchive2.gwu.edu/NSAEBB/NSAEBB326/print.htm. Accessed 22 March 2023.

New York Times. 2004. From The Editors; *The Times* and Iraq, 26 May, https://www.nytimes.com/2004/05/26/world/from-the-editors-the-times-and-iraq.html?searchResultPosition=1. Accessed 22 March 2023.

Obama, Barack. 2012. Remarks by the President to the White House Press Corps. *The White House*, 20 August, https://obamawhitehouse.archives.gov/the-press-office/2012/08/20/remarks-president-white-house-press-corps. Accessed 30 April 2023.

OPCW. 2017. Press Release on Allegations of Chemical Weapons Use in Southern Idlib, Syria, 4 April, https://www.opcw.org/media-centre/news/2017/04/opcw-press-release-allegations-chemical-weapons-use-southern-idlib-syria. Accessed 15 March 2023.

Oren, Amir. 2009. British Author: Rabin Asked Jordan to Arrange Secret Visit with Saddam. *Haaretz*, 27 February, https://www.haaretz.com/2009-02-27/ty-article/british-author-rabin-asked-jordan-to-arrange-secret-visit-with-saddam/0000017f-e127-d568-ad7f-f36f67b60000. Accessed 29 April 2023.

Ose, Hoshnag. 2008. A Secret Relationship. *Niqash*, 8 September, http://www.niqash.org/content.php?contentTypeID=75&id=2285&lang=0. Accessed March 2009.

Patterson, Graham. 2007. Alan Greenspan Claims Iraq War Was Really for Oil. *The Sunday Times*. https://www.thetimes.co.uk/article/alan-greenspan-claims-iraq-war-was-really-for-oil-5vr9rqdvbgp. Accessed 27 June 2023.

PBS. 2006. The Lost Year in Iraq, 17 October, http://www.pbs.org/wgbh/pages/frontline/yeariniraq/documents/bremermemo.pdf. Accessed 1 March 2023.

Peries, Sharmini. 2019. New Evidence Suggests 2018 Chemical Attack in Douma, Syria Was Staged. *The Real News Network*, 10 June, https://therealnews.com/new-evidence-suggests-2018-syria-chemical-attack-in-douma-was-staged. Accessed 19 May 2023.

Perle, Richard, James Colbert, Charles Fairbanks, Jr., Douglas Feith, Robert Loewenberg, David Wurmser, and Meyrav Wurmser. 1996. A Clean Break: A New Strategy for Securing the Realm, the Institute for Advanced Strategic and Political Studies, Study Group on a New Israeli Strategy Toward 2000. https:// web.archive.org/web/20140125123844/, http://www.iasps.org/strat1. htm. Accessed 3 April 2023.

Pleming, Sue. 2009. US Plans "Substantial" Pledge at Gaza Meeting. *Reuters*, 24 February, https://www.reuters.com/article/us-palestinians-clinton-idUSN2350280520090224. Accessed 29 April 2023.

Porter, Gareth. 2016. US Strikes on Syrian Troops: Report Data Contradicts "Mistake" Claims: Moscow and Damascus Cited the Attacks as the Reason for Declaring an End to the Ceasefire in Syria. *Antiwar.com*, 8 December, https:// original.antiwar.com/porter/2016/12/07/us-strikes-syrian-troops-report-data-contradicts-mistake-claims/. Accessed March 14, 2023.

Postol, Theodore. 2017. With Error Fixed, Evidence Against "Sarin Attack" Remains Convincing. *Truthdig*, 22 April, https://www.truthdig.com/articles/with-error-fixed-evidence-against-sarin-attack-remains-convincing-2/. Accessed 18 March 2023.

Powell, Jerome. 2003. *U.S. Secretary of State Colin Powell Addresses the U.N. Security Council*. National Security Archive, 5 February, https:// georgewbush-whitehouse.archives.gov/news/releases/2003/02/20030205-1.html. Accessed 21 March 2023.

———. 2005. Colin Powell on Iraq, Race, and Hurricane Relief. *ABC News*, 8 September, https://abcnews.go.com/2020/Politics/story?id= 1105979&page=1. Accessed 21 March 2023.

Riedel, Bruce. 2021. *9/11 and Iraq: The Making of a Tragedy*. Brookings, September 17, https://www.brookings.edu/blog/order-from-chaos/2021/09/17/9-11-and-iraq-the-making-of-a-tragedy/. Accessed 3 April 2023.

Ritter, Scott. 2017. Ex-Weapons Inspector: Trump's Sarin Claims Built on "Lie". *The American Conservative*, June 29, https://www.theamericanconservative. com/ex-weapons-inspector-trumps-sarin-claims-built-on-lie/. Accessed 15 March 2023.

———. 2023a. *Scott Ritter Opposing Iraq Invasion*, August 2002 (vid.). Consortium Research, March 21, 2023, https://consortiumnews. com/2023/03/21/watch-scott-ritter-opposing-iraq-invasion-august-2002/. Accessed 21 March 2023.

Rose, David. 2008. The Gaza Bombshell. *Vanity Fair*, April 2008, http://www. vanityfair.com/politics/features/2008/04/gaza200804. Accessed 29 April 2023.

Rosen, Nir. 2008. The Myth of the Surge. *Rolling Stone*, 6 May, https://www. academia.edu/969403/The_Myth_of_the_Surge. Accessed 29 April 2023.

Smith, Michael E. 2003. This Is Not the "Antiques Roadshow". 23 April, http://
www.public.asu.edu/~mesmith9/Antiquities.html. Accessed 29 April 2023.
Smith, Stephen. 2006. "Furious Envy": Baudrillard and the Looting of Baghdad.
International Journal of Baudrillard Studies 3 (2), July, https://baudrillard-
studies.ubishops.ca/furious-envy-baudrillard-and-the-looting-of-baghdad/.
Accessed 1 March 2023.
Sommerville, Quentin, and Riam Dalati. 2017. Raqqa's Dirty Secret. *BBC*, 13
November, https://www.bbc.co.uk/news/resources/idt-sh/raqqas_dirty_
secret. Accessed 16 March 2023.
Spectacles. 2024. This Will Change How You Think about the Iraq War, 4
November, https://www.youtube.com/watch?v=-cjriLK-y14. Accessed 5
February 2024.
Stein, Jonathan, and Tim Dickinson. 2006. Lie by Lie: A Timeline of How We
Got Into Iraq, Mushroom Clouds, Duct Tape, Judy Miller, Curveball. Recalling
How Americans Were Sold a Bogus Case for Invasion. *Mother Jones*, September–
October, https://www.motherjones.com/politics/2011/12/leadup-iraq-
war-timeline/. Accessed 4 April 2023.
Stephen, Linda. 2016. Iraq—Comprehensive Food Security and Vulnerability
Analysis (CFSVA). World Food Program, 1 May, https://www.wfp.org/.
Accessed 1 May 2023.
Suskind, Ron. 2004a. *The Price of Loyalty: George W. Bush, the White House, and the
Education of Paul O'Neill*. Simon & Schuster.
Susman, Tina. 2007 Poll: Civilian Toll in Iraq May Top 1M. *Los Angeles Times*, 14
September, https://www.latimes.com/world/la-fg-iraq14sep14-story.html.
Accessed 30 April 2023.
Syria Propaganda Media. 2019. Engineering Assessment of Two Cylinders
Observed at the Douma Incident, 21 February, http://syriapropagandamedia.
org/wp-content/uploads/2019/05/Engineering-assessment-of-two-
cylinders-observed-at-the-Douma-incident-27-February-2019-1.pdf. Accessed
19 May 2023.
The Cradle. 2023. Exclusive Interview with Hezbollah Commander in Iraq: 'The
Americans Did Not Fight ISIS'. *The Cradle*, 4 January, https://thecradle.co/
article-view/19989/exclusive-interview-with-hezbollah-commander-in-iraq-
the-americans-did-not-fight-isis. Accessed 11 June 2023.
Thompson, Mark. 2008. Shinseki, a Prescient General, Re-Enlists as VA Chief.
Time, 8 December, https://content.time.com/time/politics/arti-
cle/0,8599,1864915,00.html. Accessed 19 May 2023.
———. 2015. How Disbanding the Iraqi Army Fueled ISIS. *Time*, 28 May,
https://time.com/3900753/isis-iraq-syria-army-united-states-military/.
Accessed 5 February 2024.
UNICEF. 2015. Education Under Fire: How Conflict in the Middle East Is
Depriving Children of Their Schooling. UNICEF, 3 September, https://
reliefweb.int/report/syrian-arab-republic/education-under-fire-how-conflict-
middle-east-depriving-children-their. Accessed 3 May 2023.

————. 2019. *Iraq Multiple Indicator Cluster Survey*. UNICEF, 2018, https://mics.unicef.org/files?job=W1siZiIsIjIwMTkvMDMvMDEvMTkvMj MvMTgvNTg5L0VuZ2xpc2gucGRmIl1d&sha=aea1de7cc6f6ec09.Accessed 7 April 2023.

United Kingdom. 2016. The Iraq Inquiry (Chilcot Report). The National Archives, 6 July, http://blogs.bbk.ac.uk/bbkcomments/2016/07/ 06/chilcot-report-the-consequences-for-international-law/. Accessed 24 March 2023.

United Nations Assistance Mission for Iraq (UNAMI) and the Office of the United Nations High Commissioner for Human Rights (OHCHR). 2015. *Report on the Protection of Civilians in the Armed Conflict in Iraq, 1 May–31 October*, https://www.ohchr.org/en/documents/country-reports/ report-protection-civilians-armed-conflict-iraq-1-may-31-october-2015. Accessed 4 May 2023.

United Nations Security Council. 2015. Resolution 2202 (2015), Adopted by the Security Council at its 7384th Meeting, on 17 February 2015, https://www. securitycouncilreport.org/atf/cf/{65BFCF9B-6D27-4E9C-8CD3-CF6E4FF96FF9}/s_res_2202.pdf. Accessed 20 January 2024.

United States Department of State. 2003. Oil and Energy Working Group. Future of Iraq Project, https://nsarchive2.gwu.edu/NSAEBB/NSAEBB198/FOI Oil.pdf. Accessed 28 February 2023.

Webb, Gary. 1999. Dark Alliance, Seven Stories Press.

Wilhelmsen, Julie, and Geir Flikke. 2005. *"Copy That..."*: *A Russian "Bush Doctrine in the CIS?"*. Norwegian Institute of International Affairs. https://nupi.brage. unit.no/nupi-xmlui/bitstream/handle/11250/2393750/Rapport_ nr285_05_Flikke_Wilhelmsen.pdf?sequence=3. Accessed 16 March 2023.

Wolfowitz, Paul. 2001. *Interview with BBC*. Press Release, US Department of Defence, 6 November, https://www.scoop.co.nz/stories/WO0111/ S00044/deputy-secretary-wolfowitz-interview-with-bbc.htm?from-mobile=bottom-link-01. Accessed 16 March 2023.

World Bank. 2019. *Child Labour in Iraq*. World Bank. https://www.dol.gov/ agencies/ilab/resources/reports/child-labor/iraq. Accessed 2 May 2023.

————. n.d. Mortality Rate, Under-5 (per 1000 Live Births)—Middle East & North Africa. https://data.worldbank.org/indicator/SH.DYN. MORT?end=2021&locations=ZQ-KW&start=2016. Accessed 2 May 2023.

Yergin, Daniel. 2006. Ensuring Energy Security. *Foreign Affairs*, 1 March, https://www.foreignaffairs.com/world/ensuring-energy-security. Accessed 25 June.

Zerouky, Hassane. 2006. *Hamas Is a Creation of Mossad*. Global Research. http://globalresearch.ca/articles/ZER403A.html. Accessed 28 February 2023.

CHAPTER 3

Kurdistan and the Iraqi State

INTRODUCTION

Established through the Anglo-American intervention of 1991 and framed within the legacies of the longstanding conflict between Kurdish separatists and the Iraqi state, Arab-Kurdish ethnic rivalry prior to the 1991 war, and the human rights abuses of the Ba'athist regime, the KRG (Kurdistan Regional Government) was a governance project instituted to replace that of the Iraqi state in Iraq's three northern provinces from 1991. Beyond Kurdistan, it was part of a regime change-plan to put in place a post-invasion government to replace the regime of Saddam Hussein. From our present vantage point, it was a part of the Pax Americana project to destroy the Iraqi state as a regional power. The KRG became the catalyst to gather all other forces that could become the nucleus for the destruction of the Iraqi state, including the religious Shi'ite groups that were formed and supported by Iran. Among the consequences are the machinations of the opposition in exile and their effects on post-2003 governance, the establishment of federal institutions, the promotion of Islamist political factions such as the Islamic Dawa Party as legitimate representatives of the Iraqi people, and the failure to secure a democratic framework for a post-Ba'athist state. For KRG-Iraqi relations, the consequences include the constitutional framing and enshrinement of sectarianism, the emergence of the 'disputed territories' and the immense levels of criminality,

J. S. Ismael et al., *Pax Americana*, Frontiers of Globalization, https://doi.org/10.1007/978-3-031-61273-2_3

corruption and political violence, which have all played a role in undermining political authority and legitimacy.

Exploitation of Kurdish nationalism by the US was hardly an innovation for the regional politics of the Gulf: the Americans could have learned (if they needed lessons) from the efforts of Britain, Iran, Turkey, Israel, and Syria. As a restive minority with international connections, a mountainous geography, in a region accustomed to state and tribal violence, the Kurds were an attractive resource available to a foreign power intent on weakening or destroying an independent Iraq. The opportunity to use the Kurds as a proxy for this purpose came into focus during the post-1991 period, when American-managed UN sanctions remained in force, American air power controlled Iraqi skies, and a developing Kurdish insurrection, attracting sympathetic western media attention, seemed to gather together the essential components for regime change and toward realizing the Pax Americana ambition of pacifying the Middle East. Seen from the present perspective, the Kurdish revolt against the Saddam regime was the first social formation to implement the destruction of the Iraqi state and the prelude to the eventual 2003 invasion.

A divisive factor within Iraq in modern times, the Kurdish region is itself internally divided. The two groups that are the most powerful actors in KRG are Masoud Barzani's group, the Kurdistan Democratic Party (KDP), which is centered around the Barzani family, a traditional, tribal clan, which had consolidated its control over lands from state and customary lands under the British administration (Esposti 2022; Batatu 1979). The Barzanis, initially rural, took over Irbil as their city base. The Patriotic Union of Kurdistan (PUK), a breakaway movement from the KDP, founded by Jalal Talibani in the wake of the 1975 defeat of the Kurdish revolt against the Ba'ath (Esposti 2022), represent an urban constituency, centered around the city of Suleimania. Given their respective origins and environments, they are in mutual conflict in the structure of their social base, their ideological orientations and, during the course of their dual rivalry, they became further estranged until their interests were in nearly complete divergence. However, they retain some common features: both are led by their own clans, tended to engage in intra-KRG politics with a zero-sum perspective regarding their rival, and alternately pursue collaboration with Baghdad, then greater Kurdish autonomy (Ismael and Ismael 2021: 27–34; Visser 2010). However, the traditionally based leadership of the Kurdish nationalist movement opened post-Ba'athist Iraq to state collapse and massive humanitarian harm, while at the same time failing on its own terms, in the effort to craft an environment conducive to greater autonomy for—or even sovereign statehood—for Iraqi Kurdistan.

While Anglo-American designs for Iraq along with their imposed occupation policies draw deserved opprobrium, the role played by Kurdish leaders in contemporary Iraq's circumstance merits greater attention. Some 32 years following the imposition of a no-fly zone blanketing Iraq north of the 36th parallel and the founding of the KRG, and 20 years following the Anglo-American invasion and occupation of Iraq, an assessment of the Kurdish nationalist project and the decision-making of its traditional leadership reveals considerable failures on the ground. Whether on its own terms, through the establishment of an autonomous or independent Kurdish state based on democratic norms, or through its impacts on the Iraqi state and peoples across the period of maximum Anglo-American intervention that led to a failed state, the leaders of northern Iraq have played a significant role in the degradations, failures, suppression of dissent (Amnesty International 2021) and humanitarian crises that have occurred. While the decade-old threat posed by *Daesh*—the so-called Islamic State—has diminished, the reckless assertion of sovereignty through a popular referendum on September 25, 2017, opposed by the UN Security Council and all states in the region except Israel, has aggravated the crisis and directed attention to the region's leadership (Hanish 2018; Esposti 2021; Hiltermann 2023).

The absence of any substantial development of the region's economy outside petroleum rents (*New York Times* 2018; Sosnowski 2019), a public debt exceeding 100 percent of GDP which has been repudiated by the federal government in Baghdad (Snow 2018), and a chronic failure to develop institutions of democratic governance, combine to blight the record of the project for the independence led by the KDP and PUK since 1991. Most pronounced has been their role in unsuccessful attempts to develop a more favorable regional or international diplomatic landscape, especially through KRG relations with the rest of Iraq, which were necessary conditions for any potential success of the KRG project. The unwillingness or inability of the KRG to influence its environment occurred at two primary inflection points: first, during the establishment of the nascent Iraqi exile leadership sponsored by the Anglo-American regime-change framework prior to the 2003 invasion; and second, during the formative period of the occupation when the chaotic new state apparatus was embodied in Baghdad's 'Green Zone'.

No actors involved in the struggles for sovereignty, domination and survival in Iraq, not even the global hegemon, can be said to control, or even foresee, the events they seek to shape. However, the chronic instability and lack of security in Kurdistan can be attributed to some extent as consequential to positions adopted—including the Western policies supported—by the KRG leadership. Such policies, insufficient and conceptually flawed, often prompted, and at times even drove events forward. The Kurds were victims of aggression and acts of genocide by the Saddam regime, but they had also played their part in helping the Ba'athists to power, through their 1961–1963 insurrection against Baghdad, thus weakening the Qasim regime and contributing toward the CIA-enabled coup of 1963 (Aburish 1997: 98; Ismael & Ismael 2015: 222; Esposti 2022).

Since that time, from the fall of the Ba'athist regime, through the sacrifices made by Kurdish *Peshmerga* and KRG security forces in their fight against *Daesh*, KRG leaders have not successfully leveraged the positions afforded them by efforts at the popular level into any positive influence by which to secure a more stable future for Iraqi Kurdistan's residents or the wider Iraqi population.

Failure to Secure a Democratic Post-Ba'athist state

The support of much of the predominantly Kurdish population living in northern Iraq provided these traditional leaders with both the capacity to mobilize as well as considerable political legitimacy. This legitimacy proved crucial in currying favor with political leaders in Western capitals due to the comparative absence of credibility among the rest of the Iraqi opposition in exile. KDP and PUK organizational capabilities, including the ability to control terrain, were significant aspects of nascent KRG power as they embarked on state-building efforts following the 1991 war. However, their suasion as representatives of a clearly demarcated population, largely in support of their longstanding leaderships, allowed the Kurds to amplify their position in the eyes of global civil society as well as Western states over that of groups such as the Iraqi National Congress led by Ahmed Chalabi, Iraqi National Accord led by Ayad Allawi, or Islamist groups such as the Islamic Supreme Council of Iraq and Islamic Dawa Party, viewed by many observers to be associated with the Islamic Republic of Iran. While other groups and individual political actors enjoyed favorable press coverage, and in some cases demonstrated proficient deployment of their organizations toward political opposition against the Ba'athist regime, they failed to command the grounded support that could substantiate calls for regime change and the plausibility of a functioning successor regime, such as that demonstrated by the KDP and PUK. This opportunity arose less through the historic efforts of Kurdish nationalism in Iraq than as an effect of Western intervention and the post-Cold War turn against what were portrayed as authoritarian regimes wantonly abusing the human rights of their captive populations. Through their representation and leadership of these ethnically Kurdish Iraqi citizens, the KDP and PUK were able to capture and direct this newfound power and the political and financial resources it provided. The broadcasting of Iraqi refugees fleeing Ba'athist advances across the country following the end of hostilities was identified by Western authorities as a crisis, nominally brought on by the televised atrocities taking place in northern Iraq in particular. This reaction to Iraqi state forces reasserting authority in the aftermath of the 1991 Gulf War was contemporaneously identified as the 'CNN effect' by those opposed to the end of hostilities short of regime change. This understanding of the events on the ground propelled Britain, France and the US to defend their narrative of a successful prosecution of the war through provision of humanitarian assistance and the blunting of Iraqi federal forces advances into northern Iraq (Robinson 2002).

However, the emerging norms in western countries allowed the *ad hoc* policy to be later justified as humanitarian in nature, while no commensurate concern was forthcoming for Iraqis in the south of the country (Gibbons 2002), where the Ba'ath regime reasserted control through tremendous violence against popular uprisings stoked by US intervention. Thus, with the imposition of the no-fly zone (1991–2003), Iraqi federal representation was removed from northern Iraq, allowing the KDP and PUK to establish nascent state-like functions. Moreover, the connection between this quasi- sovereign status and past humanitarian sufferings at the hands of the Iraqi state—atrocities such as the March 1988 chemical weapons attack against civilians in the Iraqi city of Halabja (Human Rights Watch 1993a, 1993b), with which Western states had been complicit (Frontline 1990; Harris and Aid 2013), nonetheless provided strong emotive justification and impetus for Kurdish autonomy as well as functional entry into the emergent post-Cold War efforts, including the doctrines of liberal intervention (Whitesell 1993; McDowell 1996; Wheeler 2002) and responsibility to protect. The era's attendant norms of human rights that expanded *de jure*, as well as *de facto* supports for military intervention—framed as humanitarian protection for targeted minorities—developed over the rest of the 1990s and fit well with the Kurdish national narrative that bolstered the KRG cause (Adams 2018).

In this fashion, legitimacy flowed to the KDP and PUK as they were increasingly acknowledged (mostly through consular representation and unofficial communications) by Western governments and civil society organizations in London, Paris and New York, both for their role in speaking for the Kurdish ethnic community of Iraq as well as their ability to credibly organize northern Iraq following the withdrawal of Iraq's federal government. Critical examinations of the *bona fides* of KRG democratic practices, the independence of non-party affiliated institutions or the quality of financial or public sector management of the emerging state structures and institutions was largely absent outside Iraqi Kurdistan itself. The atrocities and human rights abuses suffered by the Kurdish community under the Ba'ath regime prior to 1991, events largely unreported and unacknowledged at the time by Western governments (Human Rights Watch 1992a, 1992b) fostered support for the 'success' of the no-fly zone and thrust the longstanding cause of Kurdish sovereignty onto the international political agenda. At the same time, the conflation of Ba'ath atrocities, especially those of the *Anfal* campaign at the end of the Iran-Iraq war (1980–1988) with previous Iraqi state efforts over the decades prior, made post-Ba'ath comity between Iraq's many communities problematic.

While the effort to build KRG capacity gained substantial support among global civil society, in their interactions with the intelligence agencies and diplomats of Western states, Kurdistan's leaders worked to put into question any reassertion of Iraqi state sovereignty over the north, while supporting calls for regime change and the end of Ba'athist rule over the rest of the country. In the Anglo-American search for additional Iraqis to act in a similar oppositional role to the regime, the KRG's leadership's capacity to navigate the labyrinthine factions of oppositional political actors proved considerably more adroit than the failed efforts of Western state agents (Tripp 2007: 283–85). This intimate knowledge of Iraq's opposition landscape, including the hosting of many leaders and activists in northern Iraq, allowed the Kurdish leaders, using the structure of the Iraqi National Council (INC), which was under the direction and aid of the US, to be in an influential position to select Iraqi interlocutors and connect them with Western efforts at regime-change (Pope 1992; Associated Press 1998). However, in the end, this leverage proved largely ephemeral, as the lack of agency and legitimacy held by many of the Arab Iraqis selected for the regime-change project prior to the 2003 invasion led to failure. More so, their defects were on greater display following the 2003 invasion, for when tasked with managing the chaotic and defective post-Ba'ath state established through Anglo-American occupation, these opposition actors proved wanton and incapable. The empowerment of such flawed Iraqi partners, while helping the Kurds in the short-term in cultivating Kurdish relations with the Western agents, in the end denied the KRG potential confederates and allies in Baghdad more positively disposed toward the KRG project. The absence of medium- and long-term selection of such parties more open to Kurdish autonomy damaged both the potential of a post-Ba'ath Iraqi regime while also negating potential friendly faces in Baghdad when the status of KRG-Iraqi relations were to be determined following the ouster of the Ba'ath regime in 2003.

As in their flawed decision-making with the selection and promotion of varied Iraqi opposition figures, similarly myopic apprehension of democratic practices informed the basic foundations of new institutions across the KRG. Political institutions, instead of being used to develop the political capacities of Kurds within and outside the political parties, were employed instead as tools for partisan advantage and for channeling oil and other revenues along partisan lines. Commitments to factional appropriation neglected inevitable emergence of alternative social and political actors; individuals and groups who would have been tied to the new arrangements with inclusive institutions. While this exclusivity denied citizens of northern Iraq viable inputs into their governance it also undermined the very popular legitimacy that had undergird Kurdish nationalist claims from 1991. The lack of institutional independence from the traditional leadership, transparent management of the resource sector (Ekurd Daily 2022) as well as the emerging political economy disarmed any attempts at reform that would have allowed for non-traditional and unarmed actors to play a role.

Beyond the KRG itself, this raises what increasingly appear to have been nonviable conceptual designs for the institutions of governance of a potential post-Ba'ath Iraq and the institutionalized relationship between the Iraqi state and the KRG. Adopting a position of ambiguity toward the goal of outright independence for a future state of Kurdistan, as well as the role to be played by the Kurdistan Region in a federal Iraq absent popular consent from the majority of the Iraqi population, allowed for considerable latitude for delay. The lack of federal agreement with the KRG vision—and more critically that of the occupying power and its CPA or post-June 2004 relations with a nominally independent Iraq—opened such designs to considerable obfuscation. Absent confederates in Baghdad who could add support to their cause, agreement enshrined prior to the ouster of the Ba'ath and especially the agreement of the US, the foundational alteration of Iraq's territorial integrity was always to be an outcome beyond the authority of the KRG alone.

Time lost during the 1994–1997 Kurdistan civil war (Associated Press 1998) and the absence of agreed support for a clear variant of regional autonomy from the Iraqi exiles prior to the 2003 invasion—US policy had consistently opposed outright Kurdish sovereignty throughout—left the question open, and therefore largely outside the influence of Kurdistan's leaders. Each day that elapsed following the overthrow of the Ba'ath diminished the prospect of a resolution, no matter the repeated appeals to humanitarian concern, fairness or fanciful provision of a stalwart ally for Western states in the Middle East region. Over the period of the Iraqi civil war and the occupation, no resolution emerged and the constitutionally mandated referendum for Kirkuk remained stillborn. This lack of political agency at the federal level increasingly undermined KRG claims to superior governance and security provision within the increasingly violent post-invasion Iraq—an assertion of capacity that finally lost credibility with the rise of *Daesh* in 2014.

Beyond the absence of contingency planning and groundwork for regional and international diplomacy with which to support the KRG cause—regional and international sponsors and support proved fleeting, with the advance of *Daesh*, and again in the face of the Iraqi state's reassertion of sovereignty in the north, as both irregular and official federal state forces advanced on Kirkuk following the September 2017 referendum on Kurdistan's independence. Such contingency planning required dexterous forethought and consideration of both the potential for anti-regime insurgency as well as a sober recognition of the growing power of the central government and its disposition toward KRG autonomy. Political positions asserted by the KRG were not in line with the tangible support of the US, regional powers or the *de jure* or *de facto* authority recognized by Baghdad. The failures of Western lobbyists and retainers were naked by 2017, though their inability to deliver support from necessary stakeholders and decision-makers in Western capitals should have been evident prior to the point of crisis (Zadeh and Kirmanj 2017).

CORRUPTION AND HUMAN RIGHTS ABUSES

More than the personalization of relationships or the KRG lobbying efforts within Western capitals, the institutional failings and lack of state- and civil-society building within the KRG stand in stark contrast to the hopes expressed from 1992. The failure to build on the opportunity to institutionalize and develop domestic state and political capacity as well as the legitimacy it would provide, both the national and the state project, testifies to the deficiencies of the past quarter-century (Wahab 2023). Across a host of human rights, good governance, United Nations and World Bank reports produced on the region the deficiencies of the state apparatus and leadership stands in stark relief.

Such state-building failures deprived the KRG leadership of both capacity as well as legitimacy when the cataclysmic emergence of *Daesh* and its so-called Islamic State rampaged across the northern *Mashriq*, challenging the personal security of the citizens of the KRG. This absence of a functional advance of the state apparatus revealed a lack of confidence in the expansion of political authority beyond the elites standing atop the traditional structures. This was made particularly acute by the demographic changes in the region that saw a population increasingly younger, aware of and attracted to alternative social, economic and political possibilities. The absence of a private sector through which to support society when state funds were imperiled by the machinations of the Turkish Republic or federal Iraqi withdrawal of support, and a lack of funds to pay state salaries, isolated the KRG leadership—but more so the population—from any resilience and potential for self-determination.

Promotion of Islamist Sectarian-Orientated Factions

Prior to the 2003 invasion, KRG efforts to provide *bona fides* and legitimacy for sectarian-orientated exile politicians gave opportunity to political actors who did not share the Kurdish leadership's vision or capacities. While this provided the cover of a wider 'Iraqi' opposition serving US efforts to cover their own campaign for regime change—it was absent the potential to provide the KRG with capable confederates and allies in the establishment and development of a post-Ba'ath Iraqi state.

Actors such as the Islamic Da'wa Party, fronted as legitimate representatives of the Iraqi people by the efforts of the KRG and their Western patrons, were assuredly Iraqi, with legitimate constituencies among both the exile community as well as those continuing to reside under Ba'athist rule. However, their popular appeal and legitimacy was centered primarily among Shi'ite activists and failed to take into account popular desires to have recourse to local trusted leadership in the event of the regime's removal. Moreover, KRG leaders failed to account for two emergent movements or factors: the immense material and organizational capacity of the Islamic Republic of Iran—which proved adroit through the Islamic Revolutionary Guard Corps (IRGC) at expeditionary deployment as well as political support to proxies across southern Iraq. While such potential hovered over exile deliberations and organizational efforts prior to the invasion—the expansive efforts, desire and capabilities of Iranian-sponsored actors deluged the occupation and played a dramatic role in post-Ba'athist Iraq outside KRG (or indeed Anglo-American) influence.

More important was the proclivity of these parties to prioritize sectarian or ethno-nationalist basis' through which to both recruit as well as frame the post-2003 political landscape (Howard 2002; Iraq Coordination and Follow-Up Committee 2003; Williams 2003; Aboud 2018; Dodge 2018). Such narrowly construed political actors were prevalent within the 'opposition' brought together by the Kurdish leaders from among the exile community rather than more cosmopolitan actors who strove for comity among Iraq's mosaic. Little voice was provided to Iraqi nationalists or others committed to a wider vision of Iraqi political identity. Following the shared anti-colonial sentiments of the wide array of Iraqi political actors following independence, support for nationalist Iraqi state-building that predated Ba'athist rule was sufficiently persuasive among the wider Iraqi population that Ba'athism was forced to infuse its program with such programs and visions—if only to coopt their popularity. These voices and the norms they embodied, however, as well as considerable support for progressive political opposition to the predations of Ba'athism, were largely absent from the Iraqi exile events brought together by Kurdish leaders and their Anglo-American sponsors, raising considerable question as to the intentionality of the project informed by 'regime change'.

The Opposition in Exile

KRG leaders, relatively secure in their stable enclave in the no-fly zone prior to the 2003 invasion, increasingly saw the exile community and associated Iraqi correlates as less robust and capable. As the Anglo-American policy of regime change drew closer to perceived action, KRG positions failed to account for how the removal of Ba'athist leadership would affect the governance of the post-2003 Iraqi polity. Establishment of federal institutions as envisioned within the 2005 Iraqi Constitution further saw a lack of attention to machinations in Baghdad. The post-invasion experience of Anglo-American occupation—regardless of the opposition of many Iraqi political actors—nonetheless failed to blunt the constitutional framing and entrenchment of sectarianism as well as ethnic divisions heretofore avoided in progressive efforts to provide comity to Iraq's varied communities (Ismael and Ismael 2021).

KRG ambiguity over its intentions regarding sovereignty and potential acceptance of autonomy within a federal Iraq brought forth the emergence of the 'disputed territories'—lands predominantly surrounding the city of Kirkuk or found along the southern reaches of the declared KRG frontier. This effort led to multiple irredentist claims and prevented any opportunity of expeditious resolution of the territorial claims during a period of KRG ascendancy and power. The absence of direct action and resolution provided alternative actors opportunity to build legitimacy, capacity and the opportunity to rebut KRG claims both within local communities as well as international *fora* examining the potential for peace building in Iraq. This entire contestation occurred over terrain long impacted—through United Nations Security Council sanctions as well as an absence of overt state authority—by immense levels of criminality, corruption and political violence. The assertion of legitimate authority based on the established nationalist calculation of political legitimacy from the 1990s was not 'fit for purpose' over the central portions of Iraq which had been outside previous KRG claims while retaining their centrality to considerations over the rise of opposition to the central government in Baghdad—an opposition not necessarily opposed to the KRG, but also one not desirous of joining the KRG project. Recognition that their southern frontier was both fluid and widely contested by an extensive array of political actors assaulted KRG notions of its efficacy, as well as international actors' grasp of what the KRG goals actually were.

Lost Opportunities to Build a Federal Iraq

Regardless of the immense humanitarian dislocation and bloodshed that followed the occupation and emergence of the 'new Iraq', the necessity of having stable, norm-enforcing and potentially democratic neighbors was lost on the KRG leadership. The public record is silent regarding how and why they failed to appreciate its importance for the viability of an autonomous or independent KRG. It was thus difficult, in the absence of the establishment of democratic institutions within the KRG, or support for like-minded actors across the rest of Iraq, for Kurdistan's democratic experiment to succeed in spite of its clear popularity among the population. The absence of effective support for democratic institution building and transparent checks on executive authority on the part of those populating the traditional leadership raises the question as to whether such discourse was meant for legitimacy purposes *outside* Iraqi Kurdistan rather than as aspirational goal setting and eventual implementation in the governance of a maturing KRG. In spite of the rhetorical commitments and deployment of numerous academic and civil society actors across the post-2003 period, the KRG was increasingly undermined through the absence of democratic legitimacy within its own praxis (Hiltermann 2023), especially evident from the absence of alternative voices and increasing calls for political freedoms by the growing number of KRG citizens questioning of the legitimacy of further traditional rule.

In the face of the challenges, first from *Daesh*, and then from federal forces, the KRG was limited, as it had been unable to pay salaries, train and recruit future state workers, while also burdened by corruption (Hiltermann 2023; Kate 2023; Wahab 2023) and the absence of a domestic economy more than a decade following the removal of Ba'athist constraints. Responsible authorities routinely ignored corruption, evidenced through growing local civil society opposition and party fractures, as well as documented by global watchdogs from NGOs as well as the UN. When addressed by KRG officials, corruption and graft allegations were instead deployed as a political weapon against opponents, rather than as a process meant to lead to routinized and predictable governance. This absence of oversight was also evident as KRG institutions and officials were seen to be outside—or above—the law (Menmy 2024). They avoided accountability leading to a shrinking political atmosphere that was increasingly closed to those opposed to the status quo. Moreover, the interconnected and systemic problems and challenges identified by global NGOs, who had been recruited earlier in the decade to audit KRG institutions and processes, were increasingly denied access and portrayed as untrustworthy in their assessments of KRG institutions.

Historical Failure of the Kurds in State-Building

Relegated by the victorious European colonial powers to the status of stateless minorities in the post-World War I settlement in the Middle East, the Kurds appeared destined to play the role of spoiler in the politics of Turkey, Syria, Iran and Iraq. As minorities, they had incentives and occasions to seek greater security in alliances, sometimes with external powers, and thereby, as in a vicious circle, intensifying suspicion and aggression on the part of dominant groups. Without the historical experience of statehood, or the role of subaltern enabler of an imperial power, the Kurds, while aspiring to control their own state, lacked opportunities to acquire the political skills and habits of statehood. Thrust by forces of imperialism and nationalism into a wider arena, the Kurds had difficulty in replacing clan loyalties with more general and more abstract norms applicable to modern states.

Within Iraq, the Kurds repeatedly found themselves at loggerheads with successive regimes in Baghdad, seeking alliances with regional and foreign powers, and thereby bringing retaliation on their heads from the national regime of the day, seemingly regardless of the loyalties or ideology of the latter. In the case of Iraq's first experiment with an anti-imperial development project, the Kurds, their leadership dominated by large landowners opposed to the Qasim land reform policies (Esposti 2022), were unable to negotiate a compromise settlement with the regime. Weakened by the Kurdish insurrection, by American and British subversion over oil concessions, and by British threats over Kuwait, Qasim's overthrow in the 1963 Ba'athist coup, while not inevitable, in view of the gathering forces arrayed against it, was not a surprising result. Considering the catastrophic consequences of their subsequent conflicts with the Ba'athists, one might say that the Kurds ought to have been more careful in what they had wished for. A broadly similar engagement then ensued between the Kurds and the Ba'athists, again leading to armed successive insurrections involving support from Iran, first under the pro-American Shah in the 1970s, then again in the 1980s under the revolutionary Islamic Republic.

In seeking to manipulate Iraqi and foreign powers to their enduring advantage, the Kurdish leadership showed themselves to be inept, bringing instead distrust, conflict and arrested development, on the KRG, and on Iraq. There is much in the Kurdish experience that suggests the tragic: the missed opportunity of the Qasim opening, the squandered opportunity afforded by the American-imposed no-fly zone of 1993–2003, and the failure to build an inter-ethnic, inter-sectional political culture and institutional framework out of their advantageous position during and following the occupation. In all three cases, the Kurds were not the most powerful actors and may not deserve the greatest share of the blame. However, it is reasonable to speculate that the results could have been more favorable to the Kurds and for all Iraqis, had the Kurdish leaders been more farsighted and pursued enduring alliances with other social groups within Iraq in building institutional arrangements that improved security for all.

To describe the Kurdish leadership as inept, would imply that they failed to achieve their goals. If their goals were to manipulate Kurdish and Iraqi politics in order to maximize economic benefit and political agency for the Kurdish population, then they would indeed have been inept. At least one journalistic source in the KRG (Ekurd Daily 2022) however, points to the Barzani clan as having amassed a fortune of approximately 55 billion USD, mostly through illegal appropriation of oil revenues and through control of trade at border crossings. To the extent that this report is reliable, the Barzani clan would not have been inept, but on the contrary, remarkably skillful in siphoning off the KRG's natural wealth for their own benefit. One can interpret some of the observations noted previously in this chapter, the lack of transparency, the exclusionary, clanish behavior in the politics of the KRG, and the stubborn insistence of KRG leaders in controlling oil revenues and border crossings as being directed at the preservation of vital clan monopoly interests. It is a harsh judgment, but in a nutshell, in being duplicitous toward their rivals and their publics, they were, within the limited scope of their anticipations, being true to themselves.

As it was, the Kurds as a collectivity served in substantially instrumental roles in the ascent of Pax Americana, as ready tools in American hands to weaken nationalist resistance to foreign oil exploitation, as collateral damage in American manipulation of the Iran-Iraq conflict, as the poster-case for humanitarian intervention against the Saddam regime, and, finally, as a spanner in the works impeding the development of any Iraqi project to build national democratic institutions and a national political culture (Ismael and Ismael 2021: 136–7) and to free itself from imperial penetration. Though not the most important factor, the Kurds, through the misdirected (or self-interested) efforts of its leaders, has served to advance the long-stated American neoconservative goal of preventing the emergence of a consolidated Iraqi state as a potential rival regional power in the Middle East.

References

Aboud, Wasn Said. 2018. London Conference of the Iraqi Opposition (14–17 December 2002) and the Role of the United States of America. *Alustath Journal for Human and Social Sciences* 226 (2): 279–310, September, https://alustath.uobaghdad.edu.iq/index.php/UJIRCO/article/view/199. Accessed 20 June 2023.

Aburish, Said K. 1997. *A Brutal Friendship: The West and The Arab Elite*. Victor Gollancz.

Adams, Simon. 2018. Halabja, Chemical Weapons and the Genocide Against the Kurds: Implications for Iraq and the World Today. Keynote address at a conference to mark the 30th anniversary of the attack on Halabja, Hosted by the Kurdistan Regional Government Representation in the United States, Washington, DC, 13 March, https://www.globalr2p.org/publications/halabja-chemical-weapons-and-the-genocide-against-the-kurds-implications-for-iraq-and-the-world-today/. Accessed 12 June 2023.

Amnesty International. 2021. *Kurdistan Region of Iraq: Arbitrary Arrests and Enforced Disappearance of Activists and Journalists*. Amnesty International. https://www.amnesty.org/en/latest/press-release/2021/06/kurdistan-region-of-iraq-arbitrary-arrests-and-enforced-disappearance-of-activists-and-journalists/. Accessed 9 June 2023.

Associated Press. 1998. *USA: Iraqi Kurd Leaders Agree to Establishing Elected Government*. Associated Press, 18 September, https://newsroom.ap.org/editorial-photos-videos/detail?itemid=39ed504c76e1eb274fd168d1d50543ad&mediatype=video&source=youtube. Accessed 19 June 2023.

Batatu, Hanna. 1979. *The Old Social Classes and the Revolutionary Movements of Iraq: A Study of Iraq's Old Landed and Commercial Classes and of Its Communists, Ba'thist, and Free Officers*. Princeton University Press.

Dodge, Toby. 2018. *Iraq and Muhasasa Ta'ifia: The External Imposition of Sectarian Politics*. The Foreign Policy Centre, November, https://fpc.org.uk/iraq-and-muhasasa-taifia-the-external-imposition-of-sectarian-politics/. Accessed 20 June 2023.

Ekurd Daily. 2022. Illegal Wealth of Massoud Barzani Estimated at $55 Billion: Ex-KRG Official—Turkish Daily. *Ekurd Daily*, 11 April, https://ekurd.net/illegal-wealth-massoud-barzani-2022-04-11. Accessed 18 June 2023.

Esposti, Nicola Degli. 2021. The 2017 Independence Referendum and the Political Economy of Kurdish Nationalism in Iraq. *Third World Quarterly*. https://www.tandfonline.com/doi/full/10.1080/01436597.2021.1949978. Accessed 21 June 2023.

———. 2022. Land Reform and Kurdish Nationalism in Postcolonial Iraq. London School of Economics & Political Science, UK. http://eprints.lse.ac.uk/114977/1/31.2.Degli_Esposti.Copyedited.pdf, and Middle East

Critique, 31:2, pp. 147–163, April, https://doi.org/10.1080/19436149.202
2.2055517. Accessed 21 June 2023.

Frontline. 1990. The Arming of Iraq. 11 September, https://www.pbs.org/
wgbh/pages/frontline/shows/longroad/etc/arming.html. Accessed 12
June 2023.

Gibbons, Phillip. 2002. *U.S. No-Fly Zones in Iraq: To What End?* Washington
Institute, 1 July, https://www.washingtoninstitute.org/policy-analysis/us-no-
fly-zones-iraq-what-end. Accessed 19 June 2023.

Hanish, Shak. 2018. The Kurdish Referendum in Iraq: An Assessment. *Journal of
Power, Politics & Governance* 6 (2): 17–29, December. http://jppgnet.com/
journals/jppg/Vol_6_No_2_December_2018/3.pdf. Accessed 10 June 2023.

Harris, Shane, and Matthew M. Aid. 2013. Exclusive: CIA Files Prove America
Helped Saddam as He Gassed Iran. *Foreign Policy*, 26 August, https://foreign-
policy.com/2013/08/26/exclusive-cia-files-prove-america-helped-saddam-
as-he-gassed-iran/. Accessed 12 June 2023.

Hiltermann, Joost. 2023. *Iraqi Kurdistan Twenty Years After*. International Crisis
Group, 23 April, https://www.crisisgroup.org/middle-east-north-africa/gulf-
and-arabian-peninsula/iraq/iraqi-kurdistan-twenty-years-after. Accessed 10
June 2023.

Howard, Michael. 2002. London Meeting for Iraqi Opposition. *The Guardian*,
20 November, https://www.theguardian.com/world/2002/nov/20/iraq.
london. Accessed 20 June 2023.

Human Rights Watch. 1992a. Unquiet Graves: The Search for the Disappeared in
Iraqi Kurdistan. *Human Rights Watch*, February, https://www.hrw.org/leg-
acy/reports/1992/iraq/iraq0292.pdf. Accessed 12 June 2023.

———. 1992b. Endless Torment: The 1991 Uprising in Iraq and Its Aftermath.
Human Rights Watch, June, https://www.hrw.org/reports/1992/Iraq926.
htm. Accessed 12 June 2023.

———. 1993a. First Anfal—The Siege of Sergalou and Bergalou, February 23—
March 19, 1988. *Human Rights Watch*, https://www.hrw.org/reports/1993/
iraqanfal/ANFAL3.htm. Accessed 11 June 2023.

———. 1993b. Genocide in Iraq—The Anfal Campaign Against the Kurds, July,
https://www.hrw.org/report/1993/07/01/genocide-iraq/anfal-campaign-
against-kurds. Accessed 20 July 2023.

Iraq Coordination and Follow-Up Committee. 2003. Iraqi Opposition
Conference: Final Statement of the Meeting of the Coordination and
Follow-Up Committee. *Relief Web*, 3 March, https://reliefweb.int/report/
iraq/iraqi-opposition-conference-final-statement-meeting-coordination-and-
follow-committee. Accessed 20 June 2023.

Ismael, Tareq Y., and Jacqueline S. Ismael. 2015. *Iraq in the Twenty-First Century:
Regime Change and the Making of a Failed State*. Routledge.

————. 2021. *Iraq in the Twenty-First Century: Regime Change and the Making of a Failed State*. Routledge.

McDowell, David. 1996. *The Kurds*. The Minority Rights Group, 1 December, https://minorityrights.org/publications/the-kurds-december-1996/. Accessed 11 June 2023.

Menmy, Dana Taib. 2024. US Court Summons Iraqi Kurdistan PM Masrour Barzani Over Multiple Charges. *The New Arab*, 19 February, https://www.newarab.com/news/us-court-summons-kurdish-pm-barzani-over-multiple-charges. Accessed 22 February 2024.

New York Times. 2018. Update: Kurdistan and the Battle over Oil, 8 October, https://www.nytimes.com/2018/10/08/business/update-kurdistan-and-the-battle-over-oil.html. Accessed 10 June 2023.

Pope, Hugh. 1992. National Agenda: Exiled Opponents of Hussein Start to Harmonize Their Voices: Salahuddin Conference Is a Watershed for the Splintered Forces Opposed to the Iraqi Dictator. *Los Angeles Times*, 33 November, https://www.latimes.com/archives/la-xpm-1992-11-03-wr-1337-story.html. Accessed 21 June 2023.

Robinson, Piers. 2002. *The CNN Effect: The Myth of News Media, Foreign Policy and Intervention*. Routledge.

Snow, Andrew. 2018. *Kurdistan Region's Debt Crisis Threatens Iraq's Economy*. United States Institute of Peace, 9 May, https://www.usip.org/publications/2018/05/kurdistan-regions-debt-crisis-threatens-iraqs-economy. Accessed 10 June 2023.

Sosnowski, Piotr. 2019. Rentier Economy of the Kurdish Region in Iraq as a Source of Barriers for the Regional Security Sector Reform. *Security & Defense Quarterly* 23 (1, Jan.). https://securityanddefence.pl/Rentier-economy-of-the-Kurdish-region-in-Iraq-as-a-source-of-barriers-for-the-regional,105429,0,2.html. Accessed 10 June 2023.

Tripp, Charles. 2007. *A History of Iraq*. 3rd ed. Cambridge University Press.

Visser, R. 2010. The Kurdish Issue in Iraq: A View from Baghdad at the Close of the Maliki Premiership. *World Affairs* 43 (1): 77–93.

Wahab, Bilal. 2023. *The Rise and Fall of Kurdish Power in Iraq*. Spring., https://www.washingtoninstitute.org/policy-analysis/rise-and-fall-kurdish-power-iraq. Accessed 13 June 2023.

Wheeler, Nicolas J. 2002. A Solidarist Moment in International Society? The Case of Safe Havens and No-Fly Zones in Iraq Get Access. In N.J. Wheeler, ed., *Saving Strangers: Humanitarian Intervention in International Society.* 139–171, Oxford. https://doi.org/10.1093/0199253102.003.0006. Accessed 11 June 2023.

Whitesell, Sarah E. 1993. The Kurdish Crisis: An International Incident Study. *Denver Journal of International Law & Policy* 21 (2): 455. https://digitalcommons.du.edu/djilp/vol21/iss2/10/. Accessed 20 July 2023.

Williams, Daniel. 2003. Summit of Iraq's Splintered Opposition Ends in Confusion. *Washington Post*, 1 March, https://www.washingtonpost.com/archive/politics/2003/03/01/summit-of-iraqs-splintered-opposition-ends-in-confusion/5d42a255-9ff6-4f51-90c5-fa765ea424de/. Accessed 20 June 2023.

Zadeh, Yoosef Abbas, and Sherko Kirmanj. 2017. The Para-Diplomacy of the Kurdistan Region in Iraq and the Kurdish Statehood Enterprise. *The Middle East Journal* 71 (4, Autumn): 587–606.

CHAPTER 4

Two Faces of Pax Americana

Introduction

The World Tribunal on Iraq (WTI), held in Istanbul in 2005, carried out a worldwide series of hearings between 2003 and 2005 on the Iraq War, and issued its jury's 'Declaration of Conscience' (Sökmen et al. 2015), which included the following:

> The invasion and occupation of Iraq was and is illegal. The reasons given by the US and UK governments for the invasion and occupation of Iraq in March 2003 have proven to be false. Much evidence supports the conclusion that a major motive for the war was to control and dominate the Middle East and its vast reserves of oil as a part of the US drive for global hegemony ... In pursuit of their agenda of empire, the Bush and Blair governments blatantly ignored the massive opposition to the war expressed by millions of people around the world. They embarked upon one of the most unjust, immoral, and cowardly wars in history.

The use of the term 'empire' in this context is appropriate, as the pursuit of empire amounts inevitably to violation of international law and of the UN Charter.

There has also been the Kuala Lumpur War Crimes Commission (KLWCC), a tribunal (the Kuala Lumpur War Crimes Tribunal, or KLWCT) consisting of five judges with judicial and academic backgrounds, which reached a unanimous verdict that George W. Bush and

J. S. Ismael et al., *Pax Americana*, Frontiers of Globalization, https://doi.org/10.1007/978-3-031-61273-2_4

Tony Blair were guilty of crimes against peace, crimes against humanity, and genocide as a result of their roles in the Iraq War (Falk 2011). Like the WTI, it was a civil society initiative, and had no legal authority to enforce its verdict.

The UK Iraq Inquiry under the chairmanship of Sir John Chilcot (2006) was charged by the successor UK government to the Blair government that had participated in the invasion, with determining, among other matters, 'whether it was right and necessary to invade Iraq'. The Inquiry declined to take a stand 'on whether military action was legal' which, 'could, of course, only be resolved by a properly constituted and internationally recognised Court' (4). Chilcot adopted instead a more procedural focus, finding that the Blair government had in several cases failed to take actions to ensure that it was acting legally. The Inquiry 'concluded that the UK chose to join the invasion of Iraq before the peaceful options for disarmament had been exhausted. Military action at that time was not a last resort' (2). Without actually saying so, the Inquiry in effect supplied the factual information that any duly constituted tribunal, if there were to be one, could employ to reach a verdict not very different to that of the Istanbul and Kuala Lumpur tribunals.

Empires generally do not find themselves in the dock to be judged on the legality of their actions, the most notable exception being Nazi Germany, arriving at Nuremberg through total defeat in war. As the United Nations is also an outcome of that same war, it is fair to describe international law as victor's justice. Civil society tribunals and official inquiries can inform us on actions taken and on the consequences of those actions, but accountability will likely have to wait until the empire submits to the jurisdiction of a competent tribunal.

THE RISE OF PAX AMERICANA

One cannot escape a sense of irony in employing the term 'empire' in speaking about the US. It was, after all, born out of a revolt against the British empire and its founding documents are steeped in European liberal Enlightenment ideas. Although it is rarely employed self-critically, the idea of anti-imperialism remains a part of American political rhetoric to this day. Just as important for its development as an empire was its practically unchallenged dominance on the North American continent. For most of the first century after it purchased the Louisiana territory in 1803 from its elder imperial cousin, France, the American empire benefitted from its cultural and technical advantage over the indigenous societies upon which it encroached and largely destroyed, its almost unimpeded access to natural resources, its potent mobilizing ideology of freedom and democracy, its representative constitution, and its extraordinarily productive capitalist economic institutions (Ismael and Ismael 2004).

The steep ascent in the American imperial trajectory toward world domination began in the spring of 1940, with the defeat of the British and French armies in the opening phase of the Second World War against Germany. The US assumed leadership of the anti-fascist coalition, and by the end of 1941, was allied with Britain, and even with the declared enemy of capitalism, the Soviet Union. American dominance in this *force majeure* coalition resulted in its commandeering of British and European imperial interests and assets, including in the Middle East.

The decisive Allied victory over the Axis powers replaced a multi-polar world with a bi-polar one, the so-called Cold War, characterized by the American empire exercising more or less effective control over most of the world's seas and territories, with the major exception of Eurasia from Central Europe to the Pacific. The ensuing competition with the USSR and Peoples' Republic of China can be viewed, in a formal sense, as retracing the essential logic of the historical conflict between the ancient Athenian maritime empire against its land-based rival of Sparta and the latter's allies in the Peloponnesian War. However, contrary to the classical Greek prototype, the modern sea-based empire had the advantage of global military reach, dominance of international economic and political institutions and the widespread credibility of its cultural and ideological production to eventually enable it to claim world hegemony. The key symbolic milestones were the fall of the Berlin Wall in 1989 and the dissolution of the USSR two years later. With the adoption by the successor Russian Federation of Western political and economic institutions and the ensuing domestic economic and social chaos, Soviet and subsequently Russian leaders found themselves dependent, like nearly all other nations, on American good will and loans from the American-controlled International Monetary Fund. This became apparent when, during the course of a September 13 1990 bilateral meeting between USSR President Gorbachev and US Secretary of State, James Baker, focusing largely on plans for dealing with Iraq's invasion of Kuwait, Gorbachev expressed his concerns about American support for a loan for the USSR. Baker responded that 'without linkage to this problem' the US would 'look at what can be done in order to obtain a loan [for the USSR] from some third country' (Gorbachev Foundation 1990).

Americans celebrated their triumph as if it were the end of the final act in the world historical drama, aptly reflected in the title of Francis Fukuyama's (1993) frequently cited bestseller *The End of History and the Last Man*. The end of ideological competition and the confirmation of the American capitalist economic model accelerated a global trend toward the homogenization of political, economic and cultural institutions, norms and practices. American models were adopted widely, and international institutions, including the United Nations, based in New York, became less distinguishable from domestic American institutions. The 1990s saw the apogee (Donnelly 2000) of the American imperial trajectory: suddenly, it was the unchallenged hegemonic norm. There were local dissenters and even rebels, such as Serbia, the Palestinians, Hizbollah in Lebanon, Iran, Libya, Cuba and North Korea, but they were on the fringe, the target of American or international sanctions and, for the most part, excluded from international society. NATO, with the Warsaw Pact disbanded, was able to bomb Belgrade and dismember Yugoslavia without authorization of the UN Security Council (Chesterman 2002; Graham 2016; Falk 2018).

In the Middle East, the US was presented with the opportunity to reshape the region without any Cold War constraints, such as had accelerated Britain's decline during and after the Suez Crisis. The biggest challenge facing the US was the hostility of the Islamic Republic of Iran, ever since the 1979 toppling of the American client regime of the Shah, who had come to power with CIA support in a 1953 coup to depose the liberal nationalist government of Mohammed Mossadegh (Kinzer 2007, 2017). To counter Iran, the US had a client in the Iraqi president, Saddam Hussein, who was among the Ba'athist party leaders in a bloody 1963 coup orchestrated by the CIA (Aburish 1997; Cockburn 1997; Sanders 2002; Morris 2003) to eliminate the leftist, nationalist regime of General Abdel Karim Qassem, and again in 1968 when Saddam seized supreme control of the Baath party in Iraq (Riedel 2019). However, both countries were vociferous supporters of the Palestinian Liberation Organization (PLO) and of Palestinian statehood, and therefore enemies of Israel. In September 1980, Iraq invaded Iran, a much larger and more populous country. This strange attack of a 'David' upon an apparent 'Goliath' was explained by some realists as an opportunistic response in a situation of perceived temporary weakness of the new Khomeini regime and the latter's ambition to export its Islamic revolution to Iraq and topple Hussein (Mearsheimer and Walt 2009), and by CIA analysts at the time in terms of 'overreach' by Saddam (Riedel). It could also be argued, however, that the chief beneficiaries of a prolonged and damaging conflict between two key supporters of Palestine would have been Israel and its American patron (Ismael and Ismael 2015: 16). There were also claims by both Iran and the Saudis, that President Jimmy Carter had given Saddam 'the green light' to attack Iran, the implication being that Carter was motivated to secure leverage over the Iranians in order secure the release of the American hostages in Teheran, an allegation that Carter denounced as 'patently false' (Parry 2015). In any case, with covert American military intelligence support and military supplies to Iraq (Frontline 1990; Chomsky 1991; Dobbs 2002), with assistance from France, and at times covert support to Iran from the US and Israel (Parry 2015), and in 1987, with military action against Iran in support of Iraqi tanker navigation in the Gulf, the combatants struggled on, as the war became, as intended by American policy (Frontline 1990) a stalemate of immense and lasting damage to both countries.

By the end of the war in 1988, both countries were seriously depleted in terms of military and economic resources. Yet, Saddam Hussein then sought concessions from neighboring Kuwait over disputed oilfields and debts to Kuwait arising out of the war with Iran. Although the interpretation of its significance remains contested (Mearsheimer and Walt 2009), eight days before his invasion of Kuwait, Hussein met American ambassador, April Glaspie, who told him the US had 'no opinion' on the Iraq-Kuwait dispute (Kinzer 2007: 287), perhaps leading the Iraqis to believe that this confirmed what they had learned earlier from the State Department, that the US still had 'no special defense or security commitments to Kuwait' (Mearsheimer and Walt 2009). Having benefitted from American support in its war with Iran, and if the allegations of President Carter's 'green light' to attack Iran in 1980 are well founded, then Saddam might have received Glaspie's non-committal position on the Iraq-Kuwait dispute as a veiled form of encouragement (Dobbs 2002; Shaibani 2024; Sciolino and Gordon 1990). This was Robert Parry's conclusion:

> Again, Saddam was looking for a signal from the U.S. president, this time George H.W. Bush. When Saddam explained his confrontation with Kuwait to U.S. Ambassador April Glaspie, he received an ambiguous reply, a reaction he apparently perceived as another 'green light'. (Parry 2015)

Regardless of what might have been in Saddam's mind at the time, with Glaspie's oddly Delphic advice of American neutrality with regard to

Kuwait, Iraqi forces invaded Kuwait and occupied it within two days, thereby giving US President George H.W. Bush the occasion to publicly affirm that the US indeed had an opinion on the dispute, and that it would use United Nations machinery to punish Iraq for its war of aggression. Although Chapter VII of the UN Charter empowers the Security Council to use armed force under its direction to prevent war, the US instead used a series of UNSC Resolutions to initially impose a strangling blockade and then to endorse unrestricted war on Iraq (Falk 1991). The irony could not have been more complete: as in the so-called Korean War, the UN Charter was manipulated, not to prevent war as per the declared purpose of the Charter, but instead to license unrestrained warfare conducted by a coalition of the willing under the command of the US (Falk 1991). The widely televised, near-total destruction of retreating Iraqi forces in what became known in as 'the duckshoot', impressed upon world opinion that the US was henceforth to be regarded as omnipotent. With the ensuing decade-long American devastation of public infrastructure, and air support for Kurdish and Shi'ite insurrections against the Saddam regime, Iraq became the second country, after Korea, to be practically destroyed with United Nations authorization.

What became known as the 'Gulf War' was the coronation of the 'New World Order' (Ismael and Ismael 1991), an optimistic-sounding phrase used by George H.W. Bush (perhaps unaware of the imperial antecedents to the Augustinian poet, Virgil) in his September 11, 1990 speech to a joint session of Congress condemning Saddam's invasion of Kuwait and the beginning of what became known to academics and journalists as the 'unipolar system'. With their founding myth clothed in anti-imperial rhetoric, Americans and their friends were for the most part reluctant to use the word 'empire' without qualification (Ignatieff 2003), although one of Bush Sr.'s advisors, was reportedly less shy (Suskind 2004b; Sullivan 2009; Switzer 2013). 'Pax Americana', the most appropriate term in our view, although at least rhetorically ruled out as a model by Bush Sr. in his 1991 UN address, was also in circulation in a descriptive sense (Hudson 1992) and was repeatedly employed in the Pentagon's 'Defense Planning Guidance' (Cheney 1992) which, when leaked to the press, was criticized by then-Senator Joseph Biden (Gellman 1992) as an unworkable 'Pax Americana'. Workable or not, the 'preservation' of Pax Americana was explicitly set out as the 'strategic goal' in the primordial defense policy manifesto of the neoconservatives (Donnelly 2000).

The post-Gulf War decade coincided for the most part with the Bill Clinton administration and may be glimpsed in the rear-view mirror as the consolidation of Pax Americana. The USSR dismantled itself and entered a decade of economic collapse and social upheaval, in a series of experimental attempts to 'learn' from the West. Meanwhile, NATO (the Warsaw Pact having disbanded) expanded incrementally eastward toward Russia (Mearsheimer 2014, 2015; Sachs 2023a, 2023b), while rejecting Russia as a member. During most of this decade, Yugoslavia was gradually dismembered though a combination of internal ethnic conflicts, Western encouragement of secessionist movements, and finally, aerial bombardment by NATO. As noted previously, as a result of the failure to secure a UNSC resolution for this military intervention, Yugoslavia cannot be listed as yet another country destroyed with UN authorization.

In Washington, many neoconservative policy wonks had left the departing Bush Sr. administration for think tanks, making this period one of ideological renewal (Perle et al. 1996; Donnelly 2000). In government and outside, the major premise uniting practically all foreign and defense policy thinking was that the new unipolar system must be made permanent (Wolfowitz 1992; Cheney 1992; Perle et al. 1996; Donnelly; Ismael and Ismael 2021: 46–7). Imperial strategizing was not limited to Republicans: former National Security Advisor to President Jimmy Carter, Zbigniew Brzezinski published (1997) one of the most widely cited books on foreign policy, *The Grand Chessboard: American Primacy and its Geostrategic Imperatives*, his guide to the modern version of what the British imperialists had dubbed its rivalry with Russia as 'the great game' (Ismael and Ismael 2004). But the status of Iraq had not been forgotten. As noted in Chap. 2, while it was being progressively strangled by UN sanctions and 'no-fly zones', the policy objective of the destruction of Iraq was becoming a bi-partisan objective. In January 1998, the neoconservative Project for a New American Century (PNAC) called on President Clinton to undertake the 'removal of Saddam Hussein's regime' (Stein and Dickinson 2006), and on October 31, Clinton (1998) signed into law the Iraq Liberation Act, which was to become a component of the domestic legal authority for the 2003 invasion.

EMPIRE OF LIES

During the 2000 presidential election campaign, the PNAC issued a defense policy planning report, 'Rebuilding America's Defenses: Strategy, Forces and Resources for a New Century' for increased military spending directed toward bolstering what they unabashedly called 'Pax Americana' (Ismael and Ismael 2021: 46). The PNAC acknowledged that this would require a major transformation in thinking, research and investment, and that 'the process of transformation, even if it brings revolutionary change, [was] likely to be a long one, absent some catastrophic and catalyzing event—like a new Pearl Harbor' (Donnelly 2000; Pilger 2002). Following G.W. Bush's electoral victory (after the Supreme Court prevented further ballot counting in Florida) regime change in Iraq was already a top item of Bush's inaugural national security meeting. As former Treasury Secretary, Paul O'Neill, recalled, 'It was all about finding a way to do it. The president saying, "Go find me a way to do this"' (Suskind 2004a). About eight months later, on the morning of September 11 in New York City, two jet liners flew out of a sunny sky and crashed into the twin towers of the World Trade Center, the opening scene in what may have become the world's most consequential morality play in nearly two millennia.

The Bush administration immediately declared a 'war on terror', to include states that 'harbor' terrorists, widely understood in Washington to include at least Afghanistan, where al Qaeda was based, and also Iraq, where there was no evidence of any connection. Regardless, Bush lumped Iraq with Iran and North Korea, into the 'axis of evil', without saying how they were cooperating to form an 'axis'. As recounted in Chap. 2, Bush's fixation on Iraq as a state sponsor of terror was apparent, at least to insiders, immediately after the September 11 attacks (Stein and Dickinson 2006) and persisted in the face of all evidence and argument to the contrary. We know from the report of Bush's phone conversation with Tony Blair only three days later, that Blair was initially doubtful of the Iraq-al Qaeda linkage (Riedel 2021).

A closely related point to the linkage the Bush Jr administration made between non-state terrorists and their alleged state sponsors, was that the latter would make available to terrorists 'weapons of mass destruction' ('WMDs'), which could be nuclear, chemical or biological. A key element of the argument was that such weapons could be unleashed by terrorists who had no fear of retaliation, making the traditional strategic concept of 'MAD'—mutually assured destruction—of no avail. The winning *quod erat demonstrandum* of the argument against doubters of this strategic syllogism appeared in Judith Miller and Michael Gordon's (2002) later-to-be notorious *New York Times* article, based on anonymous Bush administration sources, that Iraq was trying to import aluminum tubes for centrifuges for the purpose of enriching uranium. According to unnamed 'hardliners', 'the first sign of a "smoking gun" … may be a mushroom cloud'. This pithy phrase was repeated by National Security Advisor Condoleezza Rice the same day on CNN, while Vice-President Cheney confirmed the allegations (Stein and Dickinson 2006; Schwarz 2023), and repeated yet again by Bush in a speech the following month. On September 24, 2002, the UK government released a statement that Iraq could launch biological or chemical attack within 45 minutes, a report that an insider had described as 'sexed up'. When the government document on which this statement was purportedly based was finally released as a result of a freedom of information request, it contained no reference to Iraq's ability to launch a biological or chemical attack within 45 minutes (Baker et al. 2010).

AS late as March 2002 the UK government remained skeptical regarding the Bush administration claims regarding Iraq. Foreign Office political director, David Ricketts, advised his foreign secretary, Jack Straw, that 'regime change: does not stack up. It sounds like a grudge between Bush and Saddam' (Smith n.d.). Straw then wrote to Blair on March 25 that '[i]f 11 September had not happened, it is doubtful that the US would now be considering military action against Iraq' and that '[t]here has been no credible evidence to link Iraq with UBL [Osama bin Laden] and al-Qa'ida' (Smith). As late as July 2002, Chief of MI6, Richard Dearlove, had the impression that, in Washington, the 'intelligence and facts were being fixed around the policy' (Smith). Yet a UK Cabinet briefing paper dated July 21 clearly states that Blair had already told Bush when they met in April 2002 'that the UK would support military action to bring about regime change' under certain conditions (Smith). The UK War Cabinet met July 23, during which they discussed a briefing document which advised that it would be 'necessary to create the conditions in which [the UK] could legally support military action' (Smith). Chilcot (2) notes that

> by then, there had been a profound change in the UK's thinking: The Joint Intelligence Committee had concluded that Saddam Hussein could not be removed without an invasion… The [UK] Government was stating that Iraq was a threat that had to be dealt with. It had to disarm or be disarmed

[and] That implied the use of force if Iraq did not comply—and internal contingency planning for a large contribution to a military invasion had begun.

Chilcot also reports (3):

On 28 July, Mr Blair wrote to President Bush with an assurance that he would be with him 'whatever'—but, if the US wanted a coalition for military action, changes would be needed in three key areas. Those were: progress on the Middle East Peace Process; UN authority; and a shift in public opinion in the UK, Europe and the Arab world.

For these conditions to be met, however, a return to the UNSC for an additional resolution was necessary, to which Bush agreed, and on 8 November, UNSC resolution 1441 was adopted unanimously, giving 'Iraq a final opportunity to disarm or face "serious consequences", and … for any further breaches by Iraq to be reported to the Security Council "for assessment"' (Chilcot: 3). Resolution 1441 can be understood in retrospect as the means of (in the words of the UK Cabinet document) 'creating the conditions' for 'a material breach' by Saddam of the Security Council resolutions. In essence, it represents a stage in UK efforts to construct, in Chilcot's quotation of Blair's phrase, '…a "clever strategy" for regime change in Iraq, which would build over time' (2) to 'wrongfoot Saddam on the inspectors and the UNSCRs' (Smith). It was Sir Christopher Meyer, UK ambassador to the US, reporting the results of his late July meeting with Wolfowitz, who explicitly identified the idea of a clever strategy to wrongfoot Saddam into legalizing the Iraq war:

We backed regime change, but the plan had to be clever and failure was not an option. I then went through the need to wrongfoot Saddam on the inspectors and the UNSCRs [UN Security Council Resolutions]. If all this could be accomplished skilfully, we were fairly confident that a number of countries could come on board. (Smith)

The 'clever strategy' to 'wrongfoot Saddam' into legalizing his (and, as it turned out, Iraq's) destruction seemed to have emerged out of a meeting of minds between Wolfowitz and the UK ambassador six months before Colin Powell's fateful address to the Security Council. Though Powell had, early on, been skeptical of the claims advanced by Bush and the neoconservative hardliners, his carefully prepared and masterly delivered indictment was to become the final step in this plan.

By late summer of 2002, the allegations that Iraq was linked to Al Qaida and that it was developing WMDs were firm matters of doctrine. Bush had so declared, and Rumsfeld, in saying the link between Iraq and Al Qaeda was 'accurate and not debatable' (Stein and Dickinson) discouraged any dissent from the administration's groupthink. There were still dissenters, however, including within the intelligence apparatus in both the US (McGovern 2023) and the UK (Stein and Dickinson; Ross 2016, 2017) and (as noted above in Chap. 2, Ritter 2023) among the former weapons inspectors. By October, however, the overwhelming weight of opinion in Washington, with Whitehall by this time in step, was that regime change in Iraq was necessary and inevitable. A briefing paper to the UK Cabinet War Committee meeting of July 23 pointed to the connection between the sense of inevitability and acceptance of the action: 'In practice, much of the international community would find it difficult to stand in the way of the determined course of the US hegemony' (Smith). On October 16, 2002 Congress voted the President authority to use military force against Iraq (United States 107th Congress 2002). The Chilcot report concludes (5) that by March 2003, there was 'an ingrained belief in the UK policy and intelligence communities that Iraq had retained some chemical and biological capabilities; was determined to preserve and if possible enhance them—and, in the future, to acquire a nuclear capability; and was able to conceal its activities from the UN inspectors'.

The process through which millions of educated people in the twenty-first century came to fervently believe, to the point of going to war, a proposition which was contradicted by nearly all available evidence (Ismael and Ismael 2021: 55–60), is so fantastic as to invite comparisons with fiction. Hans Christian Andersen's tale (1837) of the 'Emperor's New Clothes' may be the most appropriate: a scene where all must conform, contrary to their senses and to the point of absurdity, to avoid embarrassing the naked emperor. The new Washington consensus represented, in fact, the ironic post-hoc validation of Ron Suskind's (2004b) account of what a 'senior official' in the G.W. Bush administration had to say about the journalist's expressed concern for accuracy:

> The aide said that guys like me were 'in what we call the reality-based community,' which he defined as people who 'believe that solutions emerge from your judicious study of discernible reality.' I nodded and murmured

something about enlightenment principles and empiricism. He cut me off. 'That's not the way the world really works anymore,' he continued. 'We're an empire now, and when we act, we create our own reality. And while you're studying that reality—judiciously, as you will—we'll act again, creating other new realities, which you can study too, and that's how things will sort out. We're history's actors ... and you, all of you, will be left to just study what we do.'

The Bush administration, their neoconservative friends outside government, and eventually, the Blair government as well, were indeed engaged in creating their own reality. They organized the refugees from and informants in Iraq, selected only those intelligence reports which conformed to their plans (Hersh 2003, 2004; Cook 2011; Ismael and Ismael 2021: 51–60), while suppressing inconvenient facts, fed supportive stories to cooperative journalists and media outlets, and let it be understood that the only safe option for everyone was to accept the inevitability of the official version of reality. The Blair government was brought on side by the summer of 2002, in Chilcot's words (3): 'Mr Blair sought a partnership as a way of influencing President Bush. He proposed a UN ultimatum to Iraq to readmit inspectors or face the consequences'. The price of partnership for the UK was collaboration in the 'clever strategy' to 'wrongfoot Saddam', thus rendering the invasion 'legal'.

However, problems arise in creating one's own reality: the universe, even on our small planet, is more complex than human intelligence can comprehend. No matter how smart and diligent those who see themselves as history's actors may be, it is likely that, eventually, complexity will win out, and the things we do to gain mastery come back to make us look ridiculous. One could find many fictional examples in the 'who dunits', in Shakespeare's Macbeth, or in David Hare's imaginative reconstruction in his play, 'Stuff Happens' (2004) of the Bush administration's decision making prior to the Iraq invasion. Hare has Powell make the following rebuttal to Bush regarding the evidence that Saddam was concealing WMDs:

There's an element of hypocrisy, George. We were trading with the guy! Not long ago. People keep asking, how do you know he's got weapons of mass destruction? How do we know? Because we've still got the receipts.

It is necessary to add two points to Hare's narrative. Firstly, the Americans indeed 'got the receipts', by removing them from the deposition Iraq submitted minutes earlier under direction of UNSC 1441, thereby preventing UN officials from linking materials and equipment supplied with particular locations in Iraq, which would otherwise have enabled them to confirm or refute whether Iraq had retained WMDs (Ismael and Ismael 2021: 52). Secondly, Hare understates the level of hypocrisy. During Iraq's war with Iran, the Americans supplied the Iraqis 'data on the locations of key Iranian logistics facilities, and the strength and capabilities of the Iranian air force and air defense system', knowing that Iraq would attack the targets with chemical weapons. Iraqi attacks using sarin followed, killing, according to CIA estimates, somewhere between 'hundreds' and 'thousands' (Harris and Aid 2013).

The neoconservatives in the Bush administration probably understood at least intuitively that the empire could not be caught out in a deliberate lie, or the whole fabric of the artificial reality they had created might unravel. Lies had to be concealed by more lies. As former Secretary of State in the Nixon administration, Alexander Haig, responded to Robert Parry's question whether 'he was troubled by the pattern of deceit that had become the norm among international players in the 1980s':

'Oh, no, no, no, no,' he boomed, shaking his head. 'On that kind of thing? No. Come on. Jesus! God! You know, you'd better get out and read Machiavelli or somebody else because I think you're living in a dream world! People do what their national interest tells them to do and if it means lying to a friendly nation, they're going to lie through their teeth ....' (Parry 2015)

As a credible fabric of falsehoods is woven, agnostics and skeptics are progressively won over and co-opted into further deception, until planners and onlookers alike have difficulty distinguishing truth from falsehood. But, as in Sir Walter Scott's elegant lines: 'Oh what a tangled web we weave / When first we practice to deceive', eventually, real-world complexity gets in the way and 'stuff happens', while those who set the switch that led to the train wreck can later claim they had acted in good faith on the basis of what they thought they knew at the time (Coll 2024; Malone 2024; Frontline 1990; Powell 2005; Cook 2011; Thompson 2015; Lerner 2015; Golshan and Ward 2019).

A case in point is the advice of the briefing paper presented to the July 23, 2002 meeting of the UK War Cabinet, arguing that their options were limited by the circumstances of their existing commitments and the deter-mination of the Bush administration to proceed with the invasion:

> Regime change per se is illegal under international law. US plans assume, as a minimum, the use of British bases in Cyprus and Diego Garcia. This means that legal base issues would arise virtually whatever option Ministers choose with regard to UK participation. It is necessary to create the conditions in which we could legally support military action. (Smith)

It was the assessment of the Foreign Office, in other words, that the existing fabric of lies trapped the UK into collaborating in further lies, as apt an illustration as might be found for what critics of American foreign policy and media (Cook 2011) and later, Vladimir Putin (2022a, 2022b) called 'the empire of lies'. Although it is reinforced by post-hoc assessments (Schwarz 2023), the authors of this book rejected this term while considering it for the title. Aside from the phrase being essentially tauto-logical, as all empires need to lie in order to remain empires, it is further limited in its focus on only one dimension of the phenomenon. Just as apt, though equally one-sided, is Samir Amin's (1992) descriptive label, 'empire of chaos', a term also employed by critics of empire Pepe Escobar (2023) and Chris Hedges (2023). Lies and chaos together are the essential twin features of Pax Americana: lies, combined with force, in the pro-motion of chaos on the frontiers; chaos, to obstruct processes which would otherwise threaten the state of order—the 'pax'—at the center. Lies also preserve illusions of exceptionalism and impunity at the center, and of inferiority and hopelessness at the frontier. Lies and chaos are the two faces of the imperial coin.

EMPIRE OF CHAOS

Having considered the lies, let us now turn to the chaos. An old Swahili proverb goes something like, 'When the elephants fight, the grass gets trampled' (Kensaku 2015) and although there was only one elephant in Iraq in March 2003, the grass was trampled nevertheless. As a result of the overwhelming power imbalance between Iraq and the invading force and its destructive intent, the consequences of Washington creating its own reality were born almost entirely by Iraqis. As Chilcot has it, '[t]he evidence is there for all to see. It is an account of an intervention which went badly wrong, with consequences to this day' (11). We attempted to survey the wide range of these consequences—some of the 'stuff' that has happened—in Chap. 2, from the looting of its cultural heritage, the destruction of state institutions under the guise of 'de-Ba'athification', an American-engineered constitution that entrenched sectarian politics and created sectarian and ethnic roadblocks to any future return toward a national political culture, successive waves of sectarian violence that destroyed civil society and social infrastructure, and which drove what might otherwise have become the educated professional class out of Iraq.

United Nations agencies and other non-government organizations working in Iraq have issued many factual reports, each in their respective domain, on the social and economic consequences. In an effort to preserve and facilitate wider access to this testimony, we discussed some of these briefly at the conclusion to Chap. 2. Each researched and compiled by experts in their respective domains, they include: food security and nutrition, maternal and infant welfare, education, child labor, forced displacement of populations, economic deprivation, abuse of women and violence against civilians. Individually and collectively, they describe a population which has been devastated by the series of violent assaults that began with the Iran-Iraq war in 1980, followed almost immediately by the First Gulf War in 1990–1991, and the 13 years of UN sanctions and bombing, the invasion of 2003, the chaos and sectarian conflict of the occupation, and finally, the assault of the Islamic State. Consulting any one of these expert reports leads to the same discouraging conclusion. However, as common wisdom informs us that it takes a village to raise a child, we bring to the reader's attention a single statistic representing the damning consensus of these reports. The 2018 UNICEF Iraq *Multiple Indicator Cluster Survey* (MICS) finds that the under-five mortality rate for children dying before they reach the age of five in Iraq was 26 per 1000 live births, and as high as 44 per 1000 in areas severely affected by sectarian conflict, among the highest rates in the Middle East. All the other reports noted here and in Chap. 2 document the devastation of social infrastructure that, taken together, results in this alarming fact.

Among the casualties world wide of the destruction of Iraq is the undermining of public and governmental trust in international institutions, including the UN and international law. There has been a pattern of manipulation of the UN Security Council with regard to the conflicts in Iraq (Falk 1991), Libya (Forte 2012), and of the Organization for the Prohibition of Chemical Weapons (OPCW) in the case of Syria (Falk 2018) to the extent of undermining their ability to moderate future conflicts. Although each historical antecedent can be shown to have had its own specific characteristics and circumstances, the failure of international institutions to enforce a measure of accountability against Italy for its conquest of Ethiopia may have been the last straw in the erosion of the League of Nations' authority and credibility before the Second World War. Since that time, the newly founded United Nations' credibility was dealt a serious blow, with the US and its allies exploiting a doubtful interpretation of the Security Council's procedures at the outbreak of conflict in Korea, to use the UN, not to outlaw war as envisaged in the Charter, but to conduct a war under American command (Falk 1991). Among the many enduring consequences has been the inability of the UN to play a constructive role in conflicts involving the superpowers during the Cold War. The role of the UN during the period of Pax Americana is another stage in this prolonged process of undermining of international institutions (Ismael and Ismael 2021: 151–57, 163–64), where they are not so much bypassed since 2003, but more often coopted and managed by the hegemon.

Perhaps the most entertaining demonstration of the enduring consequences of the American adventure in Iraq was in Bush Jr.'s verbal stumble, unintentionally reenacting Shakespeare's tragic hero, Macbeth, upended in public by the ghost of his murdered victim. Bush had intended to condemn Putin's invasion of Ukraine, but his words, as uttered, condemned instead 'the decision of one man to launch a wholly unjustified and brutal invasion of Iraq'. Bush immediately corrected himself: 'I mean, of Ukraine!' and joined in the audience's laughter (BBC 2022). It was a foot-in-mouth cameo appropriate to the genre of dramatist David Hare (quoted above) from his play, 'Stuff Happens'.

Both incidents, real and imaginative, are pertinent rebuttals to hypocrisy, that standard item in the American foreign policy toolkit, in the selective use of evidence to criticize and embarrass opponents. One American president found it convenient to overlook (and covertly encourage) their one-time asset, Saddam Hussein's 1980 attack on Iran. That war was hardly over, a million of so deaths later, when an American ambassador voiced a hands-off attitude toward Iraq's dispute with Kuwait, and eight days later, another American president forthrightly condemned Iraq's invasion of Kuwait as a war of aggression. No one in Washington explained why Kuwait was more deserving of international solidarity and enforcement of international law than Iran, or why international law should be an *a la carte* item, to be applied only when convenient to the hegemon. The near-destruction of Iraq by the US coalition of the willing during the Gulf War in 1991 and afterward, now viewed with the benefit of hindsight afforded by the Chilcot inquiry, looks remarkably like an earlier prototype of the 'clever strategy' of 2002 to 'wrongfoot Saddam'. One can now begin to grasp the thinking of the planners in Washington and Whitehall: if it worked so well then, why not go with it again?

The central theme surrounding discussion of the invasion of Iraq in 2003 was, of course, 'weapons of mass destruction', the so-called WMDs, where *a la carte* reasoning again goes unchallenged. In the case of chemical weapons, the US (as Hare points out through his dramatic character of Powell) did not take action against Saddam for its previous chemical attacks against Iran or the Kurds. And, if we exclude Pakistan (another *a la carte* item) from the area to be included in the Middle East, then only one state in that region, Israel, was known to possess nuclear weapons, the real McCoy of WMDs. American practice however, had been not to officially acknowledge the fact of Israel's nuclear weapons, even though (or perhaps because) the US had played a role in assisting Israel to acquire them (Hersh 1991). Moreover, the US regularly opposed the periodic proposals for making the Middle East a nuclear-free zone, which would have required Israel to divest itself of its nuclear weapons. A more logically consistent explanation for US policy between the Gulf War and the Iraq invasion is the motivation to preserve Israel's nuclear monopoly in the region and to weaken or destroy states that championed Palestinian resistance to Israel (Baker et al. 2010; Ismael and Ismael 2021). Iraq, Libya, Iran and Syria were all vocal defenders of Palestinian statehood, making them enemies of Israel, and were ostensibly suspected by Israel and the US of developing the technical capacity to produce nuclear weapons. The planners in the Bush and Blair governments considered the problem of a future Iraq government again attempting to acquire WMDs in the future. A UK Cabinet briefing document of 8 March 2002 pointed to the need for a prolonged occupation in order to prevent any future Iraqi government from developing WMDs:

> Without a continued significant allied military force on the ground, 'there would be a strong risk of the Iraqi system reverting to type. Military coup could succeed coup until an autocratic, Sunni dictator emerged who protected Sunni interests. With time he could acquire WMD.' (Smith)

There is a cunning logic in this advice: the destruction of state institutions during the invasion and occupation may have ensured Israel's nuclear monopoly for the foreseeable future.

THE DECLINE OF PAX AMERICANA

An ancient piece of wisdom, much older than Leonard Cohen, is that every human creation has within itself a fatal flaw. And so it is with empires. An examination of the emperor's coin reveals imperfections on both sides. We have previously seen how imperial strategists cannot avoid getting trapped in the contradictions and unforeseen implications of their clever strategies to deceive their enemies, their allies and their own publics. Empires long in the tooth rest on many layers of deception and self-deception, lulling them into unrealistic expectations of themselves and of their potential enemies. Pertinent examples are the productive and cognitive distortions consequent on the hegemony of global financial capitalism that has exported most industrial production to Asia, while many Americans continue to believe their own economy is bigger than China's, and that Russia is, as the late US Senator John McCain (Everett 2014) quipped, merely 'a gas station masquerading as a country'. But American self-centered concepts of magnitude and power cause them to include in such statistics as the gross domestic product (GDP) activities that have little to do with economic welfare or of military power, and hence, they are surprised that Russia is able to fire more artillery ammunition in Ukraine than all the NATO countries together can produce. Chinese leaders have taken notice of this, as *Global Times* commentator and the former editor-in-chief of the Chinese Communist Party Central Committee daily, Hu Xijin, observed:

> The US and the West have found it much more difficult than expected to defeat Russia. They know that China has not provided military aid to Russia, and the question that haunts them is: if Russia alone is already so difficult to deal with, what if China really starts to provide military aid to Russia, using its massive industrial capabilities for the Russian military? Would the situation on the Ukrainian battlefield fundamentally change? Furthermore, Russia alone can already confront the entire West in Ukraine. If they really force China and Russia to join hands, what changes will there be in the world's military situation? (Hu 2023; Bhadrakumar 2023b)

A second example is the recent announcement by Saudi Arabia that they will begin selling oil in currencies other than American dollars, thus (as Anthony Eden characterized what Nasser did to Britain in 1956) gently placing their boot on imperial America's economic throat: the vitality of the petro-dollar economy that guaranteed a large flow of dollars from the oil trade into US Treasury bills and its corporate economy, thereby financing endless government deficit spending and the world's largest military (Hudson 2021). The Saudis, probably like others in the Middle East and Africa, took note of the chaos created by the US in Iraq, Libya and Syria, and understood they finally had a safer alternative, in an assured and friendly market in a growing China, and supportive market power and potential military assistance in Russia. However, the fate of premature rebels serves as a warning to would-be regicides: 'If you shoot the king, make sure you kill him'. All players being aware of the consequences of failure and of success, can be expected to accelerate the process of dismantling the petrodollar economy and of American global financial hegemony. The Chinese brokered agreement for Saudi Arabia and Iran to re-establish diplomatic relations is the most significant of several Chinese and Russian inter-related diplomatic initiatives aimed at dispelling the chaos and illusions associated with US imperial penetration of the Middle East (Bhadrakumar 2023a; Cole 2023; Anderson 2023). Faced with the growing economic, technical and diplomatic prowess of the Russian-China strategic partnership, which its own imperial strategy of lies and chaos helped to mobilize, Pax Americana, is now threatened by their coordinated development-through-peace initiative.

REFERENCES

Aburish, Said K. 1997. *A Brutal Friendship: The West and The Arab Elite.* Victor Gollancz.

Amin, Samir. 1992. *Empire of Chaos.* New York: Monthly Review Press.

Anderson, Lisa. 2023. The Forty-Year War: How America Lost the Middle East. *Foreign Affairs*, April 18, https://www.foreignaffairs.com/reviews/middle-east-forty-year-war-china. Accessed 31 July 2023.

Baker, Raymond W., Shereen T. Ismael, and Tareq Y. Ismael. 2010. *Cultural Cleansing in Iraq: Why Museums Were Looted, Libraries Burned and Academics Murdered.* Pluto Press.

BBC. 2022. Bush Condemns Putin's Invasion of "Iraq" Instead of Ukraine, 19 May, https://www.bbc.com/news/av/world-us-canada-61505050. Accessed 19 April 2023.

Bhadrakumar, M.K. 2023a. China Steps Up, a New Era Has Dawned in World Politics. *Indian Punchline*, 11 March, https://www.indianpunchline.com/china-steps-up-a-new-era-has-dawned-in-world-politics/.   Accessed   8 April 2023.

———. 2023b. US Is Stirring Up the Syrian Cauldron. *Indian Punchline*, 26 March,   https://www.indianpunchline.com/us-is-stirring-up-the-syrian-cauldron/. Accessed 3 March 2023.

Cheney, Dick. 1992. Defense Planning Guidance. *National Archives.* https://www.archives.gov/files/declassification/iscap/pdf/2008-003-doc14.pdf. Accessed 2 May 2023.

Chesterman, Simon. 2002. *Just War or Just Peace? Humanitarian Intervention and International Law.* Oxford Academic, November, https://academic.oup.com/book/9945/chapter-abstract/157293287?redirectedFrom=fulltext. Accessed 2 April 2023.

Chilcot, Sir John. 2006. *The Iraq Inquiry,* 6 July, http://worldofstuart.excellent-content.com/uploads/ChilcotReport_Volume1.pdf. Accessed 7 April 2023.

Chomsky, Noam. 1991. What We Say Goes. *Z Magazine,* 4 April.

Clinton, Bill. 1998. Statement on Signing the Iraq Liberation Act of 1998. *The American Presidency Project,* UC Santa Barbara. https://www.presidency.ucsb.edu/documents/statement-signing-the-iraq-liberation-act-1998. Accessed 1 April 2023.

Cockburn, Patrick. 1997. Revealed: How the West Set Saddam on the Bloody Road to Power. *The Independent,* 28 June, https://www.independent.co.uk/news/world/revealed-how-the-west-set-saddam-on-the-bloody-road-to-power-1258618.html. Accessed 14 April 2023.

Cole, Juan. 2023. China Hangs Washington Out to Dry in the Middle East. *Tom Dispatch,* 16 May, https://tomdispatch.com/china-and-the-axis-of-the-sanctioned/. Accessed 19 May 2023.

Coll, Steve. 2024. *The Achilles Trap: Saddam Hussein, the C.I.A., and the Origins of America's Invasion of Iraq.* New York: Penguin Press.

Cook, Jonathan. 2011. An Empire of Lies: Why Our Media Betray Us. *Counterpunch,* 25 February, https://www.jonathan-cook.net/2011-02-28/an-empire-of-lies-why-our-media-betray-us/. Accessed 13 June 2023.

Dobbs, Michael. 2002. U.S. Had Key Role in Iraq Buildup. *Washington Post,* 30 December.

Donnelly, Thomas. 2000. *Rebuilding America's Defenses: Strategy, Forces and Resources for a New Century.* Washington: Project for a New American Century, 1   September,   https://archive.org/details/RebuildingAmericasDefenses. Accessed 28 February 2023.

Escobar, Pepe. 2023. De-dollarization Kicks into High Gear. *The Cradle*, 27 April, https://thecradle.co/article-view/24080/de-dollarization-kicks-into-high-gear. Accessed 28 April 2023.

Everett, Burgess. 2014. McCain: "Russia Is a 'Gas Station'. *Politico*, 14 March, https://www.politico.com/story/2014/03/john-mccain-russia-gas-station-105061. Accessed 8 April 2023.

Falk, Richard. 1991. Reflections on the Gulf War Experience: Force and War in the UN System. In *The Gulf War and the New World Order: International Relations of the Middle East*, ed. Tareq Y. Ismael and Jacqueline S. Ismael, 25–39. University Press of Florida.

———. 2011. Kuala Lumpur Tribunal: Bush and Blair Guilty. *Al Jazeera*, 28 November, https://www.aljazeera.com/opinions/2011/11/28/kuala-lumpur-tribunal-bush-and-blair-guilty. Accessed 28 March 2023.

———. 2018. The West, Led By the US, Has Shown as Much Contempt for International Law as Assad in the Conflict. *Middle East Eye*, 13 June, https://www.middleeasteye.net/opinion/hypocrisy-wests-syria-policy. Accessed 2 April 2023.

Forte, Maximilian C. 2012. *Slouching Towards Sirte: NATO's War on Libya and Africa*. Baraka Books.

Frontline. 1990. The Arming of Iraq. 11 September, https://www.pbs.org/wgbh/pages/frontline/shows/longroad/etc/arming.html. Accessed 12 June 2023.

Fukuyama, Francis. 1993. *The End of History and the Last Man*. Free Press.

Gellman, Barton. 1992. Keeping the US First. *Washington Post*, 11 March, https://www.washingtonpost.com/archive/politics/1992/03/11/keeping-the-us-first/31a774aa-fcd9-45be-8526-ceafc933b938/. Accessed 9 May 2023.

Golshan, Tara, and Alex Ward. 2019. Joe Biden's Iraq Problem. *Vox*, 19 October, https://www.vox.com/policy-and-politics/2019/10/15/20849072/joe-biden-iraq-history-democrats-election-2020. Accessed 9 June 2023.

Gorbachev Foundation. 1990. Document 14: Gorbachev Memcon with U.S. Secretary of State James Baker, Moscow, September 13, National Security Archive. https://nsarchive.gwu.edu/briefing-book/russia-programs/2020-09-09/inside-gorbachev-bush-partnership-first-gulf-war-1990. Accessed 20 July 2023.

Graham, Bill. 2016. *The Call of the World*. UBC Press.

Hare, David. 2004. *Stuff Happens*. Faber and Faber.

Harris, Shane, and Matthew M. Aid. 2013. Exclusive: CIA Files Prove America Helped Saddam as He Gassed Iran. *Foreign Policy*, 26 August, https://foreignpolicy.com/2013/08/26/exclusive-cia-files-prove-america-helped-saddam-as-he-gassed-iran/. Accessed 12 June 2023.

Hedges, Chris. 2023. The Lords of Chaos. *Consortium News*, 20 March, https://consortiumnews.com/2023/03/20/iraq-20-years-chris-hedges-the-lords-of-chaos/. Accessed 22 March 2023.

Hersh, Seymour M. 1991. *The Samson Option: Israel's Nuclear Arsenal and American Foreign Policy*. Random House.

———. 2003. Selective Intelligence. *The New Yorker*, 5 May, www.newyorker.com/archive/2003/05/12/030512fa_fact. Accessed 25 June 2023.

———. 2004. *Chain of Command, 1 January*. Harper Collins.

Hu, Xijin. 2023. US Gets Anxious as Russia Has Survived War of Attrition Against Entire NATO. *Global Times*, 1 March, https://www.globaltimes.cn/page/202303/1286442.shtml. Accessed 8 April 2023.

Hudson, Michael C. 1992. The Middle East under Pax Americana: How New, How Orderly? *Third World Quarterly* 13 (2): 301–316.

Hudson, Michael. 2021. *Super Imperialism. The Economic Strategy of American Empire*. 3rd ed. Islet.

Ignatieff, Michael. 2003. *Empire Lite: Nation-building in Bosnia, Kosovo and Afghanistan*. Penguin.

Ismael, Tareq Y., and Jacqueline S. Ismael, eds. 1991. *The Gulf War and the New World Order: International Relations of the Middle East*. University Press of Florida.

———. 2004. *The Iraqi Predicament*. London: Pluto Press.

———. 2015. *Iraq in the Twenty-First Century: Regime Change and the Making of a Failed State*. Routledge.

———. 2021. *Iraq in the Twenty-First Century: Regime Change and the Making of a Failed State*. Routledge.

Kensaku, Yuree. 2015. When Two Elephants Fight, the Grass Gets Trampled. Hong Kong, https://www.artbasel.com/catalog/artwork/14402/yuree-kensaku-when-two-elephants-fight-the-grass-gets-trampled. Accessed 16 April 2023.

Kinzer, Stephen. 2007. *Overthrow: America's Century of Regime Change from Hawaii to Iraq*. Times Books.

———. 2017. *The True Flag: Theodore Roosevelt, Mark Twain, and the Birth of American Empire*. Henry Holt and Co.

Lerner, Adam B. 2015. Hillary Clinton Says Her Iraq War Vote Was a "Mistake". *Politico*, 19 May, https://www.politico.com/story/2015/05/hillary-clinton-iraq-war-vote-mistake-iowa-118109. Accessed 23 June 2023.

Malone, Noreen. 2024. Is America All-Knowing and All-Powerful? Yes, Thought Saddam Hussein. *New York Times* 26 February, https://www.nytimes.com/2024/02/26/books/review/the-achilles-trap-steve-coll.html

McGovern, Ray. 2023. Iraq 20 Years: The Uses and Abuses of National Intelligence Estimates. *Consortium News*, 19 March, https://consortiumnews.

com/2023/03/19/iraq-20-years-ray-mcgovern-the-uses-and-abuses-of-national-intelligence-estimates/. Accessed 20 March 2023.

Mearsheimer, John J. 2014. Why the Ukraine Crisis Is the West's Fault: The Liberal Delusions That Provoked Putin. *Foreign Affairs* 93: 77–84, September/October, https://www.foreignaffairs.com/articles/russia-fsu/2014-08-18/why-ukraine-crisis-west-s-fault. Accessed 11 January 2024.

———. 2015. UnCommon Core: The Causes and Consequences of the Ukraine Crisis (vid.). University of Chicago, 25 September, https://www.youtube.com/watch?v=JrMiSQAGOS4. Accessed 11 January 2024.

Mearsheimer, John J., and Stephen M. Walt. 2009. An Unnecessary War. *Foreign Policy*, 3 November, https://foreignpolicy.com/2009/11/03/an-unnecessary-war-2/. Accessed 1 April 2023.

Miller, Judith, and Michael R. Gordon. 2002. Threats and Responses: The Iraqis; U.S. Says Hussein Intensifies Quest For A-Bomb Parts. *New York Times*, 8 September, https://www.nytimes.com/2002/09/08/world/threats-responses-iraqis-us-says-hussein-intensifies-quest-for-bomb-parts.html. Accessed 5 April 2023.

Morris, Roger. 2003. A Tyrant 40 Years in the Making. *New York Times*, 14 March, https://www.nytimes.com/2003/03/14/opinion/a-tyrant-40-years-in-the-making.html. Accessed 19 May 2023.

Parry, Robert. 2015. Saddam's "Green Light". *Consortium News*, 11 May, https://consortiumnews.com/2015/05/11/saddams-green-light/. Accessed 3 April 2023.

Perle, Richard, James Colbert, Charles Fairbanks, Jr., Douglas Feith, Robert Loewenberg, David Wurmser, and Meyrav Wurmser. 1996. A Clean Break: A New Strategy for Securing the Realm, the Institute for Advanced Strategic and Political Studies, Study Group on a New Israeli Strategy Toward 2000. https://web.archive.org/web/20140125123844/, http://www.iasps.org/strat1.htm. Accessed 3 April 2023.

Pilger, John. 2002. John Pilger Reveals the American Plan. *The New Statesman*, 16 December, https://www.web.archive.org/web/20110224030050/http://www.newstatesman.com/200212160005. Accessed 2 April 2023.

Powell, Jerome. 2005. Colin Powell on Iraq, Race, and Hurricane Relief. *ABC News*, 8 September, https://abcnews.go.com/2020/Politics/story?id=1105979&page=1. Accessed 21 March 2023.

Putin, Vladimir. 2022a. Address by the President of the Russian Federation, 24 February 2022, President of Russia, http://en.kremlin.ru/events/president/news/67843. Accessed 20 February 2024.

Putin, Vladimar. 2022b. Western "Empire of Lies" Has Resources, But It Cannot Defeat Truth and Justice—Putin. *TASS*, 16 March 2022, https://tass.com/world/1423145. Accessed 4 February 2023.

Riedel, Bruce. 2019. Order from Chaos: What Iran's Revolution Meant for Iraq. Brookings, 24 January, https://www.brookings.edu/blog/order-from-chaos/2019/01/24/what-irans-revolution-meant-for-iraq/. Accessed 14 April 2023.

———. 2021. *9/11 and Iraq: The Making of a Tragedy*. Brookings, September 17, https://www.brookings.edu/blog/order-from-chaos/2021/09/17/9-11-and-iraq-the-making-of-a-tragedy/. Accessed 3 April 2023.

Ritter, Scott. 2023. *Scott Ritter Opposing Iraq Invasion*, August 2002 (vid.). Consortium Research, March 21, 2023, https://consortiumnews.com/2023/03/21/watch-scott-ritter-opposing-iraq-invasion-august-2002/. Accessed 21 March 2023.

Ross, Carne. 2016. Iraq: The Story of My Evidence. *Personal Blog*, 13 June, https://www.carneross.com/index.php/2016/06/13/iraq-the-story-of-my-evidence/. Accessed 19 May 2023.

———. 2017. *Independent Diplomat: Despatches from an Unaccountable Elite*. C Hurst & Co Publishers.

Sachs, Jeffrey. 2023a. *On the Path to Peace in Ukraine* (vid.). Canadian Foreign Policy Institute, 4 May, https://www.youtube.com/watch?v=k_uyfb6OyZ8. Accessed 15 May 2023.

Sachs, Jeffrey S. 2023b. NATO Chief Admits NATO Expansion Was Key to Russian Invasion of Ukraine (vid.). *Common Dreams*, 20 September, https://www.commondreams.org/opinion/nato-chief-admits-expansion-behind--russian-invasion and https://www.jeffsachs.org/newspaper-articles/nato-chief-admits-expansion-behind-russian-invasion. Accessed 15 January 2024.

Sanders, Richard. 2002. Regime Change: How the CIA put Saddam's Party in Power, 24 October 2002, *Blog*, http://www.hartford-hwp.com/archives/51/217.html. Accessed 20 May 2023.

Schwarz, Jon. 2023. The Architects Of The Iraq War: Where Are They Now? They're All Doing Great, Thanks for Asking. *The Intercept*, 15 March, https://theintercept.com/2023/03/15/iraq-war-where-are-they-now/. Accessed 10 April 2023.

Sciolino, Elaine, and Micheal R. Gordon. 1990. Confrontation in the Gulf: US Gave Iraq Little Reason Not to Mount Iraq Assault. *New York Times*, 23 September, https://www.nytimes.com/1990/09/23/world/confrontation-in-the-gulf-us-gave-iraq-little-reason-not-to-mount-kuwait-assault.html. Accessed 15 February 2024.

Shaibani, Senan. 2024. *Indictment of the U.S. Federal Government*. Urbana, IL: AuthorHouse.

Smith, Michael. n.d. The Downing Street Memos. https://www.michaelsmith-author.com/the-downing-street-memos.html. Accessed 6 April 2023.

Sökmen, Müge Gürsoy, Roy, Arundhati and Falk, Richard (eds.) (2015), 'World Tribunal on Iraq: Making the Case Against War', Between the Lines, https:// doi.org/10.2307/j.ctt1rfzxf9

Stein, Jonathan, and Tim Dickinson. 2006. Lie by Lie: A Timeline of How We Got Into Iraq, Mushroom Clouds, Duct Tape, Judy Miller, Curveball. Recalling How Americans Were Sold a Bogus Case for Invasion. *Mother Jones*, September–October, https://www.motherjones.com/politics/2011/12/leadup-iraq-war-timeline/. Accessed 4 April 2023.

Sullivan, Andrew ('the Daily Dish'). 2009. We're an Empire Now, and When We Act, We Create Our Own Reality, *The Atlantic*, 23 April, https://www.the-atlantic.com/daily-dish/archive/2009/04/were-an-empire-now-and-when-we-act-we-create-our-own-reality/202751/. Accessed 3 April 2023.

Suskind, Ron. 2004a. *The Price of Loyalty: George W. Bush, the White House, and the Education of Paul O'Neill*. Simon & Schuster.

———. 2004b. Faith, Certainty and the Presidency of George W. Bush. *New York Times Magazine*, 17 October, https://www.nytimes.com/2004/10/17/magazine/faith-certainty-and-the-presidency-of-george-w-bush.html. Accessed 3 April 2023.

Switzer, Tom. 2013. Foreign Policy Begins at Home, by Richard N. Haass—Review. *The Spectator*, 6 July, https://www.spectator.co.uk/article/foreign-policy-begins-at-home-by-richard-n-haass-review/.

Thompson, Mark. 2015. How Disbanding the Iraqi Army Fueled ISIS. *Time*, 28 May, https://time.com/3900753/isis-iraq-syria-army-united-states-military/. Accessed 5 February 2024.

United States 107th Congress. 2002. H.J.Res.114—Authorization for Use of Military Force Against Iraq Resolution of 2002. https://www.congress.gov/bill/107th-congress/house-joint-resolution/114. Accessed 5 April 2023.

Wolfowitz, Paul. 1992. Defense Planning Guidance, 13 May, https://www.archives.gov/files/declassification/iscap/pdf/2008-003-docs1-12.pdf. Accessed 4 April 2023.

CHAPTER 5

Epilogue

This book was completed in late May 2023, just before the passing of Jacqueline Ismael, Tareq's life partner and our co-author. Delays in the publication process last autumn and the outbreak of war in the Middle East then presented us with the obligation and the opportunity to relate our conclusions to these events. Rather than revise the four chapters, we chose to retain the original text (with a few additional citations) and confine our subsequent reflections, relating to Iraq's situation in the context of intensifying conflict, in Europe and in the Middle East, to this Epilogue.

SECTARIANISM AND POLITICAL IMMOBILITY IN IRAQ

As we described in Chap. 2, 'Iraq Burning', the project of Pax Americana to destroy the Iraqi state was largely completed. The concern expressed by a staffer in the UK War Cabinet prior to the invasion (as we had noted in Chap. 4) that renewed Sunni military power might threaten the regional post-invasion status quo, now seems oddly misplaced. Given the general lack of political agency in Iraq that we observe today, one is tempted to ask how anyone could have expressed such a counterfactual concern.

From the outset of the US occupation, there were allegations and indications that the occupying forces aimed to destabilize the Iraqi state by manipulating ethnic and sectarian tensions. The introduction of a constitutional framework, starting with the Law of Administration for the State of Iraq for the Transitional Period (TAL) in March 2004, was criticized for

J. S. Ismael et al., *Pax Americana*, Frontiers of Globalization, https://doi.org/10.1007/978-3-031-61273-2_5

fostering disharmony and division among the population. The TAL was implemented by the Iraqi Governing Council, a body perceived to be under the direct influence of the US Department of Defense, and in which the Kurds also exercised powerful influence. The Council consisted of individuals associated with the US occupying army and with ties to the CIA, most originally recruited for the purpose of overthrowing Saddam Hussein. Despite chaotic conditions, a referendum on the TAL was held on October 15, 2005, and it officially took effect two months later, with the transfer of power from the Coalition Provisional Authority to the Iraqi government in May 2006. The constitution became the catalyst for the sectarian and ethnic division of Iraq, in a way, dismantling the Iraqi nation-state and weakening the harmony of its citizenry (Al-Tikriti 2008). This resulted in reduced socio-political cohesion, aligning more with antagonistic forces, where all governments and elections were essentially coalitions between the Kurds and the Shia Marjaeya, with the tendency to marginalize the Arab Sunni population.

It is peculiar that the division of Iraq into ethnic, religious, and sectarian groups appears irrational by any standard. The constitution of Iraq recognizes the Shia sect and the Kurdish ethnic group as distinct entities within the nation. This constitutional entrenchment of ethnic and sectarian divisions, combined with the system of proportional representation by electoral lists of candidates for public office, erects barriers to electoral representation by new political interests opposed to those controlling lists based on Shia or Kurdish support. Since the Shia account for nearly 60% of the Iraqi population (US Department of State 2019), Shia political leaders can regularly exclude the Arab Sunnis from participating in the governing coalition by forming a coalition with one of the Kurdish factions. As political factions tend to be based on demographic and religious sectarian criteria, political immobilism would appear to be entrenched in Iraq's political system (Ismael and Ismael 2015).

Thus, the seeds of future internal conflict are etched into the Constitution. An alliance with the Shia leaderships (the 'Marjaeya') and the Barzani clan have become dominant in Iraqi politics. The Marjaeya, serving as the paramount religious authority within the global Twelver Shia Islam community, holds a venerable position headquartered in Najaf, Iraq. Its profound influence extends across Shia populations worldwide, notably resonating deeply in particular within the hearts of Iraqi and Iranian Shia adherents. Revered for its spiritual guidance, the Marjaeya commands great influence, particularly among rural Shia communities, where its teachings hold significant sway. In its role, the Marjaeya wields considerable influence over both religious and societal matters, often shaping the perspectives and actions of its followers. However, there are instances where its influence in Iraq and Iran may lead political leadership to make decisions perceived as opportunistic, occasionally diverging from the best interests of the populace. The alliance of Marjaeya and the Barzani clan has created an environment where the dominant groups have been able to divide among themselves the spoils of government positions, eventually breeding corruption and a general inability to mobilize majority opinion in favor of resolving problems of any kind, internal or external (Jawad and Al-Assaf 2024).

In Chap. 3, 'Kurdistan and the Iraqi State', we noted that the KRG leadership behavior appeared to be more directed at the preservation of clan monopoly interests than in maximizing economic benefit and political agency for the Kurdish population. In a recent interview, Ala Talabani (Talabani and Muhsin 2024), a member of the Patriotic Union of Kurdistan party leadership in the Iraqi parliament from 2006 to 2021, essentially confirms our observations of the entrenched oligarchic structure of Kurdish politics, where familial ties continue to play a pivotal role. The interview also highlighted the trend toward increasing political repression, an obstacle to the establishment of genuine democracy and pluralism in Kurdistan.

In Chap. 2, 'Iraq Burning', in the section entitled, 'Cultural Cleansing Through Engineered Chaos', we reviewed case studies of the indifference (at best) of the occupation regime to the destruction and looting of Iraq's cultural heritage and institutions, contributing to the wiping out of cultural memory and Iraqi national identity. What survives of Iraq's rich cultural heritage is, like most collective wealth, subject to 'Muhasasa'—the sectarian quota arrangement introduced by the occupation authority and since then exploited by the sectarian and ethno-nationalist factions. A 2022 study (Kathem et al.) introduced the term 'heritage predation' to describe 'the destructive exploitation of cultural resources for political purposes' now taking place. In consequence,

> Iraq … is suffering from cultural loss at unprecedented rates. 'Intangible heritage'—an embodiment of people's identities and Iraq's rich history and shared cultures—is being eroded at a similar pace … these losses, and the appropriation of Iraq's cultural heritage by political elites, are not only the outcome of dictatorship and conflict, but also the result of the post-2003, elite-based sectarian power-sharing system, which in large part is premised

on the politicization and fracturing of the country's diverse identities and culture. (Kathem et al. 2022)

This process of heritage predation 'is designed not only to legitimize political and religious groups but ultimately to reshape Iraq itself in line with the priorities of post-2003 religious and ethno-nationalist interests' (Kathem et al. 2022).

The sectarian political structure is also congruent with a foreign policy tolerant of continued American presence in Iraq. In an interview published in the Saudi-owned newspaper *Asharq Al-Awsat* (Ghassan 2024), Hoshyar Zebari, Foreign Minister for nearly a decade, appeared to confirm his career-long alignment with the idea of tying the future of the Kurds to the continued US presence in the region, thereby weakening Iraq's independence and reinforcing Kurdish efforts to undermine Iraqi state unity and strength. Zebari also acknowledged that, as a Kurd and a member of Iraq's foreign relations elite, he allowed Iran to pursue its objectives. He understood that the Iranian leadership aimed to create what they termed an 'excess of resistance' to challenge US supremacy in Iraq, without risking direct confrontation. Iraq thus became compliant with Iranian foreign policy, while, at the same time remaining (in the context of our Chap. 3 on Kurdistan) a tool of American policy with respect to Iran. The interview suggests that the US was seemingly indifferent to this arrangement, opting to leave the handling of these militias to their agents in Iraq, while empowering the Kurds as the most influential force in any Iraqi government. Thus, even amidst the current upheaval in the Middle East, the Kurds' interests remain intertwined with those of Pax Americana.

A significant barrier to political change in Iraq is that the constitutional amending formula, which prevents any revision opposed by a two-thirds majority of voters in three governates, meaning that the three Kurdish governates are able to frustrate any attempt at constitutional amendment. This endemic political immobility has been externally imposed, not unlike the immobility imposed on Lebanon under the League of Nations mandate given to France, what we might term today, the 'Lebanonization of Iraq', or, as some critics of the constitution refer to it, 'a time bomb', likely to disrupt Iraq's political system during some future crisis, reminding us again of the imperial *force majeure* of 'divide and rule' inspiring both constitutions. In general, the constitutionalization of sectarianism works to dissolve a nation state from within, transforming its institutions and offices into negotiable assets for bargaining and diplomacy among sectional groups and external actors. This is the destination of the process we described in Chap. 2, it is the pacification of Iraq, the desolation that they call peace.

While the political immobility in Iraq can be seen to rest on 'objective' factors of ethnicity (in the case of the Kurds) and centuries-old religious divisions (between Sunnis and Shia branches of Islam), it is also true that these ethnic and religious boundaries are currently politically important at least partially as a result of the self-identification of millions of Iraqis, based on their own traumatic experience. However, many Iraqis are also aware that there was a time, in pre-Saddam Hussein Iraq, when these divisions were less salient, at least in the urban areas. One can imagine that a future era might be possible, where sectarian and ethnic divisions are perceived as being less vital than now, and where fewer inducements would be available to politicians who might otherwise be tempted to appeal to sectarian motives.

Relaxation of this immobility is unlikely to come initially from within, as the internal actors respond to the incentives established within the constitution and the social forces protected by it. Any weakening of this immobility is more likely to arise from without, as the consequence of an external shock, brought about by a confluence of global and regional changes. Among such changes might be a successful challenge mounted to Pax Americana in Europe by Russia, the growth of Chinese economic and political influence, the Sino-Russian diplomatic initiative in encouraging the growth of the BRICS countries to include the Middle East region, and, in the wake of the Hamas-led revolt against the occupation of Gaza and Israel's extreme reaction, the sudden inversion of the ideology of Zionism, from a buttress for Pax Americana, into its wrecking ball. Israel's attacks on the civilian population in Gaza and the interim ruling of the International Court of Justice (2024a, 2024b, 2024d) on the South African application, that Israel's attacks on Gaza could plausibly be genocide according to the 1948 Genocide Convention, may prove to be the game-changer in terms of the ability of the Israel and the US to employ the ideology of Zionism to bolster their combined strategic position in the Middle East (Walt 2021; Mearsheimer 2023, 2024a; Freeman 2024; Imseis 2024).

PAX AMERICANA AND THE WAR OF NATO ENLARGEMENT

As announced in the title of this book, our focus is on the impact of American imperial ambitions on the people of Iraq, not on the overall dynamics of imperial ascent and decline (Nederveen Pieterse 2024). We have said only enough about the latter to enable some understanding of why Iraqis were in the wrong place at the wrong time, and became opportune victims of American ambitions for world hegemony following the collapse of the Soviet Union. From a historical perspective, broadly similar circumstances some three generations earlier befell the Ottoman provinces that later became Iraq, when Britain succeeded in destroying the Ottoman Empire and turning the Middle East into a vital link in the lifeline of its own empire. What we have termed 'Pax Americana', is historically the successor to the British Empire, and from the point of view of present-day Iraqis, there is not all that much to distinguish the two, even to the point of the Anglo-American alliance having attacked Iraq in unison, both in 1990–1991 and again in 2003.

The concluding sentence of our quotation at the beginning of this book, of the Roman historian, Tacitus, consists of a very succinct pairing of critical assessments of ancient Roman policy and practice: the first, 'they make a desert … (or solitude)', is again taken up in our adoption in the previous chapter the rubric of 'the empire of chaos', used by some critics of American foreign policy. The completion of Tacitus' sentence: '… and call it peace', implies the second perspective we employed, 'the empire of lies'. More prosaically, the essential dynamics of the successful imperial projection of power requires the perspicacious combination of the use of force (or more frequently, the threat of force) along with an ideology of legitimation, the better to promote consent and obedience, economizing at once on the truth and on the need for the actual use of force. Hence, our short title, 'Pax Americana', reminding us of Tacitus' insight into the essential logic of empire. One reason why Tacitus' phrase is so often quoted (and deservedly so) is the implied ironic tone in the second part: we understand immediately that there is something terribly dishonest in calling a desert, which one has deliberately created through violence, to be 'peace'. We know it to be a lie.

In general, suppressing opposition and promoting internal cohesion and discipline (in the metropole) is essential to empire. While the imperial armies and covert operations (Sachs 2024c) do violence to their enemies (and, when necessary, to their subjects) the ideas implanted in their minds, can be expected, to some degree, more or less, to do violence to the truth as well. As long as the gap between the ideas promoting empire and actual realities on the ground remain relatively inconsequential, the power mobilization benefits of legitimating ideologies will tend to promote imperial success. However, the defeat, or even deterrence of one's enemies (if defeat doesn't wipe them out completely) may encourage opponents to improve their capacities, while the gap widens between what the forces of empire think they know about the threats in their environment and what may (though out of mind) be about to bite them.

One very pertinent instance of this phenomenon of imperial overreach or 'hubris' (pride) has been the overconfidence in Washington and NATO circles, from the Clinton to the Biden administrations, that Russia was too weak, militarily and politically, to mount any effective opposition to the successive waves of NATO'S eastward expansion in Europe (Mearsheimer 2014, 2015; Mearsheimer and Anderson 2023; Hahn 2023). In John Mearsheimer's view, Western leaders persisted with expansion, not because they were mistaken about the sensitivity and importance of security on their western border was for Russian leaders, but because they thought they could do so, that they could get away with it and that the Russians would not be able to stop them. Contrary to the promises of the George H.W. Bush administration not to expand NATO 'one inch' toward the Soviet Union, Western leaders persisted in the eastward expansion of NATO regardless of who was in the White House, and regardless of the advice of senior American officials not to cross Russia's very clear red line (Sachs 2023; Sachs and Hedges 2023).

While the eastward expansion of NATO was proceeding, and contemporaneously with the consolidation of Pax Americana in the Gulf region, successive American administrations took actions which undermined Russian confidence in strategic arms limitation agreements with the US. On December 13, 2001 George W. Bush announced that the US would withdraw from the Anti-Ballistic Missile (ABM) Treaty (Daalder and Lindsay 2001; Krieger 2002; Acton 2021). Part of the Russian response to this unilateral American decision, as President Putin explained at the 2007 Munich Security Conference, was to begin development of new offensive weapons that would render ineffective any future American anti-missile defense. At the same time, Putin made known his objection to NATO's eastward expansion, and this can be taken as the first clear warning to the Americans and their allies that Russia would not tolerate further NATO expansion toward Russia, which Putin (2007) described as '… a serious provocation that reduces the level of mutual trust …', a warning repeated the following year, when the NATO countries announced that Ukraine and Georgia would be on a track toward future membership in the alliance, a stern warning clearly communicated to Washington by its Ambassador in Moscow, William Burns, in his famous telegram, 'Nyet means Nyet', and subsequently made public by Wikileaks (Sachs 2023; Sachs and Hedges 2023: 44:30–45:30). With the benefit of hindsight, this fatal decision was judged by John Mearsheimer (unfortunately, we believe, quite accurately) to be '… one of the greatest strategic mistakes of modern times' (Mearsheimer et al. 2024: 1:30:48–1:31:18). In 2018, Putin announced that the new Russian weapons systems, development of which had begun around the time of the 2007 Munich conference, would soon be deployed, and once again, stating their purpose—to 'make any potential aggressor think twice, since unfriendly steps against Russia such as deploying missile defences and bringing NATO infrastructure closer to the Russian border become ineffective in military terms and entail unjustified costs, making them useless for those promoting these initiatives' (Putin 2018).

A key part of the plan to expand NATO toward the Russian border required the Ukrainian government requesting to join the alliance, at that time prohibited in its own constitution. But constitutions can be amended, given favorable political changes. American involvement in Ukrainian politics in support of anti-Russian parties, beginning as early as 2004 with the so-called 'Orange Revolution', and then participation in the violent and unconstitutional overthrow of the Viktor Yanukovych government in 2014 and the subsequent attempted violent suppression of Russian-speaking minorities in the Crimea and Donbas regions, impelled Russia toward support for a successful referendum in Crimea, authorizing union with Russia, and to support an armed rebellion against the Kiev regime by the Lugansk and Donetsk oblasts. When the Donbas rebel army surrounded and threatened to destroy the Ukrainian army, the German and French presidents appealed to Putin to intervene, resulting in two successive agreements, the 'Minsk I' and (after the Ukrainians had failed to comply with Minsk I) 'Minsk II' which required Kiev to constitutionally guarantee Russian-language minority rights and autonomous status for the Donbas oblasts, and subsequently endorsed by unanimous agreement in UN Security Council Resolution 2202. However, the German and French co-guarantors (the third being Russia) refused to ensure that Ukraine respected the agreement, and Angela Merkel, Francois Hollande, and then-Ukrainian President Petro Poroshenko even admitted later that they had never intended to comply, but rather sought to use the time to bolster the Ukrainian army for a renewed offensive (Al Mayadeen 2022; Magnier 2022; Nebenzia 2023; Mercouris 2024b). Instead, the NATO countries armed and trained an expanded Ukrainian army, which entered the Donbas region in February 2022 and began shelling the rebel-held towns. These actions were understood in Moscow as proof of bad faith and bad intentions toward Russia (Putin 2022a; Nebenzia 2023), consistent with a longstanding pattern of duplicity and aggression, beginning with the bombing of Serbia and the destruction of Libya, Syria, and Iraq. Putin notably expressed his greatest outrage for the case of Iraq:

> But the example that stands apart from the above events is, of course, the invasion of Iraq without any legal grounds. They used the pretext of allegedly reliable information available in the United States about the presence of weapons of mass destruction in Iraq. To prove that allegation, the US Secretary of State held up a vial with white power, publicly, for the whole world to see, assuring the international community that it was a chemical warfare agent created in Iraq. It later turned out that all of that was a fake and a sham, and that Iraq did not have any chemical weapons. Incredible and shocking but true. We witnessed lies made at the highest state level and voiced from the high UN rostrum. As a result we see a tremendous loss in human life, damage, destruction, and a colossal upsurge of terrorism. (Putin 2022a)

Putin then compared Russia's situation with that of the USSR shortly before the German invasion of June 1941, and vowed that they would not repeat the mistake of postponing action to counter aggression: 'Those who aspire to global dominance have publicly designated Russia as their enemy'. Putin does not see the contending forces as symmetrical in terms of the stakes: for the US, 'it is a policy of containing Russia … [but for Russia] … it is a matter of life and death, a matter of our historical future as a nation … the very existence of our state' (Putin 2022a; Lauria 2022, 2024).

Russia's initial response was to recognize the independence of the two Donbas oblasts and then to begin what it called the 'Special Military Operation', Putin citing Article 51 (Chapter VII) of the UN Charter (Putin 2022a), the 'treaties of friendship and mutual assistance with the Donetsk People's Republic and the Lugansk People's Republic, ratified by the [Russian] Federal Assembly on February 22'. Putin also specifically referred to Russia's purpose being 'to protect people who, for eight years now, have been facing humiliation and genocide perpetrated by the Kiev regime …' and '… defending Russia from those who have taken Ukraine hostage and are trying to use it against our country and our people', phrasing which, in retrospect, places the NATO-Russia war in the same context as Israel's actions in Gaza since October 7, 2023.

The NATO countries, however, declared Russia's action to be an invasion, and although Ukraine was not a member of NATO, that country has since been given the military support one might have expected in the case of a member country, including continuation of the covert cooperation between the CIA and Ukrainian intelligence that had begun in 2014 (Entous and Schwirtz 2024; Mercouris 2024d: 50:10–1:15:00; Johnson and Napolitano 2024: 4:50–10:09). The result has been an incrementally escalating undeclared war that has resulted in about 440 thousand Ukrainian casualties according to Russian estimates (Shoigu 2024), a smaller but undocumented number of Russians, and perhaps hundreds of unacknowledged combatants from NATO countries. As noted in Chap. 4, Russia has succeeded in destroying much of Ukraine's army and weaponry, including most of that supplied by NATO. In effect, the Russian objective announced by Putin of 'demilitarizing' Ukraine has also been at least partially effective with respect to depleting NATO weapons and ammunition stocks as a whole. Russia, on the other hand, has suffered no such shortage, and even announced a several-fold increase in military production during 2023.

Not mentioned in the military reports, another important casualty is that of American credibility: first, in the confidence of its current and potential allies and proxies that they have some assurance of American protection against common enemies, and second, in the confidence of Americans and Europeans that their governments and media are telling them the truth. Some observers of the European conflict might opt for Putin's stronger language, 'empire of lies' (2022a, 2022b) which we cited in Chap. 4, such as American investor and entrepreneur, David Sachs (2024; quoted by Mercouris 2024e: 1:15:00–1:17:40) in an 'X' post viewed by 2.4 million viewers, that the war in Ukraine was 'a war of lies … lies about how it started, how it's going, and how it will end'. Sachs predicted that 'the lies will succeed in dragging out the war. Congress will appropriate more funds. Russia will take more territory. Ukraine will mobilize more young men and women to feed into the meat grinder.

Discontent will mount. Eventually there will be a crisis in Kiev and the Zelensky government will be toppled'.

In spite of the descriptive accuracy of Sachs' label for this war, truth (as the saying goes) is always the first casualty, and probably all wars could be called the 'War of Lies'. Instead, we suggest that the war ought to be named after its primary cause and, in view of the dogged insistence of the US and its allies in crossing Russia's clearly identified red line, we have therefore adopted Jeffrey Sachs' (Sachs and Hedges 2023: 32:00–45:30; Sachs 2023; Lauria 2022, 2024) nomenclature for this conflict—the War of NATO Enlargement.

THE FOG OF EMPIRE

The pertinence of this geo-political conflict in Europe to the situation of Iraq lies in the weakness and increasing likelihood of the failure of Pax Americana in the Middle East and also globally, and the awareness of this weakness by all actors in the Middle East. Russian and American policy elites are both incrementally coming to the understanding that their rivalry in Europe is unlikely to be resolved through negotiation and mutual accommodation. From the Kremlin's perspective, their own repeated efforts to do so have been rebuffed and met with bad faith on the part of Washington, and there are growing fears in Russia that the US has become 'agreement incapable', or as Russian Foreign Minister, Lavrov, summed it up, 'The West is not trustworthy' (Lavrov 2024a). Readers who have followed us this far will suspect that the Foreign Minister was using understatement for effect. Fortunately for Russia, it has been able to develop a close strategic partnership with China, which has gradually come to share Russia's fears of American intentions. Russia could not wish for a better strategic partner in its circumstances, enabling it to withstand the severe economic sanctions imposed by the NATO bloc, and collaborating with Russia to strengthen and expand the BRICS countries (initially Brazil, Russia, India, China and South Africa) to include some key countries in the Middle East: Saudi Arabia, Iran, Egypt and the UAE, along with Ethiopia. The expanded BRICS now accounts for greater economic production than the G7 and dominates both oil production and consumption. With China's encouragement of African and Asian countries to join its 'Belt and Road' trading and infrastructure development initiative, the hub of global economic activity is gradually but steadily shifting from the Atlantic alliance toward China.

With the qualified and confused exception of the Trump administration, Washington has been steadfast in its opposition to Russia and, since Trump's attempted trade war against China, also toward China. It is difficult to explain this failure to seek compromise in the face of the demonstrated desire of both Russia and China toward peaceful cooperation with the US, in effect forcing them against their initial preferences, to combine their forces into a formidable obstacle to continued American dominance. 'Realist' analysts, particularly John Mearsheimer (2001, 2015, 2018; Mearsheimer and Sachs 2023) attribute this to a structural factor—that they, like all countries, are imprisoned within an unregulated global struggle for power and survival, although he considers the dominance of the Israel lobby over American policy as being 'a violation' of his realist theory (Mearsheimer 2024: 10:40). Regarding American objectives, Mearsheimer appears to be convinced (saying it twice within one minute: Mearsheimer and Anderson 2023: 39:50–40:35) that 'the United States foreign policy elite is committed to running the world'. Mearsheimer may have difficulty understanding why the US, as his realist framework would suggest, does not make greater effort to co-opt Russia in order 'to concentrate' on its competition with China. We would offer that American policy makers have come to be deceived by their own 'empire of lies', much as they had expected to deceive their presumed enemies and the majority of their fellow citizens, and are consequently unable to accurately perceive and judge what is properly in their national interest.

We would offer as additional support of this self-deception phenomenon through what we might call 'the fog of empire' (after the well-known military cliché 'fog of war') the path-breaking study of 'The Israel Lobby' (2006, 2009a) which Mearsheimer undertook with Stephen Walt. As they correctly pointed out, the Israel lobby in the US has a 'stranglehold' on Congress, on all senior government appointments requiring Senate confirmation, and is also a major factor in presidential elections. This situation is more than a little ironic for a country which never tires of insisting on its democratic credentials, that it is the very competitiveness of the American two-party system which makes the Israel lobby so effective: a potential candidate for almost any public office fears that if he or she does not conform to the lobby's wishes, the lobby will ditch him in favor of his competitor (Mearsheimer and Napolitano 2024a). The Israel lobby thus has skillfully employed its very ample financial resources to turn what might have been a democratic feature of the American constitution—the competition of political parties for the approval of the majority of voters—on its head, into a device to achieve something close to the opposite of democracy—the advantage of a wealthy minority and the policy of a foreign power.

This results in what we see now: a lack of strategic coherence in US foreign and defense policy. The pressure of partisan domestic politics perversely discourages the identification and pursuit of long-term goals supported by the majority of Americans, and which therefore tends to be dominated by other, more enduring interests, particularly those of the military-industrial complex, the finance-based oligarchy, and (as noted above) the Israel lobby. In terms of defense policy, this political imbalance has encouraged a development toward reliance on relatively expensive weapons systems and strategies which reward political constituencies and economic interests out of proportion to their contribution toward military effectiveness. As most conflicts prior to the War of NATO Enlargement have been against countries with weak militaries rather than against peer competitors, the US has experienced a lack of real-world pressure to improve war strategies and weapons systems. As a result, the American government spends about as much on defense as half the other countries in the world combined on wars which it nevertheless tends to lose, the most recent example being the NATO 'mission' in Afghanistan.

We noted in Chap. 4 the observation of a member of the Chinese Communist Party (Hu 2023) regarding the inability of the US and all of NATO to out-produce and out-fight even Russia on its own, the latter without any assistance from China. That trend has continued, with NATO leaders only now beginning to understand that they are facing defeat in their war against Russia (Macgregor and Napolitano 2024a; David Sachs 2024; Sanger and Barnes 2024; McGovern 2024; Mearsheimer et al. 2024) and to consider strategies of escalation (Amar 2024; Ritter and Napolitano 2024; Sachs and Napolitano 2024b; Anzalone and Napolitano 2024; Macgregor and Napolitano 2024b; Davis and Mearsheimer 2024). Urgings by President Macron for NATO military deployments to Ukraine and intercepted conversations of German Luftwaffe officers discussing the use of German cruise missiles to destroy the Kerch bridge linking Crimea to pre-2014 Russian territory (McGovern and Napolitano 2024c; Helmer 2024c), provoked President Putin to remind 'would-be aggressors' that all previous attempts to conquer Russia had ended in failure, and warning that 'now the consequences for potential invaders would be far more tragic' (Putin 2024; Mercouris 2024e). The publication in the New York Times of the existence of CIA bases in eastern Ukraine (Entous and Schwirtz 2024), which would probably not have been leaked if the US had intended to remain in Ukraine, and the resignation of undersecretary of state for political affairs, Victoria Nuland, widely perceived as the architect of American policy in Ukraine (Crowley; Maté and Napolitano; Sachs and Napolitano 2024c), appeared to signal to friend and foe alike that Pax Americana is looking to cut its losses in Europe (McGovern 2024; Ritter and Napolitano 2024). If, as we suggested above, truth is the first casualty of war, as the course of the War of NATO Enlargement would attest, then the credibility of the losing side will be among the hundreds of thousands of human victims. While political theorists might perceive American leaders to be belatedly following John Mearsheimer's advice that they curtail their competition with Russia in order to concentrate on China, their true peer competitor, our perspective would suggest that, in having depleted its war materiel and its credibility in Europe, Pax Americana will face China, as well as challengers in the Middle East, with fewer resources and major distractions. Mearsheimer, indeed, acknowledges that, given the reversals it faces in Ukraine and the Middle East, the US will not be in a position to focus on China:

> I think you want to understand that if you're the United States at this point in time, the last thing you want is trouble in East Asia, right? If anything you want to do everything you can to dampen the tensions in East Asia because you are up to your eyeballs and alligators in Ukraine, you were up to your eyeballs and alligators in the Middle East and we have limited industrial capacity, right? So, getting into a fight in the South China Sea or over Taiwan would be, in my opinion, catastrophic for the United States. (Mearsheimer et al. 2024: 53:24–54:00)

Dwight Eisenhower, the president who warned (1961) Americans about the military industrial complex, was also the last president to demonstrate some balance in relations with Israel and its Arab neighbors, the Israel lobby having achieved dominance over US Middle East policy since the 1967 war. The Biden administration surprised many observers when it maintained Donald Trump's unreserved pro-Israel policy, confirming that partisan affiliation makes no practical difference (Lanard 2023; Parsi 2024). Because the American political system has been promoting Zionist interests over American interests (Mearsheimer and Walt 2006, 2009; Mearsheimer and Napolitano 2024b, 2024c), Israel has benefitted handsomely from American aid to become one of the two (the other being

Iran) most powerful countries in the Middle East, while (until the current war) spending about 5 percent of its GDP on military expenditures, down from about 27 percent at the time of the 1973 war (Stockman 2024).

THE BRICS AND AXIS OF RESISTANCE CHALLENGE PAX AMERICANA

The political power of Zionism over Americans has been an important factor contributing toward lack of coherence in their foreign and defense policy since the time of Eisenhower. Going further back, it represents one of the great continuities in the historical transition from Pax Britannica, announced as policy in the Balfour Declaration of 1917, to the Pax Americana of our era, where, on occasion, even the boundaries of the American and Israeli states are sometimes difficult to distinguish. We become used to American government officials declaring more than support for, but even identification with Israel, as when Secretary of State, Antony Blinken, travels to Tel Aviv on October 13 and publicly declares himself a Jew (Blinken and Netanyahu 2023) and President Biden makes the same pilgrimage (Lanard 2023; Parsi 2024; Crooke 2024a). Blinken and Biden may have thought their protestations of support for Israel would play well with a pro-Zionist American public, but they may also have confirmed among Arab publics that the US is as responsible for Israel's genocidal actions in Gaza as the Israelis, having supplied the financial and military wherewithal as well as the diplomatic cover with its veto at the UN Security Council. The fact that South Africa, a BRICS member, took the initiative to bring accusations of genocide against Israel under the 1948 Genocide Convention before the International Court of Justice (ICJ) (International Court of Justice 2024a, 2024b, 2024c; Conley 2024), along with the energetic and persistent initiatives toward a ceasefire in Gaza by Russia and China at the United Nations, at the ICJ (Xinmin 2024; Middle East Eye (2024b) and in the region, will go some way toward identifying the BRICS as the anti-colonial 'Nemesis' to Pax Americana (Johnston 2007; Putin 2022a; Bhadrakumar 2023; Escobar 2024).

Russian Foreign Minister, Sergey Lavrov, following meetings in Arab capitals and with the ambassadors representing the Organisation for Islamic Cooperation (OIC), stated:

Everyone is firm in their determination to officially adopt a decision creating a Palestinian state as well as starting talks with the involvement of neutral and effective mediators.

The Quartet of international mediators no longer exists. The United States has done everything to undermine its work by saying that it would engage in the mediating effort on its own. We all know what came out of this. We will strongly advocate for countries from the region, primarily the Arab League member states, to take ownership of the initiative to establish a mediation mechanism. Ideally, its task would be to convene an international conference on the Palestinian issue. (Lavrov 2024b)

Lavrov had urged the OIC ambassadors to promote unity among the Palestinian factions to 'come together and declare that the Palestinian people have reunited to create a solid foundation for the future state' (Lavrov 2024b). Noting that Israeli Prime Minister Benjamin Netanyahu had already dismissed the idea of Palestinian statehood, Lavrov emphasized that: 'the negotiating process remains the only way forward to achieve a settlement … [and hoping] that those who have influence over Israel, perhaps more than we do, will play their part by ensuring that Tel Aviv takes part in the negotiating process in good faith' (Lavrov 2024b).

With Russia serving in 2024 as Chair of the BRICS, the project of de-linking world trade from the American dollar, its pace (already forced by Western sanctions on Russia and Iran and the US trade war against China, all of them BRICS members) will likely accelerate. As more countries have fewer occasions to use dollars, demand for them will decrease, bidding up the interest rates on US Treasury bills and limiting the ability of the US to fund military and other government expenditures through borrowing. Higher interest rates in turn can be expected to have negative effects for American economic growth and economic welfare generally. Since its still-unresolved dispute with revolutionary Cuba in the early 1960s, the US has tried to achieve regime change in states which did not conform to American expectations through legally questionable economic and trade sanctions not approved by the United Nations Security Council. As the number of nations subject to American sanctions increases and as the victims of sanctions learn to develop workarounds, the sanctions tool becomes less effective. If the BRICS project to break free of American currency hegemony finally succeeds, it may also promote regime change, but in Washington.

In the meantime, Israel continues its destruction of all human settlement in Gaza, with the declared objective of destroying Hamas, although about 70 percent of those killed have been women and children. There have been many published reports of the destruction caused by the conduct of intensive bombing and shelling in one of the most heavily populated areas of the world, but the most authoritative is probably the South African submission to the IJC (2024a). After more than a hundred days of Israel's military assault on Gaza, the Israeli Defence Forces (IDF) nearly all civil infrastructure on the surface had been destroyed, while the bulk of Hamas' forces remain in some 500 km of tunnels below the surface, emerging to attack the IDF. With Israeli casualties mounting, combatants and observers seemed to agree that Israel might not succeed in its declared objective of destroying Hamas. At the request of Hamas, its allies in the 'Axis of Resistance': Hezbollah in Lebanon, Ansarallah in Yemen, the PMF militias in Iraq, and Iran, each of them acting independently on a tactical level, were incrementally increasing the military pressure, 'up an escalatory ladder, step by step, increasing the pressure on Israel and on America to stop the massacre in Gaza' (Crooke and Simes, Jr. 2024), what Richard Falk (2024a) called 'the most transparent genocide in all of human history'. The absence of any clear military success for Israel, plus the interim ruling of the IJC (International Court of Justice 2024b) affirming the plausibility of the genocide allegations brought by South Africa, along with the erosion of support for Israel around the world, has undermined the previous sense of confidence within the Israeli public, with a rising fear that 'the whole Zionist project that people [in Israel] fear has been destroyed' (Crooke and Simes, Jr. 2024).

An atmosphere of fear and desperation led to further escalation, drawing in the other members of the Axis of Resistance, as Israel attacked Hezbollah forces in Lebanon and Syria and assassinated Hamas and Hezbollah leaders (Dadouch and Fahim 2024). The Ansarallah Movement in Yemen attacked shipping owned by, or in transit to or from Israel in the Red Sea, effectively threatening Israeli trade (Islamic Republic News Agency 2024a; Helmer 2024a), suffering American and British bombing in retaliation and mobilizing mass opinion in non-Western countries against Israel and the US (Nereim 2024). Hezbollah fired missiles at IDF forces near the Lebanese border, forcing the evacuation of thousands of Israelis, the PMU militias in Iraq repeatedly fired missiles at American bases in Iraq and Syria, and Iran fired missiles at Irbil to destroy targets it claimed were linked with the oil trade destined for Israel and a possible Mossad base, and also against alleged American proxy forces in the Baluchistan region of Pakistan. A missile attack on the American Ain

Al-Asad base in Iraq, presumed to be carried out by the PMF, penetrated the Patriot anti-missile defenses and was interpreted by some observers as a warning to the US that their positions in Iraq were untenable (Mercouris 2024a; Crooke and Napolitano 2024a; Benjamin and Davies 2024). Meanwhile, the New York Times reported that 'Iranian-backed militias had already carried out 140 attacks on American troops in Iraq and Syria, with nearly 70 US personnel wounded, some of them suffering traumatic brain injuries' and that, if any Americans in the region were killed in further attacks, unnamed Biden Administration officials 'privately say they may have no choice …' then quoted an expert outside the Administration (Aaron David Miller, at the Carnegie Endowment for International Peace) as being more explicit about the target of the threat: 'to respond directly against Iranian assets' (Baker 2024; Mercouris 2024a, 2024b; Moon of Alabama 2024a). That article had the effect of drawing a line in expectation that someone would cross it, as someone promptly did. A week later, the same paper reported on a drone strike on an American outpost ('Tower 22') in northern Jordan next to the Syrian border, killing three American soldiers and wounding about thirty (Schmitt 2024; Vinograd 2024), giving the Biden administration what it may have been seeking, in a *casus belli* to expand the war by striking at 'Iranian forces and the militias they support in seven sites in Syria and Iraq' (Cooper et al. 2024; Moon of Alabama 2024c; Falk 2024b). If escalation continues, it is likely to reach an explosive stage, with both sides doing their utmost to prevent or reverse a defeat.

The BRICS' initiative gathered force with the interim decision of the IJC on January 26, that South Africa had presented a plausible case that Israel was committing genocide, and that Israel must cease the specified actions that could result in genocide of the Gaza population:

THE COURT,
    Indicates the following provisional measures: (1) By fifteen votes to two,
    The State of Israel shall, in accordance with its obligations under the Convention on the Prevention and Punishment of the Crime of Genocide, in relation to Palestinians in Gaza, take all measures within its power to prevent the commission of all acts within the scope of Article II of this Convention, in particular:

(a) killing members of the group;
(b) causing serious bodily harm or mental harm to members of the group;

(c) deliberately inflicting on the group conditions of life calculated to bring about its physical destruction in whole or in part; and

(d) imposing measures intended to prevent births within the group. (International Court of Justice 2024b)

Although the Court did not endorse all of South Africa's requested interim measures, in particular, to 'immediately suspend its military operations in and against Gaza, the logic of its provisional measures indicates an intention to prohibit the worst of Israel's military operations (Moon of Alabama 2024b; Lascaris 2024). South Africa welcomed the ICJ ruling, which it expected would 'bring accountability to Israel for its acts of genocide' and that

> Third States are now on notice of the existence of a serious risk of genocide against the Palestinian people in Gaza. They must, therefore, also act independently and immediately to prevent genocide by Israel and to ensure that they are not themselves in violation of the Genocide Convention, including by aiding or assisting in the commission of genocide. This necessarily imposes an obligation on all States to cease funding and facilitating Israel's military actions, which are plausibly genocidal. (South Africa 2024)

The South African statement put into focus the culpability of Israel's allies, particularly the US, as enablers of genocide, as pointed out by numerous Western critics of Israel's actions (Sachs 2024; Sachs and Napolitano 2024a; Mokhiber and Hedges 2024; Moon of Alabama 2024b; Lascaris 2024; Murray 2024; Falk 2024b). While Israel has not complied with the Court's interim decision, given the vital stakes of the confrontation for nearly everyone, the Court's prestige, and the strength of the reasoning of its decision, we expect, that the NATO countries will have little choice but to at least register a formal assent to its judgment (The Rideau Institute 2024). There is a risk for Israel in rejecting or disregarding the decision, as this could be taken as evidence by the Court that it is, as South Africa stated, intent on an act of genocide, and therefore hasten the Court toward its final decision (Mercouris 2024c). Of potential significance for China's future participation in the resolution of the conflict, Xue Hanqin, the Chinese judge on the Court, in a separate concurring opinion, unequivocally condemned Israel's atrocities in Gaza (Lascaris 2024; International Court of Justice 2024c).

Whether Israel eventually complies or not, the Court's interim decision, which includes findings of fact confirming some of the facts claimed by South Africa in its submission (Murray 2024) will likely shift the balance against the Zionist project through force of world opinion (Crooke and Napolitano 2024b; Sachs 2024; Hudson 2024), and may finally induce the US to accept a face-saving settlement process that would result in a sovereign Palestinian state. The focus of international diplomacy returned briefly to the UN Security Council, where the US vetoed an Algerian resolution, supported by all members except the US with the UK abstaining, calling for 'a humanitarian ceasefire'(The New Arab 2024; UN News 2024), the third American veto of a UNSC resolution on Gaza.

Some of the most eloquent and informed critics of American support for Israel are retired officials of previous American governments, among them, Chas Freeman, senior diplomat, former Ambassador to Saudi Arabia, Assistant Secretary of Defense, and Director of National Intelligence. Freeman is direct and unreserved in his denunciation of Biden's defense of Israel, a country with the 'values of the Ku Klux Klan':

> We supported [Israel] because we thought they were useful to us strategically, but they are taking us down with them, totally. And, in effect, we have made a choice. We prefer to back Israel over backing the international system, the rule of law, the United Nations system that we created after the World War II, the rule bound order, if you will, not the one that is dictated by Washington, but the one that reflects the common aspirations of mankind. We have chosen Israel over that international system. We're prepared to destroy the international system in order to allow Israel to continue to conduct genocide. I think that is truly sick and if the president wanted to have a place in history, he would take decisive action to bring Israel to heel. (Davis and Freeman 2024)

Freeman's articulate condemnation of Biden's 'complicity in genocide' from the standpoint of liberal internationalism, an article of faith for the Democratic Party since the Second World War, may have identified a point of vulnerability for Biden. While opinion among many Democrats is shifting against Israel, with a January 2024 poll reporting that more than half of Americans who had voted for Biden in 2020 believed Israel was committing genocide (Robertson 2024), there is little evidence as yet that it had moved the Biden administration (McGovern and Napolitano 2024b; McGovern et al. 2024b). Given the record of Donald Trump's Middle

East policy during his presidency, little hope can be expected from that quarter. However, candidate Biden (or whoever replaces him should he not remain in the race) will continue to experience electoral pressure to court dissident Democrats, especially in states where Arab and Muslim opinion is significant, such as the important 'swing' state of Michigan (Epstein 2024; Epstein and Goldmacher 2024) where 100 thousand Democratic voters refused to support Biden as the Democratic presidential candidate in the state primary, followed a week later by Vice-President Kamala Harris calling for an 'an immediate cease-fire, for at least the next six weeks' (Green 2024). Dissent among Democratic voters continued to grow, reaching 19 percent in the Minnesota primary, even though campaign organizers had a budget of only $20,000 and began a week before voting (Nehamas and Epstein 2024). Although state voting rules differ in how 'uncommitted' votes are registered, dissent among Democratic voters was also significant in other 'Super Tuesday' primaries. The significance of the erosion of political support for Biden and the extent of his identification with Israel lies, less in a viable domestic alternative to Pax Americana (both Biden and Trump are agreed on world hegemony and support for Israel, if on little else), than on revealing to the global majority that large numbers of Americans do not support the empire. Even without military conscription, its domestic support is weakening, recalling the 1968 anti-war popular mobilization against the war in Vietnam. As in that war, a major change in domestic opinion, though insufficient on its own, was linked to changing global factors, political, economic and military.

Our recollection of the historical parallel of the American anti-war movement of 1968 inevitably includes the surprise announcement of President Lyndon Johnson at the end of March that year, that he would end the bombing of North Vietnam and not seek re-election (Elving 2018). It would not be a greater surprise if today's wartime president, conflicted between the Israel lobby and the growing demands of Democratic voters to end the Gaza genocide, amid the impending debacle in Ukraine, and as his prospects of re-election fade, might come to understand that his best hope of leaving a positive legacy would be to heed the growing number of dissident Democrats, the global majority and the ICJ.

Even in the absence of a last-minute reversal of policy, if the shift in world opinion against the genocide in Gaza maintains the strength and breadth of its momentum (Johnson 2024; Wong and Stevis-Gridneff 2024) while the Israeli military is fought into a quagmire (Crooke 2024e), there is a possibility for the majority of states supporting Palestine to secure United Nations authority through the General Assembly under the 'Uniting for Peace' precedent to make the perpetrators and their enablers accountable (Boyle et al. 2024; Murray 2024; Mokhiber and Hedges 2024; Boyle and Blevens 2024). Should American military and political hegemony in the Middle East continue to weaken, a potential strategy using the forum and authority of the General Assembly could open new avenues for redress for violations of international and humanitarian law in Palestine and the region, and bring relief to the victims, including compensation through reparations (Shaibani 2024; Al-Azzawi 2024; Gordon 2024). As Senan Shaibani points out, the heinous crimes committed, even against the children of those resisting occupation, makes the logical case for reparations very strong: 'If the White House justifies the murder of an Arab child as a descendent of Al-Qaeda, then what penalty will redress the … [descendants] from white supremacists guilty of genocide and slavery?' (Shaibani: 91)

United Nations meetings and resolutions, and an ICJ final decision, however, all take time, which neither the embattled population of Gaza, nor the combatants may have. The time bomb of escalation in the Middle East therefore goes on ticking. Iran and Russia, preparing perhaps for the worst, have initialed a strategic defense agreement, which Russian defense minister, '[Sergei] Shoigu conveyed that Russia's commitment to Iran's sovereignty and territorial integrity will be explicitly stated in the pact' (Bhadrakumar 2024a). The Iranian press report added that 'the two ministers also pointed out the importance of issues related to regional security and emphasised that Moscow and Tehran will continue their joint efforts in establishing a multipolar world order and negating the unilateralism of the United States' (Islamic Republic News Agency 2024b; Bhadrakumar 2024a).

Notwithstanding their disparate geopolitical status and tactics, there is a general alignment in strategic intent of Ansarallah's position on the question of the Israeli genocide of the Palestinians, the South African position set out in its submission to the ICJ, as well as other members of the Axis of Resistance, the BRICS and the other states supporting Palestine: all aim to 'stop the genocide', putting them, in spite of the American re-listing of Ansarallah as a 'terrorist organization', within the growing mainstream of international opinion (Al-Bukhaiti and Blumenthal 2024; Mokhiber and Hedges 2024; Crooke 2024d; Crooke and Napolitano 2024e). Of the range of military actions undertaken by the Axis of Resistance, that of Ansarallah appears to be among the more successful, effectively closing the Suez Canal to shipping to or from Israel (Smith 2024) and effectively giving Chinese shipping companies an advantage in insurance costs and ability to use the shorter Suez Canal route (Longley and Quinn 2024). Combined with the continued fierce resistance of Hamas and the rising Israeli casualties, it is not apparent at this point that a viable military resolution exists for Israel and the US.

As missile attacks on Irbil and on the Ain Al-Asad base, and the American retaliatory bombing of sites in Syria and Iraq and assassination of an Iraqi Shi'ite militia leader in Baghdad (Falk 2024b; Crooke 2024d) in declared retaliation for the 'Tower 22' attack might portend, Iraq could once again, find itself in the wrong place at the wrong time. Aware of the potential danger even before the attacks, President Mohammed Shia' Al Sudani issued a statement that Iraq would work with the Americans to remove their armed forces from Iraq. His statement, a model of diplomatic ambiguity, is as good an indicator as any of Iraq's continued political immobilism. In an interview with Reuters, Sudani said he wanted 'a process of understanding and dialogue ... [with] a time frame ... that is, honestly, quick, so that they don't remain long and the attacks keep happening'. Sudani then seemed to leave the door open, adding, that Iraq 'was open to establishing bilateral relations and engaging in security cooperation with coalition nations, including ... training and advising Iraqi security forces as well as weapons purchases'. The same Reuters dispatch reported however, that the Pentagon 'had no plans to withdraw US troops, which are in Iraq at the invitation of its government' (AhlulBayt News Agency 2024a, 2024b; Azhari 2024; Salem 2024; Moon of Alabama 2024c). Nor was it acknowledged that Sudani's announcement marked the third attempt since 2008 for Iraq to have American forces withdrawn. However, this time will likely be different, as the American lethal attacks on the Hashd militias forced Sudani to condemn the American action and reinforce his opposition to the continued presence of American forces in Iraq (Schenker 2024). The Russian-assisted recovery of Syrian territory by the Assad government by 2018 had placed American forces in both Syria and Iraq in an exposed position, causing former President Trump to publicly announce his intention to withdraw them (Landler et al. 2018). While Trump's plan was ultimately shelved by elements of his own administration, the pressing logic of such a withdrawal is finally becoming apparent to the current administration (Schenker). From the Iraqi perspective, there remains the fear that their country will again become (analogous to Ukraine) a zone of conflict between Pax Americana and its challengers.

Pax Americana has already been significantly weakened since 2003, when it stood astride the Middle East like a colossus. The US and the UK were unable to secure UN Security Council endorsement of their invasion of Iraq but no state was so bold at that time as to challenge the invaders before the ICJ. The UN Secretary General, Kofi Annan, had, when confronted by a BBC interviewer the year after the invasion, seemingly reluctantly acknowledged that it was, 'not in conformity with the UN Charter, from our point of view, and from the Charter point of view it was illegal' (Annan 2004; MacAskill and Borger 2004). Unlike the interim ruling of the ICJ regarding Israel, the Court, in the absence of any submission from a member state, remained silent on whether the killings of hundreds of thousands of Iraqis as a result of the sanctions after 1991, during the invasion and occupation should likewise be judged as plausible evidence for the commission of genocide (Falk 2024b). As long as the world's most powerful state can act with total impunity, it is doubtful whether we can regard international law as being more than aspiration.

The fact that the Court has directed Israel to take specific actions and is deliberating on whether it has in fact committed genocide according to the 1948 Convention implies that the US will, if the Court's final decision goes against Israel, face the risk of having to accept legal responsibility for enabling Israel's slaughter of the civilian population of Gaza. Nicaragua's submission to the ICJ (International Court of Justice 2024e) accusing Germany of complicity in the genocide will be seen as a precedent applicable to the US and its allies, likely having the effect of the Court deciding almost simultaneously on the question of genocide and of complicity. In the event that, as we expect, these decisions will be in the affirmative, it will no longer be credible for the many states condemning the genocide in Gaza to look the other way with regard to the prior invasion and destruction of Iraq. Iraqis, including those in the diaspora, therefore have a more pronounced moral standing in the Israel genocide case than many other states. As South Africa comes to the defense of Palestine before the ICJ, the destruction of Iraq will increasingly be understood as a conspicuous anomaly in terms of international law, and Iraqis can begin to take some hope in future support from one or more of the BRICS states in appealing on their behalf for justice and restitution (Al-Azzawi 2024; Gordon 2024).

Irrespective of which specific diplomatic measures are taken, and even if hostilities continue, the formal acceptance by most countries of the Court's judgment will set in motion a sea change in world opinion concerning Zionism, raising the costs for Pax Americana of maintaining its

Middle East outpost (Helmer 2024c), and threatening the viability of that historical project. With the global credibility of the US and Europe, historical patrons of the Zionist project, seriously impaired, future diplomatic initiative would shift to one of the BRICS countries, most probably China, to mediate the conflict and, in concert with the OIC and the Arab League, manage the process toward a negotiated resolution. Whether the juridical form of the solution emerges as two states or one, we would anticipate that, as Israelis begin to vote with their feet, the Zionist state would eventually wither demographically, ultimately leaving in its place a single Palestinian-majority state in which all residents have the same rights.

If, on the other hand, the social elements supporting Pax Americana, do as they have regularly done before—'double down' and 'go for broke'—then the two wars, in the Middle East and Europe, would become more closely linked (Helmer 2024b), escalating into a very intense, global conflict, without any second prize. All parties, believing they had everything to lose, would collaborate as far as necessary with the enemies of their enemies (Bhadrakumar 2024b; Crooke 2024b; Priebe and Charap 2024; Messina 2024). The forces opposing Pax Americana—primarily the BRICS countries and the anti-Zionist forces in the Middle East—appear to have substantially come to the conclusion that they must (in the popular American parlance) either hang together, or hang separately (Nasrallah 2023a, 2023b; Crooke and Napolitano 2024a, 2024c, 2024d). Although (as this book went to press) we do not regard such a widely destructive scenario as the most likely outcome, we would surmise that what we have referred to as 'the fog of empire' to describe the self-imposed inability of American leaders to understand the strength of the forces arrayed against them (McGovern et al. 2024a; McGovern and Napolitano 2024a) would, in the case of uncontrolled escalation, probably lead to the defeat of Pax Americana, though at great cost to all.

The opposition to Pax Americana is a diverse and ill-defined coalition of states and non-state actors that coordinate their actions, less in terms of specific tactics, than of overall strategy and objectives, to overcome Israeli genocide of the Palestinians and to expel American military power from the region. We see this most clearly in the speeches of Hassan Nasrallah (2023a, 2023b) and in the statements of Ansarallah (Al-Bukhaiti and Blumenthal 2024), but also in the submissions of South Africa to the ICJ (2024a, 2024d), and the forthright denunciation of the genocide at the African Union summit by Brazil's President Luiz Inacio Lula da Silva, who also spoke in favor of the South African ICJ submission and condemned the 'rich nations' for suspending their contributions to Palestinian emergency aid through the UNRWA (Livni 2024; Middle East Eye 2024a). More nuanced and indirect, are the initiatives undertaken by China and Russia to encourage regional dialogue and collaboration on a range of longstanding divisive issues (Bhadrakumar 2024c; Crooke 2024c), including the plight of Palestine. There have already been some prominent successes, including the re-establishment of Iranian-Saudi diplomatic relations, the inclusion of Iran, Saudi Arabia, UAE and Egypt into the expanded BRICS, the emergency OIC-Arab League summit in Riyadh, and the Russian and Chinese diplomatic initiatives, particularly at the UN Security Council (Crooke 2024b) and China's statement at the ICJ that the 'Palestinian people's use of force to resist foreign oppression and complete the establishment of an independent state is [an] inalienable right well founded in international law' (Xinmin 2024; Middle East Eye 2024b). The overall BRICS strategy can be characterized as the polar opposite of Pax Americana: instead of 'divide and rule', encouraging cooperation toward common goals, in essence, the oft-repeated Chinese slogan of 'win-win'.

Renowned Lebanese commentator, Sharahra (2023), emphasized the contrasting mode of operation of Russia and China in the Middle East compared to the Americans. According to Sharahra, America's foreign policy in the region is intricately woven with a strategy aimed at destabilization, perpetuating a climate of fear among Arab political leaderships regarding change and public engagement. Central to this strategy is the premise that democratic input from the populace would likely result in the rejection of incumbent leaderships. Consequently, the US extends offers of stability and security to these regimes, contingent upon their alignment with American foreign policy objectives. Sharahra contends that America's primary aim is dominance, manifested through a deliberate erosion of stability to assert control. In stark contrast, the BRICS nations, particularly China and Russia, adopt a nuanced approach devoid of direct control ambitions. Their focus lies in advancing their interests through collaborative partnerships with regional states, rather than imposition or manipulation. Sharahra highlights their role in fostering dialogue and reconciliation among conflicting parties as a testament to their commitment to harmony and cooperation. Chinese initiatives, such as advocating for Saudi-Iranian dialogue, have facilitated significant diplomatic breakthroughs, while Russian efforts have encouraged engagement between Syrian and Turkish stakeholders, and (we would add) among Palestinian factions, encouraging them to work together within the umbrella of the PLO (The Cradle 2024).

The neutrality and impartiality exhibited by the BRICS nations in their dealings with the Middle East endear them to both state leaderships and populations alike. Unlike the perceived hegemonic intentions of the US, China, and Russia are viewed as partners seeking mutual benefit and stability in the region. This portrayal enhances their credibility and diminishes any sense of threat, positioning them as facilitators of peace and progress.

In his insightful exploration, Sharahra underscores the divergent approaches of Pax Americana and the BRICS nations in navigating the complexities of the Middle East. While one seeks control through instability (what we have characterized as 'empire of chaos'), the BRICS countries prioritize cooperation and diplomacy, earning them the trust and favor of regional actors. As the dynamics continue to evolve, understanding these contrasting paradigms is paramount to comprehending the unfolding geopolitical landscape of the Middle East.

Sharahra's blunt portrayal of the American presence in the Middle East, what we have termed Pax Americana, is an apt summation of where we have arrived in this book. What he describes as the motivation and approach of the BRICS countries recalls for us an earlier American president who, in his first two years in the White House, had learned from his experience with the confrontations of the Cold War, the necessity of appreciating the humanity of his adversaries and understanding their motivations. In his June 1963 commencement address at American University, John F. Kennedy mentioned the idea of Pax Americana, but unequivocally disavowed any intention of seeking it:

> What kind of peace do we seek? Not a Pax Americana enforced on the world by American weapons of war. Not the peace of the grave or the security of the slave. I am talking about genuine peace, the kind of peace that makes life on earth worth living, the kind of peace that enables men and nations to grow and to hope and to build a better life for their children—not merely peace for Americans but peace for all men and women—not merely peace in our time but peace for all time. (Kennedy 1963; Sachs 2013: 74; Sachs and Hedges 2023: 24:50–25:21)

Kennedy's theme was revived by George H.W. Bush (1991) at the moment that Pax American became a reality, and also Barack Obama

(Times of Israel 2015), in promoting his agreement with Iran to regulate Iran's development of atomic weapons, only to see it disowned by President Trump and finally abandoned by Biden. Although the evidence is mixed, we are persuaded that Kennedy (unlike Bush Sr.) meant what he said. Unfortunately, good intentions and successful diplomacy were not a match for the imperatives of the security state. It is a sobering reality that one hesitates to compare the president who uttered those words in 1963 to the current incumbent, or any likely successor. Who would have the courage and fortitude to curb today's equivalents of Curtis Lemay and Allan Dulles? Even if an enlightened American president were to offer an olive branch to Iran and Russia, given the experience of those leaders in their previous dealings with their American counterparts, would they be able to summon the trust to shake hands?

References

Acton, James M. 2021. *The U.S. Exit From the Anti-ballistic Missile Treaty Has Fueled a New Arms Race.* Carnegie Endowment for International Peace, 13 December, https://carnegieendowment. org/2021/12/13/u.s.-exit-from-anti-ballistic-missile-treaty-has-fueled-new-arms-race-pub-85977. Accessed 19 January 2024.

AhlulBayt News Agency. 2024a. Iraq Decision to End US Military Presence "Irreversible": Sudani. *AhlulBayt News Agency,* 6 January, https://en.abna24.com/story/1426987. Accessed 19 January 2024.

———. 2024b. Iraq Seeks Quick Exit of US forces: Sudani. *AhlulBayt News Agency,* 11 January, https://en.abna24.com/story/1428375. Accessed 19 January 2024.

Al Mayadeen. 2022. Russia Fooled on Minsk Agreements: Putin. *Al Mayadeen English,* 22 December, https://english.almayadeen.net/news/politics/russia-fooled-on-minsk-agreements:-putin. Accessed 20 January 2024.

Al-Azzawi, Souad N. 2024. The Occupation of Iraq, and Two Decades of Environmental Degradation. *Journal of Contemporary Iraq & the Arab World* 18 (2-3), pp. 167-197.

Al-Bukhaiti, Mohammed, and Max Blumenthal. 2024. "Our Goal Is To Stop the Genocide": The Grayzone Interviews Houthi Spokesman (vid.), trans. Hekmat Aboukhater, *The Greyzone,* 25 January, https://thegrayzone.com/2024/01/25/interview-houthi-spokesman/. Accessed 28 January 2024.

Al-Tikriti, Nabil. 2008. *US Policy and the Creation of a Sectarian Iraq.* Middle East Institute, 2 July, https://www.mei.edu/publications/us-policy-and-creation-sectarian-iraq. Accessed 29 January 2024.

Amar, Tarik Cyril. 2024. Here's Why the West Can't Be Trusted to Observe Its Own 'Red Lines' in Ukraine. *RT*, 2 March, https://www.rt.com/news/593616-macron-scholz-ukraine-troops/. Accessed 2 March 2024.

Annan, Kofi. 2004. UN News, 'Lessons of Iraq War Underscore Importance of UN Charter—Annan'. *UN News*, 16 September, https://news.un.org/en/story/2004/09/115352. Accessed 8 February 2024.

Anzalone, Kyle, and Andrew Napolitano. 2024. Unseen Battlefronts and the True Cost of Military Support. *Judging Freedom*, 4 March, https://www.youtube.com/watch?v=qlev_AZywFg. Accessed 7 March 2024.

Azhari, Timour. 2024. Exclusive-Iraq Seeks Quick Exit of US Forces But No Deadline Set, PM Says. *Reuters*, 10 January, https://www.aol.co.uk/news/exclusive-iraq-seeks-quick-exit-100145329.html. Accessed 19 January 2024.

Baker, Peter. 2024. As U.S. and Militias Engage, White House Worries About a Tipping Point. *New York Times*, 21 January, https://www.nytimes.com/2024/01/21/us/politics/us-militias-tipping-point.html. Accessed 22 January 2024.

Benjamin, Medea, and Nicolas J.S. Davies. 2024. Biden Must Choose Between a Ceasefire in Gaza and a Regional War. *Counterpunch*, 26 January, https://www.counterpunch.org/2024/01/26/biden-must-choose-between-a-ceasefire-in-gaza-and-a-regional-war/. Accessed 26 January 2024.

Bhadrakumar, M.K. 2023. US Faces Defeat in Geopolitical War in Gaza. *Indian Punchline*, 16 October, https://www.indianpunchline.com/us-faces-defeat-in-geopolitical-war-in-gaza/. Accessed 17 October 2023.

———. 2024a. Decoding Iran's Missile, Drone Strikes. *Indian Punchline*, 18 January, https://www.indianpunchline.com/, and *Consortium News*, 19 January, https://consortiumnews.com/2024/01/19/decoding-irans-missile-drone-strikes/. Accessed 20 January 2024.

———. 2024b. Geopolitics Is Moving North Korea's Way. *Indian Punchline*, 23 January, https://www.indianpunchline.com/geopolitics-is-moving-north-koreas-way/. Accessed 24 January 2024.

———. 2024c. 'Swarming' the US in West Asia, Until It Folds. *The Cradle*, 29 January, https://thecradle.co/articles/swarming-the-us-in-west-asia-until-it-folds. Accessed 3 February 2024.

Blinken, Antony J., and Benjamin Netanyahu. 2023. Secretary Antony J. Blinken and Israeli Prime Minister Benjamin Netanyahu After Their Meeting. U.S. Department of State, 12 October, https://www.state.gov/secretary-antony-j-blinken-and-israeli-prime-minister-benjamin-netanyahu-after-their-meeting-2/. Accessed 20 January 2024.

Boyle, Frances, and Rachel Blevens. 2024. U.S. Vetoes Gaza Ceasefire Resolution + the Genocide Case Against Israel w/ Prof. Francis Boyle, 20 February, https://www.youtube.com/watch?v=1TPhe2j7MNM. Accessed 22 February 2024.

Boyle, Frances, Joe Lauria, Ray McGovern, Alexander Mercouris, Craig Murray, and Elizabeth Vos. 2024. ICJ Rules on Israel, (vid.), *Consortium News*, 27 January, https://consortiumnews.com/2024/01/27/watch-cn-live-icj-rules-on-israel/. Accessed 28 January 2024.

Bush, George H.W. 1991. President Bush Annual UN Address, 23 September, 46th session of the UN General Assembly. https://2009-2017.state.gov/p/io/potusunga/207269.htm. Accessed 18 May 2023.

Conley, Julia. 2024. South Africa Calls on ICJ to Stop Israel's Rafah Assault. *Consortium News*, 13 February, https://consortiumnews.com/2024/02/13/south-africa-calls-on-icj-to-stop-israels-rafah-assault/.   Accessed   17 February 2024.

Cooper, Helene, Eric Schmitt, and Julian E. Barnes. 2024. U.S. Conducts Retaliatory Strikes Against Iranian Proxies as War Deepens. *New York Times*, 2 February, https://www.nytimes.com/2024/02/02/us/politics/us-strikes-iranian-proxies.html. Accessed 3 February 2024.

Crooke, Alastair. 2024a. Gut Feelings Make for Strategic Errors—U.S. Lured Into Battlescape in Gaza, Yemen and Now Iraq. 15 January, https://www.unz.com/article/gut-feelings-make-for-strategic-errors-u-s-lured-into-battlescape-in-gaza-yemen-and-now-iraq/. Accessed 16 January 2024.

Crooke, Alistair. 2024b. *The Tragic Self-destruction of an Enraged Israel*. Strategic Culture   Foundation,   29   January,   https://strategic-culture.su/news/2024/01/29/the-tragic-self-destruction-of-an-enraged-israel/. Accessed 30 January 2024.

———. 2024c. *The Three Strands to the 'Swarming of Biden'*. Strategic Culture Foundation, 2 February, https://strategic-culture.su/news/2024/02/02/the-three-strands-to-the-swarming-of-biden/. Accessed 3 February 2024.

———. 2024d. The World's Gyre, 12 February, https://strategic-culture.su/news/2024/02/12/the-worlds-gyre/. Accessed 14 February 2024.

———. 2024e. *U.S. Seeks to Cap Middle East Violence; In This, Iran Is (a Kind of) "Ally"*. Strategic Culture Foundation, 26 February, https://strategic-culture.su/news/2024/02/26/us-seeks-cap-middle-east-violence-in-this-iran-kind-ally/. Accessed 10 March 2024.

Crooke, Alastair, and Napolitano, Andrew. 2024a. Alastair Crooke: Netanyahu: Ploy or Reversion? (vid.). *Judging Freedom*, 22 January, https://www.youtube.com/watch?v=OPHmovWe2ts. Accessed 22 January 2024.

Crooke, Alastair, and Andrew Napolitano. 2024b. Alastair Crooke: Will Israel Self-Destruct? (vid.). *Judging Freedom*, 29 January, https://www.youtube.com/watch?v=pvKJ6oFS7sE. Accessed 29 January 2024.

Crooke, Alastair, and Napolitano, Andrew. 2024c. Washington's Theater of the Absurd! (vid.). *Judging Freedom*, 5 February, https://www.youtube.com/watch?v=LAUWnrgcZdM&t=1353s. Accessed 12 February 2024.

———. 2024d. Regional Armageddon in Middle East (vid.). *Judging Freedom*. https://www.youtube.com/watch?v=Fj6ZwBknwjg. Accessed 12 February 2024.

Crooke, Alastair, and Andrew Napolitano. 2024e. Israel/US Fatal Mistakes (vid.). *Judging Freedom*, 19 February, https://www.youtube.com/watch?v=4od1eL4-tBY. Accessed 19 February 2024.

Crooke, Alastair, and Dimitry Simes, Jr. 2024. Netanyahu's Gamble: Is Israel Preparing for Another War? (vid.). *New Rules*, 18 January, https://rumble.com/v47q2wr-live-new-rules-podcast-w-alastair-crooke.html. Accessed 21 January 2024.

Daalder, Ivo H., and James M. Lindsay. 2001. *Unilateral Withdrawal From the ABM Treaty Is a Bad Idea*. Brookings Institution, 30 April, https://www.brookings.edu/articles/unilateral-withdrawal-from-the-abm-treaty-is-a-bad-idea/. Accessed 19 January 2024.

Dadouch, Sarah, and Kareem Fahim. 2024. Hezbollah Leader Vows 'Punishment' After Killing of Hamas Official in Lebanon. *Washington Post*, 3 January, https://www.washingtonpost.com/world/2024/01/03/hezbollah-leader-speak-after-killing-hamas-official-lebanon/. Accessed 24 January 2024.

Davis, Daniel, and Chas Freeman. 2024. 'Israel May Lose This War w/ fmr US Ambassador Chas Freeman (vid.). *Deep Dive*, 6 March, https://www.youtube.com/watch?v=URTKZkdipHU. Accessed 9 March 2024.

Davis, Daniel, and John Mearsheimer. 2024. John Mearsheimer—U.S. Blind Support of Ukraine / The West: Collective Suicide (vid.). *Deep Dive*, 6 March, https://www.youtube.com/watch?v=8lvN1IKOwzY. Accessed 8 March 2024.

Eisenhower, Dwight D. 1961. Farewell Address by President Dwight D. Eisenhower, January 17, 1961; Final TV Talk 1/17/61 (1), Box 38, Speech Series, Papers of Dwight D. Eisenhower as President, 1953–61, Eisenhower Library; National Archives and Records Administration. https://www.archives.gov/milestone-documents/president-dwight-d-eisenhowers-farewell-address. Accessed 19 January 2024.

Elving, Ron. 2018. Remembering 1968: LBJ Surprises Nation with Announcement He Won't Seek Re-Election, NPR, 25 March, https://www.npr.org/2018/03/25/596805375/president-johnson-made-a-bombshell-announcement-50-years-ago

Entous, Adam, and Michael Schwirtz. 2024. The Spy War: How the C.I.A. Secretly Helps Ukraine Fight Putin. *New York Times*, 25 February, https://www.nytimes.com/2024/02/25/world/europe/cia-ukraine-intelligence-russia-war.html. Accessed 26 February 2024.

Epstein, Reid J. 2024. Will Biden's Gaza Stance Hurt Him in 2024? Michigan Is the First Test. *New York Times*, 25 February, https://www.nytimes.com/2024/02/22/us/politics/biden-michigan-gaza.html. Accessed 25 February 2024.

Epstein, Reid J., and Goldmacher, Shane. 2024. 'Michigan Primary Takeaways: 'Uncommitted' Makes Itself Heard'. *New York Times*, 28 February, https://www.nytimes.com/2024/02/28/us/politics/michigan-primary-biden-trump.html. Accessed 28 February 2024.

Escobar, Pepe. 2024. Pepe Escobar: Five Variables Defining Our Future. *Sputnik*, 25 January, https://sputnikglobe.com/20240125/pepe-escobar-five-variables-defining-our-future-1116381887.html. Accessed 25 January 2024.

Falk, Richard. 2024a. Western Media Bias, Israeli Apologetics, and Ongoing Genocide. *Counterpunch*, 22 January, https://www.counterpunch.org/2024/01/22/western-media-bias-israeli-apologetics-and-ongoing-genocide/. Accessed 25 January 2024.

———. 2024b. Introduction. *Journal of Contemporary Iraq & the Arab World* 18 (2-3), pp. 97-100.

Freeman, Chas. 2024. 'Former Ambassador Chas Freeman Interviewed by Thomas Karat About Gaza' (vid.). *Non-corporate News*, 7 January, https://www.youtube.com/watch?v=2qymBMLVikI. Accessed 8 January 2024.

Ghassan, Charbel. 2024. Zebari for "Middle East": We Heard in Tehran Frank Words Explaining the Role of Militias (Arabic), Asharq Al-Awsat (The Arab World), 20 February.

Gordon, Joy. 2024. The Legacy of the UN Security Council Sanctions on Iraq. *Journal of Contemporary Iraq & the Arab World* 18 (2-3), pp. 135-145.

Green, Erica L. 2024. Harris Calls for an 'Immediate Cease-Fire' in Gaza. *New York Times*. https://www.nytimes.com/2024/03/03/world/middleeast/kamala-harris-cease-fire.html. Accessed 5 March 2024.

Hahn, Gordon. 2023. 'In Putin's Russia Politics is War by Other Means and War is Revolutionizing Russian Military Affairs', *RUSSIAN & EURASIAN POLITICS*, 16 November, https://gordonhahn.com/category/russian-military-strategy/

Helmer, John. 2024a. The US, Israel Have Lost Battlefield Control—Houthis Have Attacked US Destroyer, Hit Greek-US Owned Bulker; Iran Has Hit US Base in Kurdish Capital, Erbil. *Dances with Bears*, 16 January, https://johnhelmer.org/the-us-israel-have-lost-battlefield-control-houthis-have-attacked-us-destroyer-hit-greek-us-owned-bulker-iran-has-hit-us-base-in-kurdish-capital-erbil/. Accessed 16 January 2024.

———. 2024b. The Tower-22 Strike in Jordan Triggers US, Israel into All-front War—The Arabs and Iran Are Ready, the Russians too. *Dances with Bears*, 28 January, https://johnhelmer.net/the-tower-22-strike-in-jordan-triggers-us-israel-into-all-front-war-the-arabs-and-iran-are-ready-the-russians-too/#more-89274. Accessed 31 January 2024.

———. 2024c. Moody's Just Told You So—Downgrades Israel, Warns That Weaker US Backing for Israel, War with Hezbollah Would Trigger Crash. *Dances with Bears*, 11 February, https://johnhelmer.net/moodys-just-told-you-so-downgrades-israel-warns-that-weaker-us-backing-for-israel-war-with-hezbollah-would-trigger-crash/. Accessed 14 February 2024.

Hu, Xijin. 2023. US Gets Anxious as Russia Has Survived War of Attrition Against Entire NATO. *Global Times*, 1 March, https://www.globaltimes.cn/page/202303/1286442.shtml. Accessed 8 April 2023.

Hudson, John. 2024. USAID's Samantha Power, Genocide Scholar, Confronted by Staff on Gaza. *Washington Post*, 31 January, https://www.washingtonpost.com/national-security/2024/01/31/samantha-power-usaid-confronted-gaza/?campaign_id=9&emc=edit_nn_20240201&instance_id=114027&nl=the-morning&regi_id=7062190&segment_id=156981&te=1&user_id=e1ddf1d17d81e96d432c42ea2c1367b5. Accessed 1 February 2024.

Imseis, Ardi. 2024. Gaza Genocide: International Justice? With Ardi Imseis. *Connections Episode* 83, (vid.), https://www.youtube.com/watch?v=I3KErJkZf_Y.

International Court of Justice. 2024a. Application Instituting Proceedings. https://www.icj-cij.org/sites/default/files/case-related/192/192-20231228-app-01-00-en.pdf. Accessed 8 January 2024.

———. 2024b. Application of the Convention on the Prevention and Punishment of the Crime of Genocide in the Gaza Strip (South Africa v. Israel), 26 January, https://www.icj-cij.org/sites/default/files/case-related/192/192-20240126-ord-01-00-en.pdf. Accessed 26 January 2024.

———. 2024c. Declaration of Judge Xue, 26 January, https://www.icj-cij.org/node/203448. Accessed 28 January 2024.

———. 2024d. Urgent Request for Additional Measures Under Article 75(1) of the Rules of the Court of the International Court of Justice, 12 February, https://www.icj-cij.org/sites/default/files/case-related/192/192-20240212-wri-01-00-en.pdf. Accessed 14 February 2024.

———. 2024e. *The Republic of Nicaragua Institutes Proceedings Against the Federal Republic of Germany and Requests the Court to Indicate Provisional Measures.* International Court of Justice, 1 March, https://www.icj-cij.org/sites/default/files/case-related/193/193-20240301-pre-01-00-en.pdf. Accessed 4 March 2024.

Islamic Republic News Agency. 2024a. Yemen's Ansarullah Warns Regional States Against US Deception, 11 January, https://en.irna.ir/news/85361444/Yemen-s-Ansarullah-warns-regional-states-against-US-deception. Accessed 21 January 2024.

———. 2024b. Russia's Adherence to Iran's Sovereignty to Be Included in Bilateral Deal: DM. *Islamic Republic News Agency (IRNA)*, 15 January, https://en.irna.ir/news/85355443/Russia-s-adherence-to-Iran-s-overeignty-included-in-bilateral. Accessed 21 January 2024.

Ismael, Tareq Y., and Jacqueline S. Ismael. 2015. *Iraq in the Twenty-First Century: Regime Change and the Making of a Failed State*. Routledge.

Jawad, Saad Naji, and Sawsan Ismail Al-Assaf. 2024. The Iraqi Youth October 2019 Uprising (Tishreen Intifada): Reality and Prospects. *Journal of Contemporary Iraq & the Arab World* 18 (2-3), pp. 147-165.

Johnson, Jake. 2024. Western Officials Warn of War-Crimes Complicity. *Consortium News*, 2 February, https://consortiumnews.com/2024/02/02/western-officials-warn-of-war-crimes-complicity/. Accessed 3 February 2024.

Johnson, Larry, and Andrew Napolitano. 2024. Larry Johnson: Ukraine War Viewed from MOSCOW! (vid.). *Judging Freedom*, 26 February, https://www.youtube.com/watch?v=Acwrv4KIblc. Accessed 27 February 2024.

Johnston, Chalmers. 2007. *Nemesis: The Last Days of the American Republic*. Metropolitan Books.

Kathem, Mehiyar, Eleanor Robson, Lina G. Tahan. 2022. Cultural Heritage Predation in Iraq. *Chatham House*, 24 March, https://www.chathamhouse.org/2022/03/cultural-heritage-predation-iraq/02-historical-context-conflict-and-destabilization. Accessed 2 March 2024.

Kennedy, John F. 1963. World Peace, 10 June, John F. Kennedy Presidential Library and Museum. https://www.jfklibrary.org/asset-viewer/archives/usg-01-07. Accessed 29 January 2024.

Krieger, David. 2002. Farewell to the ABM Treaty, 13 June, Nuclear Age for Peace Foundation, https://www.wagingpeace.org/farewell-to-the-abm-treaty/. Accessed 19 January 2024.

Lanard, Noah. 2023. How Joe Biden Became America's Top Israel Hawk. *Mother Jones*, 22 December, https://www.motherjones.com/politics/2023/12/how-joe-biden-became-americas-top-israel-hawk/. Accessed 9 January 2024.

Landler, Mark, Helene Cooper, and Eric Schmitt. 2018. Trump to Withdraw U.S. Forces From Syria, Declaring "We Have Won Against ISIS". *New York Times*, 19 December, https://www.nytimes.com/2018/12/19/us/politics/trump-syria-turkey-troop-withdrawal.html. Accessed 23 June 2024.

Lascaris, Dimitri. 2024. What Now, Genocide Justin? 26 January, https://dimitrilascaris.org/2024/01/26/what-now-genocide-justin/#respond. Accessed 27 January 2024.

Lauria, Joe. 2022. Why Putin Went to War. *Consortium News*, 24 February, https://consortiumnews.com/2024/02/24/why-putin-went-to-war/. Accessed 25 February 2024.

———. 2024. Why Putin Went to War. *Consortium News*, 24 February, https://consortiumnews.com/2024/02/24/why-putin-went-to-war/. Accessed 25 February 2024.

Lavrov, Sergey. 2024a. Russia Now Knows West Cannot Be Trusted, Says Lavrov. *Tass*, 18 January, https://tass.com/politics/1734063. Accessed 18 January 2024.

———. 2024b. *Foreign Minister Sergey Lavrov's Remarks and Answers to Media Questions Following a UN Security Council meeting on Ukraine and an Open Debate on "The Situation in the Middle East, Including the Palestinian Question.* Ministry of Foreign Affairs of the Russian Federation, New York, January 24, 2024, https://mid.ru/en/press_service/photos/meropriyatiya_s_uchastiem_ministra/1927568/?TSPD_101_R0=08765fb817ab2000d728a27cbc3df5c6 ddbaea464004396d27e2085e70894fab3b130986b8375c1908566a0b7314 3 0 0 0 0 4 2 a 4 d 9 e 3 6 8 c 4 9 c 6 b 2 3 7 8 d 8 a 4 9 0 c 0 1 6 0 c e 7 3 6 e b 6 e f-d1922ad0cd95daf79fb772fb05e4aee76430326ab52be6300b081f

Livni, Ephrat. 2024. Brazil's President Angers Israel After Comparing War in Gaza to the Holocaust. *New York Times*, 18 February, https://www.nytimes.com/2024/02/18/world/middleeast/brazil-lula-israel-gaza-holocaust.html. Accessed 18 February 2024.

Longley, Alex, and Quinn Áine. 2024. Chinese Ships Get Insurance Edge Navigating Red Sea, GCaptain, Bloomberg, 6 February, https://gcaptain.com/chinese-ships-get-insurance-edge-navigating-red-sea/

MacAskill, Ewin, and Julian Borger. 2004. Iraq War Was Illegal and Breached UN Charter, Says Annan. *The Guardian*, 16 September, https://www.theguardian.com/world/2004/sep/16/iraq.iraq. Accessed 16 February 2024.

Macgregor, Douglas, and Andrew Napolitano. 2024a. Wrongheaded US Military Priorities (vid.), *Judging Freedom*, 3 January, https://www.youtube.com/watch?v=GqNWKJENDLY. Accessed 6 January 2024.

———. 2024b. NATO's Misguided Actions Towards Russia. *Judging Freedom*, 4 March, https://www.youtube.com/watch?v=Gpi5sJHpOkY. Accessed 7 March 2024.

Magnier, Eliajah. 2022. François Hollande Confirms Minsk Agreements Were a Western Ploy. *Voltaire Network*, 31 December, https://www.voltairenet.org/article218584.html. Accessed 20 January 2024.

McGovern, Ray. 2024. Nuland's Game Is Up as Russia Smashed Ukraine's Army—History Matters! (vid.). *Dialogue Works*, https://www.youtube.com/watch?v=uw_wap0sqDk. Accessed 11 March 2024.

McGovern, Ray, and Andrew Napolitano. 2024a. Ray McGovern: Will CIA help BiBi? (vid.). *Judging Freedom*, https://www.youtube.com/watch?v=kRkUx4Kbv6E. Accessed 11 January, 2024.

———. 2024b. Ray McGovern: Neocons and Wider Middle East War (vid.). *Judging Freedom*, 22 January, https://www.youtube.com/watch?v=fgQTsTX 6r7g&list=TLPQMjMwMTIwMjSLKFcfFWfDag&index=3. Accessed 22 January 2024.

———. 2024c. Ray McGovern: Germany Caught Off-guard by Leak of Secret Ukraine War Talks. *Judging Freedom*, 4 March, https://www.youtube.com/watch?v=M-jWZQ72qFo&t=11s. Accessed 5 March 2024.

McGovern, Ray, Larry Johnson, and Andrew Napolitano. 2024a. INTEL Roundtable: Johnson & McGovern: CIA and Neocon Intransigence. (vid.). *Judging Freedom*, 19 January, https://www.youtube.com/watch?v= jRGkoBSFLRA. Accessed 20 January 2024.

———. 2024b. INTEL Roundtable: Johnson & McGovern: Ukraine's Last Gasp; ICJ Analysis. (vid.). *Judging Freedom*, 26 January, https://www.youtube. com/watch?v=T_IH3y_Q0-Y. Accessed 26 January 2024.

Mearsheimer, John J. 2001. *The Tragedy of Great Power Politics*. W. W. Norton & Company.

———. 2014. Why the Ukraine Crisis Is the West's Fault: The Liberal Delusions That Provoked Putin. *Foreign Affairs* 93: 77–84, September/October, https://www.foreignaffairs.com/articles/russia-fsu/2014-08-18/why-ukraine-crisis-west-s-fault. Accessed 11 January 2024.

———. 2015. UnCommon Core: The Causes and Consequences of the Ukraine Crisis (vid.). University of Chicago, 25 September, https://www.youtube. com/watch?v=JrMiSQAGOS4. Accessed 11 January 2024.

———. 2018. *The Great Delusion: Liberal Dreams and International Realities*. Yale University Press.

———. 2023. *Death and Destruction in Gaza*. John's Substack, 11 December, https://mearsheimer.substack.com/p/death-and-destruction-in-gaza. Accessed 12 December 2023.

———. 2024a. 'Genocide in Gaza', John's Substack, 4 January, https:// mearsheimer.substack.com/p/genocide-in-gaza. Accessed 9 January 2024.

———. 2024b. *The Death of Ideology* (vid.). Institute of Art and Ideas, 24 January, https://www.youtube.com/watch?v=ClitqYW8HVk.   Accessed   18 February 2024.

Mearsheimer, John J., and John Anderson. 2023. Ukraine, Taiwan and The True Cause of War (vid.), 7 December, https://www.youtube.com/ watch?v=huDriv7IAa0. Accessed 10 January 2024.

Mearsheimer, John J., and Andrew Napolitano. 2024a. Is Armageddon Coming in the Middle East? (vid.). *Judging Freedom*, 15 February, https://www.youtube. com/watch?v=HAOB8g63tDc. Accessed 15 February 2024.

———. 2024b. US and the Unipolar Moment (vid.). *Judging Freedom*, 22 February 2024, https://www.youtube.com/watch?v=P0zLXaO48eY. Accessed 22 February 2024.

———. 2024c. Prof. John Mearsheimer: When Will Middle East and Ukraine Explode (vid.). *Judging Freedom*, 29 February, https://www.youtube.com/ watch?v=nqxgnrR20gs&t=1286s. Accessed 1 March 2024.

Mearsheimer, John J., and Jeffrey Sachs. 2023. A Missed Opportunity for Peace (vid.). *Jeffrey Sachs of Fans*, 16 November, https://www.youtube.com/ watch?v=sWmWWxsrBAY. Accessed 16 November 2023.

Mearsheimer, John J. and Stephen M. Walt. 2006. The Israel Lobby. *London Review of Books*, 23 March, https://www.lrb.co.uk/the-paper/v28/n06/john-mearsheimer/the-israel-lobby. Accessed 17 January 2024.

Mearsheimer, John J., and Stephen M. Walt. 2009. *The Israel Lobby and U.S. Foreign Policy*. Macmillan.

Mearsheimer, John, Mercouris, Alexander and Diesen, Glenn. 2024. The West in Decline, The Duran, 16 March, https://www.youtube.com/watch?v=UNoUHzd1LcM. Accessed 16 March 2024.

Mercouris, Alexander. 2024a. Crisis Ukraine: Avdeyevka Collapse, Reports Zaluzhny Sacked Budanov Taking Over; Al-Asad Base Attack (vid.). *Alexander Mercouris*, 21 January, https://rumble.com/v48dn6w-crisis-ukraine-avdeyevka-collapse-reports-zaluzhny-sacked-budanov-taking-ov.html. Accessed 21 January 2024.

———. 2024b. Ukraine Terrible Day: Missiles Rock Kiev, South Avdeyevka Lost, 18 Tanks Lost; NYT US-Iran War Coming (vid.). *Alexander Mercouris*, 23 January, https://rumble.com/v48sza9-ukraine-terrible-day-missiles-rock-kiev-south-avdeyevka-lost18-tanks-lost-n.html. Accessed 24 January 2024.

———. 2024c. ICJ Rules Against Israel; Shock Decision; Texas Defies Biden, Prospect of US Funds For Ukraine Fade (vid.), 26 January, https://rumble.com/v49hthk-icj-rules-against-israel-shock-decision-texas-defies-biden-prospect-of-us-f.html. Accessed 26 January 2024.

———. 2024d. Rus Advance Quickens Patriots' Destroyed; 8 Year Anti Rus CIA Ukr Operation; G7 Asset Seize Backs Off (vid.), 26 February, https://rumble.com/v4fullk-rus-advance-quickens-patriots-destroyed-8-year-anti-rus-cia-ukr-operation-g.html. Accessed 26 February 2024.

———. 2024e. EU Leaders Isolate Macron, Scrounge MidEast/Africa for Shells; Ukr May Coup Rumours; Rus Orlovka, 28 February, https://rumble.com/v4g88x3-eu-leaders-isolate-macron-scrounge-mideastafrica-for-shells-ukr-may-coup-ru.html. Accessed 28 February 2024.

Messina, Piero. 2024. *Planning the Aftermath, Rand Corporation Evokes a Nuclear Clash between Russia, China and the United States*. South Front, 18 February, https://southfront.press/planning-the-aftermath-rand-corporation-evokes-a-nuclear-clash-between-russia-china-and-the-united-states/. Accessed 18 February 2024.

Middle East Eye. 2024a. 'It's a Genocide': Brazil's Lula Compares War on Gaza to Holocaust, Sparking Controversy. *Middle East Eye*, https://www.middleeasteye.net/news/its-genocide-brazils-lula-compares-war-gaza-holocaust. Accessed 19 February 2024.

———. 2024b. Palestinians' Use of Force to Resist Foreign Oppression 'Well Founded' in International Law: China', Middle East Eye, 22 February, https://www.middleeastmonitor.com/20240222-palestinians-use-of-force-to-resist-foreign-oppression-well-founded-in-international-law-china/. Accessed 29 February 2024.

Mokhiber, Craig, and Chris Hedges. 2024. Gaza: ICJ Ruling, UN Failures, and US Complicity (vid). *The Chris Hedges Report, The Real News Network*, 26 January, https://www.youtube.com/watch?v=aQUopbLHOtg. Accessed 27 January 2024.

Moon of Alabama. 2024a. U.S. Claims No Alternative to Larger Middle East War, 22 January, https://www.moonofalabama.org/2024/01/us-claims-no-alternative-to-larger-middle-east-war.html#more. Accessed 22 January 2024.

———. 2024b. The ICJ Could Not Order a General Ceasefire. It Ordered Israel to Cease Fire, 26 January, https://www.moonofalabama.org/2024/01/the-icj-could-not-order-a-general-ceasefire-it-ordered-israel-to-cease-fire.html#more. Accessed 27 January 2024.

———. 2024c. Ending The U.S. Presence in Middle East, 3 February, https://www.moonofalabama.org/2024/02/ending-us-presence-in-middle-east.html. Accessed 3 February 2024.

Murray, Craig. 2024. Murray: UN Court Spurned Israel's Key Argument. *Consortium News*, 29 January, https://consortiumnews.com/2024/01/29/craig-murray-un-court-spurned-israels-key-argument/. Accessed 29 January 2024.

Nasrallah, Hassan. 2023a. Hezbollah's Hassan Nasrallah Speech on Israel-Hamas War: Key Takeaways. *Al-Jazeera*, 3 November, https://www.aljazeera.com/news/2023/11/3/hezbollahs-hassan-nasrallah-speech-on-israel-hamas-war-key-takeaways. Accessed 22 January 2024.

———. 2023b. Hezbollah Leader Nasrallah: October 7 Proves Israel Is as "Fragile as a Spider's Web," Why Else Would U.S. Send Aircraft Carrier? *Real Clear Politics*, https://www.realclearpolitics.com/video/2023/11/03/hezbollah_leader_hassan_nasrallah_to_prevent_a_regional_war_israel_must_stop_attack_on_gaza.html. Accessed 28 January 2024.

Nebenzia, Vassily. 2023. Statement by Permanent Representative Vassily Nebenzia at UNSC Briefing Dedicated to the Anniversary of Resolution 2202 That Endorsed the Minsk Package of Measures. Permanent Mission of the Russian Federation to the United Nations, 17 February, https://russiaun.ru/en/news/170223_n. Accessed 20 January 2024.

Nehamas, Nicholas, and Reid J. Epstein. 2024. "Uncommitted" Draws Strong Support Against Biden in Minnesota. *New York Times*, 5 March, https://www.nytimes.com/2024/03/05/us/politics/biden-uncommitted-protest-vote-minnesota.html. Accessed 6 March 2024.

Nereim, Vivian. 2024. Honed at Home in Yemen, Houthi Propaganda Is Going Global. *New York Times*, 24 January, https://www.nytimes.com/2024/01/24/world/middleeast/yemen-houthis-propaganda.html?campaign_id=9&emc=edit_nn_20240124&instance_id=113315&nl=the-morning&regi_id=7062190&segment_id=156155&te=1&user_id=e1ddf1d17d81e96d432c42ea2c1367b5. Accessed 24 January 2024.

Parsi, Trita. 2024. Will Israel Drag the US Into Another Ruinous War President Biden Refuses to Pursue the Most Obvious Way of De-escalating Tensions and Avoid American Deaths: A Cease-fire in Gaza. *The Nation*, 3 January, https://www.thenation.com/article/world/israel-hamas-hezbollah-iran/. Accessed 5 January 2024.

Nederveen Pieterse, Jan. 2024. Iraq, Afghanistan, Pakistan: Patterns Old and New. *Journal of Contemporary Iraq & the Arab World* 18 (2-3), pp. 117-133.

Priebe, Miranda, and Samuel Charap. 2024. *The Day After: Postwar U.S. Strategy Toward Russia*. Rand Corporation, 9 February, https://www.rand.org/pubs/research_briefs/RBA2510-1.html. Accessed 18 February 2024.

Putin, Vladimir. 2007. *Speech and the Following Discussion at the Munich Conference on Security Policy*. President of Russia, 10 February, http://en.kremlin.ru/events/president/transcripts/24034. Accessed 15 January 2024.

———. 2018. *Presidential Address to the Federal Assembly*. President of Russia, 1 March, http://en.kremlin.ru/events/president/transcripts/messages/56957. Accessed 20 January 2024.

———. 2022a. Address by the President of the Russian Federation, 24 February 2022, President of Russia, http://en.kremlin.ru/events/president/news/67843. Accessed 20 February 2024.

Putin, Vladimar. 2022b. Western "Empire of Lies" Has Resources, But It Cannot Defeat Truth and Justice—Putin. *TASS*, 16 March 2022, https://tass.com/world/1423145. Accessed 4 February 2023.

Putin, Vladimir. 2024. West Flirting with Nuclear War—Putin. *RT*, 29 February, https://www.rt.com/russia/593443-putin-west-flirting-nuclear-war/. Accessed 2 March 2024.

Rideau Institute. 2024. US Allies Must Demand Decisive Action to Stop the Gaza Carnage, 21 January, https://www.ceasefire.ca/us-allies-must-demand-decisive-action-to-stop-the-gaza-carnage/. Accessed 23 January 2024.

Ritter, Scott, and Andrew Napolitano. 2024. Scott Ritter: How Close Is US to War? (vid.). *Judging Freedom*, 11 March, https://www.youtube.com/watch?v=w3C8ihfeQ_w. Accessed 13 March 2024.

Robertson, Nick. 2024. Half of Biden Voters Say Israel Committing Genocide in Gaza: Poll. *The Hill*, 25 January, https://thehill.com/policy/defense/4429906-half-biden-voters-israel-committing-genocide-in-gaza-poll/. Accessed 13 March 2024.

Sachs, David. 2024. A War of Lies. *X*, 17 February, https://twitter.com/DavidSacks/status/1758976951744897179?lang=en. Accessed 28 February 2024.

Sachs, Jeffrey. 2013. *To Move the World: JFK's Quest for Peace*. New York: Random House.

Sachs, Jeffrey S. 2023. NATO Chief Admits NATO Expansion Was Key to Russian Invasion of Ukraine (vid.). *Common Dreams*, 20 September, https://www.

commondreams.org/opinion/nato-chief-admits-expansion-behind-russian-invasion and https://www.jeffsachs.org/newspaper-articles/nato-chief-admits-expansion-behind-russian-invasion. Accessed 15 January 2024.

Sachs, Jeffrey S. 2024b. Israel Cannot Hide From the UN Court. *Consortium News*, 31 January, https://consortiumnews.com/2024/01/31/israel-cannot-hide-from-the-un-court/. Accessed 31 January 2024.

———. 2024c. How the CIA Destabilizes the World. *Consortium News*, 15 February, https://consortiumnews.com/2024/02/15/how-the-cia-destabilizes-the-world/. Common Dreams, 12 February, https://www.commondreams.org/opinion/cia-destablizes-the-world.   Accessed   17 February 2024.

Sachs, Jeffrey, and Chris Hedges. 2023. What JFK Tried to Do Before His Assassination (vid.). *The Chris Hedges Report, The Real News Network*, 29 September, https://www.youtube.com/watch?v=Wqm9Yl1gGEY. Accessed 29 January 2024.

Sachs, Jeffrey, and Andrew Napolitano. 2024a. Prof. Jeffery Sachs: A Deep Dive into the ICJ Ruling and Diplomacy (vid.). *Judging Freedom*, 26 January, https://www.youtube.com/watch?v=iUNrUclBnsA. Accessed 26 January 2024.

———. 2024b. Prof. Jeffrey Sachs: US Misunderstands Russia (vid.). *Judging Freedom*, 29 February, https://www.youtube.com/watch?v=p8L1Y2APY9E. Accessed 7 March 2024.

———. 2024c. Prof. Jeffrey Sachs: US/Russia/China: Worst Tensions in 30 Years (vid.). *Judging Freedom*, 14 March, https://www.youtube.com/watch?v=2EZg8mPatv4. Accessed 14 March 2024.

Salem, Amr. 2024. Iraq Discusses Security Cooperation with NATO. *Iraqi News*, 17 January, https://www.iraqinews.com/iraq/iraq-discusses-security-cooperation-with-nato/. Accessed 19 January 2024.

Sanger, David E., & Julian E. Barnes. 2024. Intelligence Officials Warn of Losses for Ukraine Without More U.S. Aid. *New York Times*, 11 March, https://www.nytimes.com/2024/03/11/us/politics/intelligence-officials-ukraine-aid.html. Accessed 13 March 2024.

Schenker, David. 2024. Leaving Iraq May Be Washington's Best Choice. *Foreign Policy*, 26 February, https://foreignpolicy.com/2024/02/26/us-iraq-iran-military-militia-attacks-sudani/. Accessed 27 February 2024.

Schmitt, Eric. 2024. Mix-Up Preceded Deadly Drone Strike in Jordan, U.S. Officials Say. *New York Times*, 29 January, https://www.nytimes.com/2024/01/29/world/middleeast/jordan-drone-strike-us-soldiers.html. Accessed 30 January 2024.

Shaibani, Senan. 2024. *Indictment of the U.S. Federal Government*. Urbana, IL: AuthorHouse.

Sharahra. 2023. The Sponsorship of International Powers Competing with the United States for Reconciliations and Rapprochement Processes in the Region

Pushes the Latter to Adopt Policies of Sabotage and Arson (vid, Arabic). Al-Akhbar, 31 March, https://www.youtube.com/watch?v=itI_zy9Cnm4. Accessed 29 January 2024.

Shoigu, Sergei. 2024. Ukrainian Army Loses 444,000 Troops during Military Operation—Shoigu. *Tass*, 26 February, https://tass.com/politics/1752183. Accessed 28 February 2024.

Smith, Yves. 2024. International Court of Justice Rules Forcefully Against Israel in Landmark Genocide Ruling, Including Restricting Military Action. *Naked Capitalism*, 26 January, https://www.nakedcapitalism.com/2024/01/international-court-of-justice-rules-forcefully-against-israel-in-landmark-genocide-ruling-including-restricting-military-action.html. Accessed 27 January 2024.

Stockman, David. 2024. To Hell With Fighting the Houthis! *Anti-War.com*, 15 January, https://original.antiwar.com/david_stockman/2024/01/14/to-hell-with-fighting-the-houthis/. Accessed 16 January 2024.

Talabani, Ala, and Mohammed Sayyed Muhsin. 2024. Unresolved Issues (vid., Arabic), 20 March, https://www.youtube.com/watch?v=3qcz2xx-mik. Accessed 20 March 2024.

The Cradle. 2024. Palestinian Factions Strive for 'National Unity' in Moscow. *The Cradle*, 1 March, https://thecradle.co/articles-id/23699. Accessed 9 March 2024.

The New Arab. 2024. Key Differences in Algeria, US's UN Resolution Text on Gaza Ceasefire, 20 February, https://www.newarab.com/news/gaza-key-differences-algeria-us-un-resolution-text. Accessed 22 February 2024.

Times of Israel. 2015. The Kennedy Speech that Obama Hopes to Echo. *Times of Israel*, 5 August, https://www.timesofisrael.com/liveblog_entry/the-kennedy-speech-that-obama-hopes-to-echo/. Accessed 29 January 2024.

U.S. Department of State, Office of International Religious Freedom. 2019. 2019 Report on International Religious Freedom: Iraq. https://www.state.gov/reports/2019-report-on-international-religious-freedom/iraq/#:~:text=Restrictions%20on%20freedom%20of%20religion,of%20non-governmental%20organizations%20(NGOs). Accessed 28 January 2024.

UN News. 2024. US Vetoes Algerian Resolution Demanding Immediate Ceasefire in Gaza, 20 February, https://news.un.org/en/story/2024/02/1146697. Accessed 15 March 2024.

Vinograd, Cassandra. 2024. Iran Denies Ordering Drone Strike as Biden Weighs a Response. *New York Times*, 29 January, https://www.nytimes.com/2024/01/29/world/middleeast/iran-us-troops-jordan.html?campaign_id=9&emc=edit_nn_20240130&instance_id=113843&nl=the-morning&regi_id=7062190&segment_id=156791&smid=url-share&te=1&user_id=e1ddf1d17d81e96d432c42ea2c1367b5. Accessed 30 January 2024.

Walt, Stephen M. 2021. It's Time to End the 'Special Relationship' With Israel: The benefits of U.S. support no longer outweigh the costs. *Foreign Policy*, 27 May, https://foreignpolicy.com/2021/05/27/its-time-to-end-the-special-relationship-with-israel/. Accessed 1 January 2024.

Wong, Edward, and Matina Stevis-Gridneff. 2024. Over 800 Officials in U.S. and Europe Sign Letter Protesting Israel Policies. *New York Times*, 2 February, https://www.nytimes.com/2024/02/02/us/politics/protest-letter-israel-gaza.html. Accessed 3 February 2024.

Xinmin, Ma. 2024. China's Legal Representative at ICJ Emphasises Rights to Palestinian Self-determination (vid). *Middle East Eye*, 22 February, https://www.youtube.com/watch?v=wmJUkWfIzTM. Accessed 25 February 2024.

REFERENCES

ABC News. 2004. Official Confirms O'Neill's Iraq Claim. *ABC News*, 13 January, https://abcnews.go.com/WNT/story?id=129250&page=1. Accessed 4 April 2023.

Abdullah, Hamid. 2023. Tilk al-Ayam (Arabic), 15 June, (vid.) https://www.youtube.com/watch?v=r-d-xbnoyG4. Accessed 2 July 2023.

Abizaid, John. 2007. Gen. Abizaid on Iraq War: "Of Course It's About Oil". *Democracy Now*, 16 October, https://www.democracynow.org/2007/10/16/headlines/gen_abizaid_on_iraq_war_of_course_its_about_oil. Accessed 29 April 2023.

Aboud, Wasn Said. 2018. London Conference of the Iraqi Opposition (14–17 December 2002) and the Role of the United States of America. *Alustath Journal for Human and Social Sciences* 226 (2): 279–310, September, https://alustath.uobaghdad.edu.iq/index.php/UJIRCO/article/view/199. Accessed 20 June 2023.

Abouzeid, Rania. 2012. Meet the Islamist Militants Fighting Alongside Syria's Rebels. *Time*, 26 July, https://world.time.com/2012/07/26/time-exclusive-meet-the-islamist-militants-fighting-alongside-syrias-rebels/. Accessed 9 March 2023.

Aburish, Said K. 1997. *A Brutal Friendship: The West and The Arab Elite*. Victor Gollancz.

Acton, James M. 2021. *The U.S. Exit From the Anti-ballistic Missile Treaty Has Fueled a New Arms Race*. Carnegie Endowment for International Peace, 13 December, https://carnegieendowment.org/2021/12/13/u.s.-exit-from-anti-ballistic-missile-treaty-has-fueled-new-arms-race-pub-85977. Accessed 19 January 2024.

Adams, Simon. 2018. Halabja, Chemical Weapons and the Genocide Against the Kurds: Implications for Iraq and the World Today. Keynote address at a conference to mark the 30th anniversary of the attack on Halabja, Hosted by the Kurdistan Regional Government Representation in the United States, Washington, DC, 13 March, https://www.globalr2p.org/publications/halabja-chemical-weapons-and-the-genocide-against-the-kurds-implications-for-iraq-and-the-world-today/. Accessed 12 June 2023.

Adriaensens, Dirk. 2010.'Ending States that Sponsor Terrorism: Dismantling the Iraqi State, Destroying an Entire Country, Destroying Iraqi culture, erasing collective memory. *Global Research*, 5 November, https://www.globalresearch.ca/ending-states-that-sponsor-terrorism-dismantling-the-iraqi-state-destroying-an-entire-country/21781. Accessed 16 March 2023.

AhlulBayt News Agency. 2024a. Iraq Decision to End US Military Presence "Irreversible": Sudani. *AhlulBayt News Agency*, 6 January, https://en.abna24.com/story/1426987. Accessed 19 January 2024.

———. 2024b. Iraq Seeks Quick Exit of US forces: Sudani. *AhlulBayt News Agency*, 11 January, https://en.abna24.com/story/1428375. Accessed 19 January 2024.

Ahmatovic, Sejla. 2024. EU's Top Diplomat Accuses Israel of Funding Hamas. *Politico*, 20 January, https://www.politico.eu/article/israel-funded-hamas-claims-eu-top-diplomat-josep-borrell/. Accessed 21 January 2024.

Al Mayadeen. 2022. Russia Fooled on Minsk Agreements: Putin. *Al Mayadeen English*, 22 December, https://english.almayadeen.net/news/politics/russia-fooled-on-minsk-agreements:-putin. Accessed 20 January 2024.

Alaaldin, Farhad. 2021. *A State in Collapse: Iraq's Security and Governance Failures.* Washington Institute, 2 June, https://www.washingtoninstitute.org/policy-analysis/state-collapse-iraqs-security-and-governance-failures. Accessed 14 August 2023.

Al-Azzawi, Souad N. 2024. The Occupation of Iraq, and Two Decades of Environmental Degradation. *Journal of Contemporary Iraq & the Arab World* 18(2–3), 167–197.

Al-Bukhaiti, Mohammed, and Max Blumenthal. 2024. "Our Goal Is To Stop the Genocide": The Grayzone Interviews Houthi Spokesman (vid.), trans. Hekmat Aboukhater, *The Greyzone*, 25 January, https://thegrayzone.com/2024/01/25/interview-houthi-spokesman/. Accessed 28 January 2024.

Longley Alex, and Áine Quinn. 2024. Chinese Ships Get Insurance Edge Navigating Red Sea. GCaptain, Bloomberg, 6 February, https://gcaptain.com/chinese-ships-get-insurance-edge-navigating-red-sea/. Accessed 11 February 2024.

Alpher, David. 2017. *Past Is Prologue: Abroad in Syria with the Ghosts of Iraq.* United States Department of the Army, Peacekeeping and Stability Operations Institute (PKSOI), January, https://apps.dtic.mil/sti/trecms/pdf/AD1058528.pdf. Accessed 1 March 2023.

Al-Tikriti, Nabil. 2008. *US Policy and the Creation of a Sectarian Iraq.* Middle East Institute, 2 July, https://www.mei.edu/publications/us-policy-and-creation-sectarian-iraq. Accessed 29 January 2024.

Amar, Tarik Cyril. 2024. Here's Why the West Can't Be Trusted to Observe Its Own 'Red Lines' in Ukraine. *RT,* 2 March, https://www.rt.com/news/593616-macron-scholz-ukraine-troops/. Accessed 2 March 2024.

Amin, Samir. 1992. *Empire of Chaos.* New York: Monthly Review Press.

Amnesty International. 2016. *Banished and Dispossessed: Forced Displacement and Deliberate Destruction in Northern Iraq.* Amnesty International. https://www.amnesty.org/en/documents/mde14/3229/2016/en/. Accessed 3 May 2023.

———. 2021. *Kurdistan Region of Iraq: Arbitrary Arrests and Enforced Disappearance of Activists and Journalists.* Amnesty International. https://www.amnesty.org/en/latest/press-release/2021/06/kurdistan-region-of-iraq-arbitrary-arrests-and-enforced-disappearance-of-activists-and-journalists/. Accessed 9 June 2023.

Andersen, Hans Christian. 1837. *The Emperor's New Clothes.* Translated by Jean Hersholt. The Hans Christian Center. https://andersen.sdu.dk/vaerk/hersholt/TheEmperorsNewClothes_e.html. Accessed 5 April 2023.

Anderson, Grey. 2023a. Weapon of Power, Matrix of Management: NATO's Hegemonic Formula. *New Left Review,* March–June, https://newleftreview.org/issues/ii140/articles/grey-anderson-weapon-of-power-matrix-of-management?pc=1510. Accessed 4 May 2023.

Anderson, Lisa. 2023b. The Forty-Year War: How America Lost the Middle East. *Foreign Affairs,* April 18, https://www.foreignaffairs.com/reviews/middle-east-forty-year-war-china. Accessed 31 July 2023.

Annan, Kofi. 2004. UN News, 'Lessons of Iraq War Underscore Importance of UN Charter—Annan'. *UN News,* 16 September, https://news.un.org/en/story/2004/09/115352. Accessed 8 February 2024.

Anzalone, Kyle, and Andrew Napolitano. 2024. Unseen Battlefronts and the True Cost of Military Support. *Judging Freedom,* 4 March, https://www.youtube.com/watch?v=qlev_AZywFg. Accessed 7 March 2024.

Arbuthnot, Felicity. 2008. Iraq: Erasing History. *Global Research,* 14 April, 2007, https://www.globalresearch.ca/iraq-erasing-history/5384. Accessed 30 April 2023.

Arraf, Jane. 2021. Iraq Reclaims 17,000 Looted Artifacts, Its Biggest-Ever Repatriation. *New York Times,* 3 August, https://www.nytimes.com/2021/08/03/world/middleeast/iraq-looted-artifacts-return.html. Accessed 18 May 2023.

Ashton, Nigel. 2010. *Hussein: A Political Life.* Yale University Press.

Asia Sentinel. 2019. Paul Wolfowitz's Neocon Blueprint for US Strategic Action. *Asia Sentinel,* 21 May, https://www.asiasentinel.com/p/paul-wolfowitz-neocon-blueprint-us-strategic-action. Accessed 4 April 2023.

Associated Press. 1998. *USA: Iraqi Kurd Leaders Agree to Establishing Elected Government*. Associated Press, 18 September, https://newsroom.ap.org/editorial-photos-videos/detail?itemid=39ed504c76e1eb274fd168d1d50543a d&mediatype=video&source=youtube. Accessed 19 June 2023.

———. 2008. Historic Handshake: Barak Meets Iraq's President in Athens. *Haaretz*, 1 July, 2008, https://www.haaretz.com/2008-07-01/ty-article/historic-handshake-barak-meets-iraqs-president-in-athens/0000017f-f110-df98-a5ff-f3bdde660000. Accessed 29 April 2023.

Aydoğan, Bekir. 2020. *The Iraqi Kurds' Destructive Infighting: Causes and Consequences*. London School of Economics and Political Science, 15 April, https://blogs.lse.ac.uk/mec/2020/04/15/the-iraqi-kurds-destructive-infighting-causes-and-consequences/. Accessed 19 June 2023.

Azhari, Timour. 2024. Exclusive-Iraq Seeks Quick Exit of US Forces But No Deadline Set, PM Says. *Reuters*, 10 January, https://www.aol.co.uk/news/exclusive-iraq-seeks-quick-exit-100145329.html. Accessed 19 January 2024.

Bacevich, Andrew J. 2013. *The New American Militarism: How Americans Are Seduced by War*. Oxford University Press.

———. 2016. *America's War for the Greater Middle East: A Military History*. Random House.

Bahrani, Zainab. 2003. Looting and Conquest. *The Nation*, 14 May, http://www.thenation.com/doc/20030526/bahrani. Accessed December 2008.

Baker, Luke. 2008. Britain Releases Secret File from Before Iraq War. *Reuters*, 19 February, https://www.reuters.com/article/us-britain-iraq-dossier-idUKL1858955920080219. Accessed 5 April 2023.

Baker, Peter. 2024. As U.S. and Militias Engage, White House Worries About a Tipping Point. *New York Times*, 21 January, https://www.nytimes.com/2024/01/21/us/politics/us-militias-tipping-point.html. Accessed 22 January 2024.

Baker, Raymond W., Shereen T. Ismael, and Tareq Y. Ismael. 2010. *Cultural Cleansing in Iraq: Why Museums Were Looted, Libraries Burned and Academics Murdered*. Pluto Press.

Baroud, Ramzy. 2008. The Not-so-Historic Barak-Talabani Handshake. *Counterpunch*, 11 July, http://www.counterpunch.org/baroud07112008.html. Accessed 15 March 2009.

Batatu, Hanna. 1979. *The Old Social Classes and the Revolutionary Movements of Iraq: A Study of Iraq's Old Landed and Commercial Classes and of Its Communists, Ba'thist, and Free Officers*. Princeton University Press.

BBC. 2017. Syria War: Raqqa Deal Agreed to Evacuate Civilians, 14 October, https://www.bbc.com/news/world-middle-east-41620009. Accessed 15 March 2023.

———. 2022. Bush Condemns Putin's Invasion of "Iraq" Instead of Ukraine, 19 May, https://www.bbc.com/news/av/world-us-canada-61505050. Accessed 19 April 2023.

BBC News. 2006. Iraq 'Death Squad Caught in Act, 16 February, http://news.bbc.co.uk/2/hi/middle_east/4719252.stm. Accessed March 2009.

Beier, J. Marshall. 2003. Discriminating Tastes: "Smart" Bombs, Non-Combatants, and Notions of Legitimacy in Warfare. *Security Dialogue* 34: 4.

Bellinger, John. 2016. The Chilcot Inquiry and the Legal Basis for the Iraq War. *Lawfare*, 11 July, https://www.lawfareblog.com/chilcot-inquiry-and-legal-basis-iraq-war. Accessed 24 March.

Benhorin, Yitzhak. 2008. Doug Feith: Israel Didn'T Push for Iraq War. *Ynet*, 13 May, https://www.ynetnews.com/articles/0,7340,L-3542925,00.html. Accessed 18 May 2023.

Benjamin, Medea, and Nicolas J.S. Davies. 2024. Biden Must Choose Between a Ceasefire in Gaza and a Regional War. *Counterpunch*, 26 January, https://www.counterpunch.org/2024/01/26/biden-must-choose-between-a-ceasefire-in-gaza-and-a-regional-war/. Accessed 26 January 2024.

Beri, Navya. 2024. Iraq Preparing to End Presence of US-led Coalition, Says PM Mohamed Shia al-Sudani, 5 January, https://www.msn.com/en-in/news/other/iraq-preparing-to-end-presence-of-us-led-coalition-says-pm-mohamed-shia-al-sudani/ar-AA1mxiEk. Accessed 19 January 2024.

Bhadrakumar, M.K. 2023a. Russia's Gas Union Eyes Pakistan, India. *Indian Punchline*, 30 January, https://www.indianpunchline.com/russias-gas-union-eyes-pakistan-india/. Accessed 18 May 2023.

———. 2023b. China Steps Up, a New Era Has Dawned in World Politics. *Indian Punchline*, 11 March, https://www.indianpunchline.com/china-steps-up-a-new-era-has-dawned-in-world-politics/. Accessed 8 April 2023.

———. 2023c. Foreign Devils on the Road to Afghanistan. *Indian Punchline*, 12 March, https://www.indianpunchline.com/foreign-devils-on-the-road-to-afghanistan/. Accessed 12 March 2023.

———. 2023d. US Paranoid about Russia-China Summit. *Indian Punchline*, 19 March, https://www.indianpunchline.com/us-paranoid-about-russia-china-summit/. Accessed 31 March 2023.

———. 2023e. US Is Stirring Up the Syrian Cauldron. *Indian Punchline*, 26 March, https://www.indianpunchline.com/us-is-stirring-up-the-syrian-cauldron/. Accessed 3 March 2023.

———. 2023f. Russia Alone Can Already Confront the Entire West.... *Indian Punchline*, 30 March, https://www.indianpunchline.com/russia-alone-can-already-confront-the-entire-west/. Accessed 31 March 2023.

———. 2023g. Erdogan Weighs Up Russia, Dares Biden, 3 April, https://www.indianpunchline.com/erdogan-weighs-up-russia-dares-biden/. Accessed 3 April 2023.

———. 2023h. US Faces Defeat in Geopolitical War in Gaza. *Indian Punchline*, 16 October, https://www.indianpunchline.com/us-faces-defeat-in-geopolitical-war-in-gaza/. Accessed 17 October 2023.

———. 2024a. Decoding Iran's Missile, Drone Strikes. *Indian Punchline*, 18 January, https://www.indianpunchline.com/, and *Consortium News*, 19 January, https://consortiumnews.com/2024/01/19/decoding-irans-missile-drone-strikes/. Accessed 20 January 2024.

———. 2024b. Geopolitics Is Moving North Korea's Way. *Indian Punchline*, 23 January, https://www.indianpunchline.com/geopolitics-is-moving-north-koreas-way/. Accessed 24 January 2024.

———. 2024c. ICJ Ruling on Gaza Is on the Way. *Indian Punchline*, 26 January, https://www.indianpunchline.com/icj-ruling-on-gaza-is-on-the-way/. Accessed 26 January 2024.

———. 2024d. 'Swarming' the US in West Asia, Until It Folds. *The Cradle*, 29 January, https://thecradle.co/articles/swarming-the-us-in-west-asia-until-it-folds. Accessed 3 February 2024.

———. 2024e. Is Ground Beneath Biden's Russia Policy Shifting? *Indian Punchline*, 6 March, https://www.indianpunchline.com/is-ground-beneath-bidens-russia-policy-shifting/. Accessed 10 March 2024.

Blinken, Antony J., and Benjamin Netanyahu. 2023. Secretary Antony J. Blinken and Israeli Prime Minister Benjamin Netanyahu After Their Meeting. U.S. Department of State, 12 October, https://www.state.gov/secretary-antony-j-blinken-and-israeli-prime-minister-benjamin-netanyahu-after-their-meeting-2/. Accessed 20 January 2024.

Blum, William. 2000. *Rogue State: A Guide to the World's Only Superpower.* Common Courage Press.

———. 2005. *Rogue State: A Guide to the World's Only Superpower.* Common Courage Press.

———. 2012. The U.S. and Its Comrade in Arms, Al Qaeda. *Foreign Policy Journal*, 11 August, https://www.foreignpolicyjournal.com/2012/08/11/the-u-s-and-its-comrade-in-arms-al-qaeda/. Accessed 18 May 2023.

Blumenthal, Max. 2019. *The Management of Savagery: How America's National Security State Fueled the Rise of Al Qaeda, ISIS, and Donald Trump.* Verso.

Blumi, Isa. 2018. *Destroying Yemen.* University of California Press.

Bolger, Daniel P. 2014. *Why We Lost: A General's Inside Account of the Iraq and Afghanistan Wars.* Mariner Books.

Boot, Max. 2023. What the Neocons Got Wrong: And How the Iraq War Taught Me About the Limits of American Power. *Foreign Affairs*, 10 March, https://www.foreignaffairs.com/iraq/what-neocons-got-wrong. Accessed 23 June 2023.

Borger, Julian. 2003. The Spies Who Pushed for War. *Guardian*, 17 July, http://www.guardian.co.uk/world/2003/jul/17/iraq.usa. Accessed March 2009.

Boyle, Frances, and Rachel Blevens. 2024. U.S. Vetoes Gaza Ceasefire Resolution + the Genocide Case Against Israel w/ Prof. Francis Boyle, 20 February, https://www.youtube.com/watch?v=1TPhe2j7MNM. Accessed 22 February 2024.

Boyle, Frances, Joe Lauria, Ray McGovern, Alexander Mercouris, Craig Murray, and Elizabeth Vos. 2024. ICJ Rules on Israel, (vid.), *Consortium News*, 27 January, https://consortiumnews.com/2024/01/27/watch-cn-live-icj-rules-on-israel/. Accessed 28 January 2024.

Brands, Hal. 2018. Choosing Primacy: U.S. Strategy and Global Order at the Dawn of the Post-Cold War Era. *Texas National Security Review* 1 (2, Feb.). https://doi.org/10.15781/T2VH5D166. Accessed 7 May 2023.

Brownlee, Jason. 2012. *Democracy Prevention: The Politics of the U.S.-Egyptian Alliance*. Cambridge University Press.

Brzezinski, Zbigniew. 1997. *The Grand Chessboard: American Primacy and its Geostrategic Imperatives*. Basic Books.

Buckley, Cara. 2007. Rare Look Inside Baghdad Museum. *New York Times*, 12 December, https://www.nytimes.com/2007/12/12/world/middleeast/12iraq.html. Accessed 29 April 2023.

Bush, George H.W. 1991. President Bush Annual UN Address, 23 September, 46th session of the UN General Assembly. https://2009-2017.state.gov/p/io/potusunga/207269.htm. Accessed 18 May 2023.

Bush, George W. 2001a. Statement by the President in His Address to the Nation. *The White House*, 11 September, https://georgewbush-whitehouse.archives.gov/news/releases/2001/09/20010911-16.html. Accessed 4 April 2023.

Bush, George W. 2001b. Address to a Joint Session of Congress and the American People, 20 September, https://georgewbush-whitehouse.archives.gov/news/releases/2001/09/20010920-8.html. Accessed 3 April 2023.

———. 2002a. State of the Union Address, 20 January, National Security Archive. https://nsarchive.gwu.edu/document/28048-document-08-george-w-bush-state-union-address-january-20-2002. Accessed 21 March 2023.

Bush, George W. 2002b. President Bush Delivers Graduation Speech at West Point United States Military Academy, West Point, New York. *The White House*, 1 June, https://georgewbush-whitehouse.archives.gov/news/releases/2002/06/20020601-3.html. Accessed 22 March 2023.

Bush, George H.W. 2017. The Other 9/11: George H.W. Bush's 1990 New World Order speech: Out of These Troubled Times, a New World Order Can Emerge. *Dallas Morning News*, 8 September, https://www.dallasnews.com/opinion/commentary/2017/09/08/the-other-9-11-george-h-w-bush-s-1990-new-world-order-speech/. Accessed 1 April 2023.

Camu, Cyril, and Louet, Sophie. 2017. French Military Says Coalition Opposed IS Withdrawal from Raqqa, 16 November, https://www.reuters.com/article/us-mideast-crisis-syria-france/french-military-says-coalition-opposed-is-withdrawal-from-raqqa-idUSKBN1DG1VP. Accessed 16 March 2023.

Charbel, Ghassan. 2024. Zebari for "Middle East": We Heard in Tehran Frank Words Explaining the Role of Militias, (Arabic), Aawsat, 20 February, https://aawsat.com/%D8%A7%D9%84%D8%B9 %D8%A7%D9%84%D9%85-%D8%A7%D9%84%D8%B9%D8%B1%D8% A8%D9%8A/%D8%A7%D9%84%D9%85%D8%B4%D8%B1%D9%82- %D8%A7%D9%84%D8%B9%D8%B1%D8%A8%D9%8A/4864221-%D8%B2% D9%8A%D8%A8%D8%A7%D8%B1%D9%8A-%D9%84%D9%80%D8%A7%D9 %84%D8%B4%D8%B1%D9%82-%D8%A7%D9%84%D8%A3%D9%88%D8%B 3%D8%B7-%D8%B3%D9%85%D8%B9%D9%86%D8%A7-%D9%81%D9%8A- %D8%B7%D9%87%D8%B1%D8%A7%D9%86-%D9%83%D9%84%D8%A7% D9%85%D8%A7%D9%8B-%D8%B5%D8%B1%D9%8A%D8%AD%D8%A7% D9%8B-%D9%8A%D9%81%D8%B3%D8%B1-%D8%AF%D9%88%D8%B1. Accessed 22 February 2024.

Cheney, Dick. 1992. Defense Planning Guidance. *National Archives*. https://www.archives.gov/files/declassification/iscap/pdf/2008-003-doc14.pdf. Accessed 2 May 2023.

———. 2003. The War Behind Closed Doors: Excerpts from 1992 Draft "Defense Planning Guidance". In *PBS: Frontline*, ed. Michael Kirk. https://www.pbs.org/wgbh/pages/frontline/shows/iraq/etc/script.html.   Accessed   3 April 2023.

———. 2004. *Full Text of Dick Cheney's Speech at the Institute of Petroleum Autumn Lunch 1999*. London Institute of Petroleum, 8 June, http://www.energybulletin.net/559.html. Accessed December 2008.

Chesterman, Simon. 2002. *Just War or Just Peace? Humanitarian Intervention and International Law*. Oxford Academic, November, https://academic.oup.com/book/9945/chapter-abstract/157293287?redirectedFrom=fulltext. Accessed 2 April 2023.

Chilcot, Sir John. 2006. *The Iraq Inquiry*, 6 July, http://worldofstuart.excellent-content.com/uploads/ChilcotReport_Volume1.pdf. Accessed 7 April 2023.

Chomsky, Noam. 1991. What We Say Goes. *Z Magazine*, 4 April.

Chossudovsky, Michel. 2023. Twelve Years Ago: The US-NATO-Israel Sponsored Al Qaeda Insurgency in Syria. Who Was Behind The 2011 "Protest Movement"? *Global Research*, 17 March 2023, https://www.globalresearch.ca/syria-who-is-behind-the-protest-movement-fabricating-a-pretext-for-a-us-nato-humanitarian-intervention/24591. Accessed 8 May 2023.

Chung, Cynthia. 2023. *The Machiavellians: James Burnham's Fascist Italian Defenders of Freedom*. Strategic Culture Foundation, 25 January, https://strategic-culture.org/news/2023/01/25/machiavellians-james-burnham-fascist-italian-defenders-freedom/. Accessed 18 May 2023.

Clark, Wesley. 2007. Gen. Wesley Clark Weighs Presidential Bid: "I Think About It Every Day. *Democracy Now*, 2 March, https://www.democracynow.org/2007/3/2/gen_wesley_clark_weighs_presidential_bid.   Accessed   13 March 2023.

Clark, Kate. 2008. Corruption in Iraqi Kurdistan. *BBC*, 10 January, http://news. bbc.co.uk/2/hi/programmes/crossing_continents/7178820.stm. Accessed 13 June 2023.

Clinton, Bill. 1998. Statement on Signing the Iraq Liberation Act of 1998. *The American Presidency Project*, UC Santa Barbara. https://www.presidency.ucsb. edu/documents/statement-signing-the-iraq-liberation-act-1998. Accessed 1 April 2023.

Clinton, Hillary. 2011. Hillary Clinton Laughing About Muammar Gaddafi's Death. *YouTube Video*. https://www.youtube.com/watch?v=7voBEfcHfJg. Accessed 1 May 2023.

Cockburn, Patrick. 1997. Revealed: How the West Set Saddam on the Bloody Road to Power. *The Independent*, 28 June, https://www.independent.co.uk/ news/world/revealed-how-the-west-set-saddam-on-the-bloody-road-to-power-1258618.html. Accessed 14 April 2023.

———. 2014. MI6, the CIA and Turkey's Rogue Game in Syria: World View: New Claims Say Ankara Worked with the US and Britain to Smuggle Gaddafi's Guns to Rebel Groups. *The Independent*, 13 April, https://www.independent. co.uk/voices/comment/mi6-the-cia-and-turkey-s-rogue-game-in-syria-9256551.html. Accessed 18 March 2023.

———. 2015. *The Rise of Islamic State: ISIS and the New Sunni Revolution*. Verso.

Cockburn, Andrew, and Patrick Cockburn. 2000. *Out of the Ashes, the Resurrection of Saddam Hussein*. London: Harper Perennial.

Cole, Juan. 2007. Informed Comment, 20 December, http://www.juancole. com. Accessed December 2008.

———. 2023. China Hangs Washington Out to Dry in the Middle East. *Tom Dispatch*, 16 May, https://tomdispatch.com/china-and-the-axis-of-the-sanctioned/. Accessed 19 May 2023.

Conley, Julia. 2024. South Africa Calls on ICJ to Stop Israel's Rafah Assault. *Consortium News*, 13 February, https://consortiumnews.com/2024/02/13/ south-africa-calls-on-icj-to-stop-israels-rafah-assault/. Accessed 17 February 2024.

Cook, Jonathan. 2011. An Empire of Lies: Why Our Media Betray Us. *Counterpunch*, 25 February, https://www.jonathan-cook.net/2011-02-28/ an-empire-of-lies-why-our-media-betray-us/. Accessed 13 June 2023.

Cooper, Helene, Eric Schmitt, and Julian E. Barnes. 2024. U.S. Conducts Retaliatory Strikes Against Iranian Proxies as War Deepens. *New York Times*, 2 February, https://www.nytimes.com/2024/02/02/us/politics/us-strikes-iranian-proxies.html. Accessed 3 February 2024.

Corn, David. 2005. From Iran-Contra to Iraq. *The Nation*, 6 May, https://www. thenation.com/article/archive/iran-contra-iraq/. Accessed 29 April 2023.

Cowell, Frederick. 2016. *Chilcot Report: The Consequences for International Law*. Birbeck University of London. http://blogs.bbk.ac.uk/bbkcomments/2016/07/06/chilcot-report-the-consequences-for-international-law/. Accessed 24 March 2023.

184   REFERENCES

Crane, Susan A., ed. 2000. *Museums and Memory*. Stanford University Press.
Crooke, Alastair. 2023. *How Could Western Intelligence Have Got It Wrong, Again? They Didn't. They Had Other Purposes*. Strategic Culture Foundation, 6 March, https://strategic-culture.org/news/2023/03/06/how-could-western-intelligence-have-got-it-wrong-again-they-didnt-they-had-other-purposes/. Accessed 9 March 2023.
———. 2024a. Gut Feelings Make for Strategic Errors—U.S. Lured Into Battlescape in Gaza, Yemen and Now Iraq. 15 January, https://www.unz.com/article/gut-feelings-make-for-strategic-errors-u-s-lured-into-battlescape-in-gaza-yemen-and-now-iraq/. Accessed 16 January 2024.
———. 2024b. *Netanyahu's Shape-shifting 'Endgame'—It Is No Ploy, But a Reversion to Earlier Zionist Strategy*. Strategic Culture Foundation, 22 January, https://strategic-culture.su/news/2024/01/22/netanyahu-shape-shifting-endgame-ino-ploy-but-reversion-earlier-zionist-strategy/. Accessed 22 January 2024.
Crooke, Alistair. 2024c. *The Tragic Self-destruction of an Enraged Israel*. Strategic Culture Foundation, 29 January, https://strategic-culture.su/news/2024/01/29/the-tragic-self-destruction-of-an-enraged-israel/. Accessed 30 January 2024.
———. 2024d. *The Three Strands to the 'Swarming of Biden'*. Strategic Culture Foundation, 2 February, https://strategic-culture.su/news/2024/02/02/the-three-strands-to-the-swarming-of-biden/. Accessed 3 February 2024.
———. 2024e. The World's Gyre, 12 February, https://strategic-culture.su/news/2024/02/12/the-worlds-gyre/. Accessed 14 February 2024.
———. 2024f. *U.S. Seeks to Cap Middle East Violence; In This, Iran Is (a Kind of) "Ally"*. Strategic Culture Foundation, 26 February, https://strategic-culture.su/news/2024/02/26/us-seeks-cap-middle-east-violence-in-this-iran-kind-ally/. Accessed 10 March 2024.
———. 2024g. *'Out of Touch With Reality'—White House Fails to Navigate the Israeli Re-calibration*. Strategic Culture Foundation, 11 March, https://strategic-culture.su/news/2024/03/11/out-of-touch-with-reality-white-house-fails-to-navigate-the-israeli-re-calibration/. Accessed 11 March 2024.
Crooke, Alastair, and Napolitano, Andrew. 2024a. Alastair Crooke: Netanyahu: Ploy or Reversion? (vid.). *Judging Freedom*, 22 January, https://www.youtube.com/watch?v=OPHmovWe2ts. Accessed 22 January 2024.
Crooke, Alastair, and Andrew Napolitano. 2024b. Alastair Crooke: Will Israel Self-Destruct? (vid.). *Judging Freedom*, 29 January, https://www.youtube.com/watch?v=pvKJ6oFS7sE. Accessed 29 January 2024.
Crooke, Alastair, and Napolitano, Andrew. 2024c. Washington's Theater of the Absurd! (vid.). *Judging Freedom*, 5 February, https://www.youtube.com/watch?v=LAUWnrgcZdM&t=1353s. Accessed 12 February 2024.

————. 2024d. Regional Armageddon in Middle East (vid.). *Judging Freedom*. https://www.youtube.com/watch?v=Fj6ZwBknwjg. Accessed 12 February 2024.

Crooke, Alastair, and Andrew Napolitano. 2024e. Israel/US Fatal Mistakes (vid.). *Judging Freedom*, 19 February, https://www.youtube.com/watch?v=4od1eL4-tBY. Accessed 19 February 2024.

Crooke, Alastair, and Dimitry Simes, Jr. 2024. Netanyahu's Gamble: Is Israel Preparing for Another War? (vid.). *New Rules*, 18 January, https://rumble.com/v47q2wr-live-new-rules-podcast-w-alastair-crooke.html. Accessed 21 January 2024.

Crowley, Michael. 2024. Victoria Nuland, Veteran Russia Hawk, to Leave the State Department. *New York Times*, 5 March, https://www.nytimes.com/2024/03/05/us/politics/victoria-nuland-state-department.html. Accessed 13 March 2024.

Daalder, Ivo H., and James M. Lindsay. 2001. *Unilateral Withdrawal From the ABM Treaty Is a Bad Idea*. Brookings Institution, 30 April, https://www.brookings.edu/articles/unilateral-withdrawal-from-the-abm-treaty-is-a-bad-idea/. Accessed 19 January 2024.

Dadouch, Sarah, and Kareem Fahim. 2024. Hezbollah Leader Vows 'Punishment' After Killing of Hamas Official in Lebanon. *Washington Post*, 3 January, https://www.washingtonpost.com/world/2024/01/03/hezbollah-leader-speak-after-killing-hamas-official-lebanon/. Accessed 24 January 2024.

Daher, Joseph. 2019. *Syria after the Uprisings: The Political Economy of State Resilience*. Haymarket Books.

Daily Sabah. 2017. US Watched Daesh Gaining Power, Kerry Admits in Leaked Audio, 7 January, https://www.dailysabah.com/syrian-crisis/2017/01/07/us-watched-daesh-gaining-power-kerry-admits-in-leaked-audio. Accessed 9 March 2023.

Daly, Corbett. 2011. Clinton on Qaddafi: "We Came, We Saw, He Died", (vid.), *CBS News*, 20 October, https://www.cbsnews.com/news/clinton-on-qaddafi-we-came-we-saw-he-died/. Accessed 18 May 2023.

Davis, Daniel, and Chas Freeman. 2024. 'Israel May Lose This War w/ fmr US Ambassador Chas Freeman (vid.). *Deep Dive*, 6 March, https://www.youtube.com/watch?v=URTKZkdipHU. Accessed 9 March 2024.

Davis, Daniel, and John Mearsheimer. 2024. John Mearsheimer—U.S. Blind Support of Ukraine / The West: Collective Suicide (vid.). *Deep Dive*, 6 March, https://www.youtube.com/watch?v=8lvN1IKOwzY. Accessed 8 March 2024.

Dawisha, Adeed. 2003. *Arab Nationalism in the Twentieth Century: From Triumph to Despair*. Princeton University Press. https://epdf.pub/arab-nationalism-in-the-twentieth-century-from-triumph-to-despair.html. Accessed 6 June 2023.

Deblauwe, Francis. 2003. Plundering the Past: The Rape of Iraq's National Museum. *Archaeology Odyssey*, July–August, https://www.academia. edu/241385/Plundering_the_Past_The_Rape_of_Iraq_s_National_ Museum?email_work_card=view-paper. Accessed 7 March 2023.

———. 2005. Mesopotamian Ruins and American Scholars, August, http://www.bibleinterp.com/articles/Deblauwe_   Mesopotamian_Scholars.htm. Accessed December 2008.

DeGhett, Torie Rose. 2014. The War Photo No One Would Publish. *Atlantic Magazine*, 8 August 2014, https://www.theatlantic.com/international/archive/2014/08/the-war-photo-no-one-would-publish/375762/. Accessed 18 May 2023.

Der Derian, James. 2009. *Virtuous War: Mapping the Military-Industrial-Media-Entertainment-Network*. 2nd ed. Routledge.

Dickinson, Elizabeth. 2008. Study: Surge of Violence Led to Peace in Iraq. *Foreign Policy: Passport*, 19 September, https://foreignpolicy.com/2008/09/19/study-surge-of-violence-led-to-peace-in-iraq/. Accessed 29 April 2023.

Diplomatic Magazine. n.d. List of 13 Billionaires in the Kurdistan Region. *Diplomatic Magazine*, 4 August, https://diplomaticmagazine.net/detail/4546#:~:text=1. Accessed 7 June 2023.

Dobbins, James, Raphael S. Cohen, Nathan Chandler, Frederick Bryan, Edward Geist, Paul DeLuca, Forrest E. Morgan, Howard J. Shatz, and Brent Williams. 2019. *Extending Russia Competing from Advantageous Ground*. Rand Corp. https://www.rand.org/content/dam/rand/pubs/research_reports/RR3000/RR3063/RAND_RR3063.pdf. Accessed 28 January 2023.

Dobbs, Michael. 2002. U.S. Had Key Role in Iraq Buildup. *Washington Post*, 30 December.

Dodge, Toby. 2018. *Iraq and Muhasasa Ta'ifia: The External Imposition of Sectarian Politics*. The Foreign Policy Centre, November, https://fpc.org.uk/iraq-and-muhasasa-taifia-the-external-imposition-of-sectarian-politics/. Accessed 20 June 2023.

Donnelly, Thomas. 2000. *Rebuilding America's Defenses: Strategy, Forces and Resources for a New Century*. Washington: Project for a New American Century, 1 September, https://archive.org/details/RebuildingAmericasDefenses. Accessed 28 February 2023.

Dower, John W. 2018. *The Violent American Century: War and Terror Since World War II*. Haymarket Books.

Eisenhower, Dwight D. 1961. Farewell Address by President Dwight D. Eisenhower, January 17, 1961; Final TV Talk 1/17/61 (1), Box 38, Speech Series, Papers of Dwight D. Eisenhower as President, 1953–61, Eisenhower Library; National Archives and Records Administration. https://www.archives.gov/milestone-documents/president-dwight-d-eisenhowers-farewell-address. Accessed 19 January 2024.

Ekurd Daily. 2022. Illegal Wealth of Massoud Barzani Estimated at $55 Billion: Ex-KRG Official—Turkish Daily. *Ekurd Daily*, 11 April, https://ekurd.net/illegal-wealth-massoud-barzani-2022-04-11. Accessed 18 June 2023.

Elving, Ron. 2018. Remembering 1968: LBJ Surprises Nation with Announcement He Won't Seek Re-Election, NPR, 25 March, https://www.npr.org/2018/03/25/596805375/president-johnson-made-a-bombshellannouncement-50-years-ago

———. 2024. Remembering 1968: LBJ Surprises Nation With Announcement He Won't Seek Re-Election. NPR, 25 March, https://www.npr.org/2018/03/25/596805375/president-johnson-made-a-bombshell-announcement-50-years-ago. Accessed 15 March 2024.

Entous, Adam, and Michael Schwirtz. 2024. The Spy War: How the C.I.A. Secretly Helps Ukraine Fight Putin. *New York Times*, 25 February, https://www.nytimes.com/2024/02/25/world/europe/cia-ukraine-intelligence-russia-war.html. Accessed 26 February 2024.

Epstein, Reid J. 2024. Will Biden's Gaza Stance Hurt Him in 2024? Michigan Is the First Test. *New York Times*, 25 February, https://www.nytimes.com/2024/02/22/us/politics/biden-michigan-gaza.html. Accessed 25 February 2024.

Epstein, Reid J., and Goldmacher, Shane. 2024. 'Michigan Primary Takeaways: 'Uncommitted' Makes Itself Heard'. *New York Times*, 28 February, https://www.nytimes.com/2024/02/28/us/politics/michigan-primary-biden-trump.html. Accessed 28 February 2024.

Escobar, Pepe. 2014. *Empire of Chaos*. Nimble Pluribus.

———. 2023. De-dollarization Kicks into High Gear. *The Cradle*, 27 April, https://thecradle.co/article-view/24080/de-dollarization-kicks-into-high-gear. Accessed 28 April 2023.

———. 2024. Pepe Escobar: Five Variables Defining Our Future. *Sputnik*, 25 January, https://sputnikglobe.com/20240125/pepe-escobar-five-variables-defining-our-future-1116381887.html. Accessed 25 January 2024.

Esposti, Nicola Degli. 2021. The 2017 Independence Referendum and the Political Economy of Kurdish Nationalism in Iraq. *Third World Quarterly*. https://www.tandfonline.com/doi/full/10.1080/01436597.2021.1949978. Accessed 21 June 2023.

———. 2022. Land Reform and Kurdish Nationalism in Postcolonial Iraq. London School of Economics & Political Science, UK. http://eprints.lse.ac.uk/114977/1/31.2.Degli_Esposti.Copyedited.pdf, and Middle East Critique, 31:2, pp. 147–163, April, https://doi.org/10.1080/19436149.2022.2055517. Accessed 21 June 2023.

Evans, Dominic, and Orhan Coskun. 2017. Defector Says Thousands of Islamic State Fighters Left Raqqa in Secret Deal. *Reuters*, 7 December, https://www.reuters.com/article/us-mideast-crisis-syria-defector-idUSKBN1E12AP. Accessed 15 March 2023.

Everett, Burgess. 2014. McCain: "Russia Is a 'Gas Station'. *Politico*, 14 March, https://www.politico.com/story/2014/03/john-mccain-russia-gas-station-105061. Accessed 8 April 2023.

Falk, Richard. 1991. Reflections on the Gulf War Experience: Force and War in the UN System. In *The Gulf War and the New World Order: International Relations of the Middle East*, ed. Tareq Y. Ismael and Jacqueline S. Ismael, 25–39. University Press of Florida.

———. 2009. Israeli War Crimes. *Le Monde diplomatique*, March. https://mondediplo.com/2009/03/03warcrimes. Accessed 30 April 2023.

———. 2011. Kuala Lumpur Tribunal: Bush and Blair Guilty. *Al Jazeera*, 28 November, https://www.aljazeera.com/opinions/2011/11/28/kuala-lumpur-tribunal-bush-and-blair-guilty. Accessed 28 March 2023.

———. 2015. *Humanitarian Intervention and Legitimacy Wars: Seeking Peace and Justice in the 21st Century.* Routledge.

———. 2017. What the Chilcot Report Teaches Us. *International Journal of Contemporary Iraqi Studies* 11 (1): 13–22, March, https://intellectdiscover.com/content/journals/10.1386/ijcis.11.1-2.13_1. Accessed 24 March 2023.

———. 2018. The West, Led By the US, Has Shown as Much Contempt for International Law as Assad in the Conflict. *Middle East Eye*, 13 June, https://www.middleeasteye.net/opinion/hypocrisy-wests-syria-policy. Accessed 2 April 2023.

———. 2024a. Western Media Bias, Israeli Apologetics, and Ongoing Genocide. *Counterpunch*, 22 January, https://www.counterpunch.org/2024/01/22/western-media-bias-israeli-apologetics-and-ongoing-genocide/. Accessed 25 January 2024.

———. 2024b. Introduction. *Journal of Contemporary Iraq & the Arab World 18* (2–3), pp. 97–100.

Feinstein, Andrew. 2012. *Shadow World: Inside the Global Arms Trade.* Picador.

Fisk, Robert. 2007a. It Is the Death of History. *The Independent*, 17 September, http://www.independent.co.uk/opinion/commentators/fisk/robert-fisk-it-is-the-death-of-history-402571.html. Accessed March 2008.

———. 2007b. Another Crime of Occupation Iraq: Cultural Heritage Looted, Pillaged. *The Independent*, 17 September 2007, http://www. alternet.org/waroniraq/62810/. Accessed December 2008.

———. 2016. After Mosul Falls, ISIS Will Flee to Syria. Then What? *Consortium News*, 18 October, https://www.counterpunch.org/2016/10/18/after-mosul-falls-isis-will-flee-to-syria-then-what/. Accessed 18 May 2023.

Forte, Maximilian C. 2012. *Slouching Towards Sirte: NATO's War on Libya and Africa.* Baraka Books.

Foster, John Bellamy, and Robert W. McChesney, eds. 2004. *Pox Americana: Exposing the American Empire.* Monthly Review Press.

Freeman, Chas. 2024. 'Former Ambassador Chas Freeman Interviewed by Thomas Karat About Gaza' (vid.). *Non-corporate News*, 7 January, https://www.youtube.com/watch?v=2qymBMLVikI. Accessed 8 January 2024.

Freeman, Chas, and Rostami Alkhorshid. 2023. NATO Unity Has Cracked (vid.). *Dialogue Works*, 23 December, https://m.youtube.com/watch?v=58DptJJ8kQc. Accessed 30 December 2023.

Freier, Nathan P., Christopher M. Bado, Christopher J. Bolan Colonel, and Robert S. Hume. 2017. At Our Own Peril: DoD Risk Assessment in a Post-Primacy World. SSI The U.S. Army War College, June, https://ssi.armywarcollege.edu/pubs/display.cfm?pubID=1358.

Frontline. 1990. The Arming of Iraq. 11 September, https://www.pbs.org/wgbh/pages/frontline/shows/longroad/etc/arming.html. Accessed 12 June 2023.

———. n.d. PBS, Lost year in Iraq. https://www.pbs.org/wgbh/pages/frontline/yeariniraq/documents/. Accessed 20 July 2023.

Fukuyama, Francis. 1993. *The End of History and the Last Man*. Free Press.

Gani, Jasmine. 2019. US Policy Towards the Syrian Conflict Under Obama: Strategic Patience and Miscalculation. In *The War for Syria: Regional and International Dimensions of the Syrian Uprising*, ed. Raymond Hinnebusch and Adham Saouli. Routledge.

Gellman, Barton. 1992. Keeping the US First. *Washington Post*, 11 March, https://www.washingtonpost.com/archive/politics/1992/03/11/keeping-the-us-first/31a774aa-fcd9-45be-8526-ceafc933b938/. Accessed 9 May 2023.

Gerstein, Josh. 2014. Biden Sorry for ISIL Funding Remarks That Echoed Obama. *Politico*, 6 October, https://www.politico.com/blogs/under-the-radar/2014/10/biden-sorry-for-isil-funding-remarks-that-echoed-obama-196622. Accessed 20 May 2023.

Ghassan, Charbel. 2024. Zebari for "Middle East": We Heard in Tehran Frank Words Explaining the Role of Militias (Arabic), Asharq Al-Awsat (The Arab World), 20 February.

Gibbons, Phillip. 2002. *U.S. No-Fly Zones in Iraq: To What End?* Washington Institute, 1 July, https://www.washingtoninstitute.org/policy-analysis/us-no-fly-zones-iraq-what-end. Accessed 19 June 2023.

Global Times. 2022. Xi's Mideast Trip Ushers in a New Era of Relations between China and Arab Countries: FM. *Global Times-Xinhua*, 11 December, https://www.globaltimes.cn/page/202212/1281586.shtml. Accessed 15 December 2022.

Goldberg, Geoffrey. 2016. The Obama Doctrine. *The Atlantic*, April, https://www.theatlantic.com/magazine/archive/2016/04/the-obama-doctrine/471525/. Accessed 15 March 2023.

Golshan, Tara, and Alex Ward. 2019. Joe Biden's Iraq Problem. *Vox*, 19 October, https://www.vox.com/policy-and-politics/2019/10/15/20849072/joe-biden-iraq-history-democrats-election-2020. Accessed 9 June 2023.

Gorbachev Foundation. 1990. Document 14: Gorbachev Memcon with U.S. Secretary of State James Baker, Moscow, September 13, National Security Archive. https://nsarchive.gwu.edu/briefing-book/russia-programs/2020-09-09/inside-gorbachev-bush-partnership-first-gulf-war-1990. Accessed 20 July 2023.

Gordon, Joy. 2012. *Invisible War: The United States and the Iraq Sanctions.* Harvard University Press.

———. 2024. The Legacy of the UN Security Council Sanctions on Iraq. *Journal of Contemporary Iraq & the Arab World 18* (2–3), pp. 135–145.

Graham, Bill. 2016. *The Call of the World*. UBC Press.

Green, Erica L. 2024. Harris Calls for an 'Immediate Cease-Fire' in Gaza. *New York Times*. https://www.nytimes.com/2024/03/03/world/middleeast/kamala-harris-cease-fire.html. Accessed 5 March 2024.

Greenspan, Alan. 2007. *Age of Turbulence: Adventures in a New World*. Penguin.

Gugliotta, Guy. 2005. Looted Iraqi Relics Slow to Resurface; Some Famous Pieces Unlikely to Re-appear. *Washington Post*, 8 November, http://www.washingtonpost.com/wp-dyn/content/article/2005/11/07/AR2005110701479.html. Accessed December 2008.

Guyer, Jonathan. 2023. How Ukraine Could Become America's Next Forever War. *Vox*, 24 February, https://www.vox.com/world-politics/2023/2/24/23600166/ukraine-war-biden-russia-afghanistan-iraq-aid. Accessed 22 March 2023.

Haass, Richard N. 2010. *War of Necessity, War of Choice: A Memoir of Two Iraq Wars*. Simon & Schuster.

Hahn, Gordon. 2023. 'In Putin's Russia Politics is War by Other Means and War is Revolutionizing Russian Military Affairs', *RUSSIAN & EURASIAN POLITICS*, 16 November, https://gordonhahn.com/category/russian-military-strategy/

Hallion, Richard. 1997. *Storm over Iraq: Air Power and the Gulf War*. Smithsonian Institution.

Hanieh, Adam. 2018. *Money, Markets, and Monarchies: The Gulf Cooperation Council and the Political Economy of the Contemporary Middle East*. Cambridge University Press.

Hanish, Shak. 2018. The Kurdish Referendum in Iraq: An Assessment. *Journal of Power, Politics & Governance* 6 (2): 17–29, December. http://jppgnet.com/journals/jppg/Vol_6_No_2_December_2018/3.pdf. Accessed 10 June 2023.

Hare, David. 2004. *Stuff Happens*. Faber and Faber.

Harris, Shane, and Matthew M. Aid. 2013. Exclusive: CIA Files Prove America Helped Saddam as He Gassed Iran. *Foreign Policy*, 26 August, https://foreignpolicy.com/2013/08/26/exclusive-cia-files-prove-america-helped-saddam-as-he-gassed-iran/. Accessed 12 June 2023.

Hassan, Ghali. 2005. The Destruction of Iraq's Educational System Under US Occupation, 11 May, http://www.globalresearch.ca/articles/HAS505B.html. Accessed December 2008.

Hathaway, Oona A. 2016. What the Chilcot Report Teaches Us About National Security Lawyering. *Just Security*, 11 July, https://www.justsecurity.org/31946/chilcot-report-teaches-national-security-lawyering/. Accessed 18 May 2023.

Hedges, Chris. 2023. The Lords of Chaos. *Consortium News*, 20 March, https://consortiumnews.com/2023/03/20/iraq-20-years-chris-hedges-the-lords-of-chaos/. Accessed 22 March 2023.

Helmer, John. 2024a. The US, Israel Have Lost Battlefield Control—Houthis Have Attacked US Destroyer, Hit Greek-US Owned Bulker; Iran Has Hit US Base in Kurdish Capital, Erbil. *Dances with Bears*, 16 January, https://johnhelmer.org/the-us-israel-have-lost-battlefield-control-houthis-have-attacked-us-destroyer-hit-greek-us-owned-bulker-iran-has-hit-us-base-in-kurdish-capital-erbil/. Accessed 16 January 2024.

———. 2024b. The Tower-22 Strike in Jordan Triggers US, Israel into All-front War—The Arabs and Iran Are Ready, the Russians too. *Dances with Bears*, 28 January, https://johnhelmer.net/the-tower-22-strike-in-jordan-triggers-us-israel-into-all-front-war-the-arabs-and-iran-are-ready-the-russians-too/#more-89274. Accessed 31 January 2024.

———. 2024c. Moody's Just Told You So—Downgrades Israel, Warns That Weaker US Backing for Israel, War with Hezbollah Would Trigger Crash. *Dances with Bears*, 11 February, https://johnhelmer.net/moodys-just-told-you-so-downgrades-israel-warns-that-weaker-us-backing-for-israel-war-with-hezbollah-would-trigger-crash/. Accessed 14 February 2024.

———. 2024d. New Evidence the German Taurus Attack Plan Was Leaked by the US Air Force. *Dances with Bears*, 15 March, https://johnhelmer.net/new-evidence-the-german-taurus-attack-plan-was-leaked-by-the-us-air-force/#more-89562. Accessed 16 March 2024.

Henry, C.K. 2004. Geopolitics in Iraq an Old Game. *Asia Times*, 3 September, reposted at: http://henryckliu.com/page65.html. Accessed 7 June 2023.

Hersh, Seymour M. 1991. *The Samson Option: Israel's Nuclear Arsenal and American Foreign Policy*. Random House.

Hersh, Seymour. 2000. Overwhelming Force: What Happened in the Final Days of the Gulf War? *The New Yorker*, 22 May.

Hersh, Seymour M. 2003a. Selective Intelligence. *The New Yorker*, 5 May, www.newyorker.com/archive/2003/05/12/030512fa_fact. Accessed 25 June 2023.

———. 2003b. Moving Targets. *The New Yorker*, 15 December, http://www.newyorker.com/archive/2003/12/15/031215fa_fact. Accessed March 2009.

———. 2004a. *Chain of Command, 1 January*. Harper Collins.

———. 2004b. Plan B. *The New Yorker*, June 28, http://www.newyorker.com/archive/2004/06/28/040628fa_fact. Accessed March 2009.

Hersh, Seymour M. 2007. The Redirection: Is the Administration's New Policy Benefitting Our Enemies in the War on Terrorism? *The New Yorker*, 25 February, https://www.newyorker.com/magazine/2007/03/05/the-redirection. Accessed 9 March 2023.

Hersh, Seymour M. 2014. The Red Line and the Rat Line. *London Review of Books*, April.

———. 2016. Military to Military. *London Review of Books*, 7 January, https://www.lrb.co.uk/the-paper/v38/n01/seymour-m.-hersh/military-to-military. Accessed 15 March 2023.

Hersh, Seymour M. 2023. My Meeting with Pakistan's Pervez Musharraf: What the General Told Me about Pakistan's Nuclear Arsenal in the Early Days of the Obama Administration, 3 May, https://seymourhersh.substack.com/p/was-it-self-censorship?utm_source=substack&utm_medium=email.   Accessed 3 May 2023.

Hersh, Seymour. 2024a. The Political Costs of Biden's Wars. *Substack*, 17 January, https://seymourhersh.substack.com/p/the-political-costs-of-bidens-wars?utm_campaign=email-post&r=2241lj&utm_source=substack&utm_medium=email. Accessed 18 January 2024.

———. 2024b. A Unified Theory of Presidential Folly, 25 January, https://seymourhersh.substack.com/p/a-unified-theory-of-presidential?utm_campaign=email-post&r=2241lj&utm_source=substack&utm_medium=email. Accessed 25 January 2024.

Hiltermann, Joost. 2016. The Kurds: A Divided Future? *The New York Review*, 19 May,   https://www.nybooks.com/online/2016/05/19/kurds-syria-iraq-divided-future/. Accessed 10 June 2023.

———. 2023. *Iraqi Kurdistan Twenty Years After*. International Crisis Group, 23 April, https://www.crisisgroup.org/middle-east-north-africa/gulf-and-arabian-peninsula/iraq/iraqi-kurdistan-twenty-years-after.   Accessed   10 June 2023.

Hinnebusch, Raymond A. 2007. The US Invasion of Iraq: Explanations and Implications. *Critique: Critical Middle Eastern Studies* 16 (3, Oct. 1), 209–228. https://www.tandfonline.com/doi/full/10.1080/10669920701616443#_i6. Accessed 14 April 2023.

———. 2016. Egypt, Syria and the Arab State System in the New World Order. In *The Middle East in the New World Order*, ed. Haifaa A. Jawad, 2nd ed., 162–182. Springer.

Hirsh, Michael. 2023. The Lessons Not Learned From Iraq: Twenty Years On, the War Still Shapes Policy—Mostly for the Worse. *Foreign Policy*, 17 March, https://foreignpolicy.com/2023/03/17/iraq-war-anniversary-lessons-bush-biden-afghanistan/. Accessed 18 May 2023.

Hoff, Brad. 2012. Defense Intelligence Agency Document: West Will Facilitate Rise of Islamic State "In Order to Isolate the Syrian Regime", Levant Report. https://levantreport.com/2015/05/19/2012-defense-intelligence-agency-document-west-will-facilitate-rise-of-islamic-state-in-order-to-isolate-the-syrian-regime/. Accessed 15 March 2023.

Hove, Mediel. 2018. The Origins of the 'Islamic State (ISIS). *Conflict Studies Quarterly*, April. http://www.csq.ro/wp-content/uploads/Mediel-HOVE.pdf. Accessed 8 March 2023.

Howard, Michael. 2002. London Meeting for Iraqi Opposition. *The Guardian*, 20 November, https://www.theguardian.com/world/2002/nov/20/iraq.london. Accessed 20 June 2023.

Hu, Xijin. 2023. US Gets Anxious as Russia Has Survived War of Attrition Against Entire NATO. *Global Times*, 1 March, https://www.globaltimes.cn/page/202303/1286442.shtml. Accessed 8 April 2023.

Hudson, Michael C. 1992. The Middle East under Pax Americana: How New, How Orderly? *Third World Quarterly* 13 (2): 301–316.

Hudson, Michael. 2003. *Super Imperialism: The Origin and Fundamentals of US World Dominance*. London: Pluto Press.

———. 2021. *Super Imperialism. The Economic Strategy of American Empire*. 3rd ed. Islet.

———. 2023. What Can the World Expect from China's Economic Recovery? CGTN, 28 April 2023, (vid.), https://globalsouth.co/2023/04/28/michael-hudson-on-cgtn-what-can-the-world-expect-from-chinas-economic-recovery/. Accessed 29 April 2023.

Hudson, John. 2024. USAID's Samantha Power, Genocide Scholar, Confronted by Staff on Gaza. *Washington Post*, 31 January, https://www.washingtonpost.com/national-security/2024/01/31/samantha-power-usaid-confronted-gaza/?campaign_id=9&emc=edit_nn_20240201&instance_id=114027&nl=the-morning&regi_id=7062190&segment_id=156981&te=1&user_id=e1ddf1d17d81e96d432c42ea2c1367b5. Accessed 1 February 2024.

Hughes, David. 2016. Chilcot Report: John Prescott Says Iraq War Was Illegal. *The Independent*, 9 July, https://www.independent.co.uk/news/uk/politics/chilcot-report-john-prescott-says-tony-blair-led-uk-into-illegal-war-in-iraq-a7129106.html. Accessed 24 March 2023.

Human Rights First. 2008. How to Confront the Iraqi Refugee Crisis: A Blueprint for the New Administration, December, https://reliefweb.int/report/iraq/how-confront-iraqi-refugee-crisis-blueprint-new-administration. Accessed 30 March 2023.

Human Rights Watch. 1992a. Unquiet Graves: The Search for the Disappeared in Iraqi Kurdistan. *Human Rights Watch*, February, https://www.hrw.org/legacy/reports/1992/iraq/iraq0292.pdf. Accessed 12 June 2023.

———. 1992b. Endless Torment: The 1991 Uprising in Iraq and Its Aftermath. *Human Rights Watch*, June, https://www.hrw.org/reports/1992/Iraq926.htm. Accessed 12 June 2023.

———. 1993a. First Anfal—The Siege of Sergalou and Bergalou, February 23—March 19, 1988. *Human Rights Watch*, https://www.hrw.org/reports/1993/iraqanfal/ANFAL3.htm. Accessed 11 June 2023.

———. 1993b. Genocide in Iraq—The Anfal Campaign Against the Kurds, July, https://www.hrw.org/report/1993/07/01/genocide-iraq/anfal-campaign-against-kurds. Accessed 20 July 2023.

———. 2014. "No-One is Safe": The Abuse of Women in Iraq's Criminal Justice System. *Human Rights Watch*, February, https://www.hrw.org/report/2014/02/06/no-one-safe/abuse-women-iraqs-criminal-justice-system. Accessed 4 May 2023.

Hussain, Hannan R. 2023. Eyes on the Future: The China-Palestine Strategic Partnership. *China.org.cn*, 18 June, http://www.china.org.cn/opinion/2023-06/19/content_88213867.htm. Accessed 20 June 2023.

Hussein, Mohammed, and Kate Dourian. 2023. Parliament Passes Budget after Gutting KRG Revenue Guarantees. *Iraq Oil Report*, 13 June, https://www.iraqoilreport.com/news/parliament-passes-budget-after-gutting-krg-revenue-guarantees-45794/#:~:text=SULAIMANIYA. Accessed 14 June 2023.

Husseini, Sam. 2023. The Lies, and Lies About the Lies, About the Invasion. *Consortium News*, March 20, https://consortiumnews.com/2023/03/20/iraq-20-years-sam-husseini-the-lies-and-lies-about-the-lies-about-the-invasion/. Accessed 22 March 2023.

IDMC. 2019. *Global Report on Internal Displacement 2019*. The Internal Displacement Monitoring Centre (IDMC). www.internal-displacement.org/global-report/grid2019. Accessed 18 May 2023.

Ignatieff, Michael. 2003. *Empire Lite: Nation-building in Bosnia, Kosovo and Afghanistan*. Penguin.

Illaik, Hasan. 2023. The Hidden Security Clauses of the Iran-Saudi Deal. *The Cradle*, 12 March, https://thecradle.co/article-view/22445/exclusive-the-hidden-security-clauses-of-the-iran-saudi-deal. Accessed 13 March 2023.

Immerwahr, Daniel. 2019. *How to Hide an Empire: A History of the Greater United States*. Farrar, Straus and Giroux.

Imseis, Ardi. 2024. Gaza Genocide: International Justice? With Ardi Imseis. *Connections Episode* 83, (vid.), https://www.youtube.com/watch?v=I3KErJkZf_Y.

Institut Kurde de Paris. 2006. Iraqi Kurdistan Unifies its Administration with a Single Government. Institut Kurde de Paris 254, May, p. 2, http://www.institutkurde.org/en/publications/bulletins/254.html. Accessed March 2009.

Institute for Public Accuracy. 2019. *Postol: Newly Revealed Documents Show Syrian Chemical "Attacks Were Staged".* Institute for Public Accuracy, 21 May 2019, https://accuracy.org/release/postol-newly-revealed-documents-show-syrian-chemical-attacks-were-staged. Accessed 18 March 2023.

International Court of Justice. 2024a. Application Instituting Proceedings. https://www.icj-cij.org/sites/default/files/case-related/192/192-20231228-app-01-00-en.pdf. Accessed 8 January 2024.

———. 2024b. Press Release, 12 January, https://www.ceasefire.ca/wp-content/uploads/2024/01/192-20240112-pre-01-00-en.pdf.   Accessed   22 January 2024.

———. 2024c. Application of the Convention on the Prevention and Punishment of the Crime of Genocide in the Gaza Strip (South Africa v. Israel), 26 January, https://www.icj-cij.org/sites/default/files/case-related/192/192-20240126-ord-01-00-en.pdf. Accessed 26 January 2024.

———. 2024d. Declaration of Judge Xue, 26 January, https://www.icj-cij.org/node/203448. Accessed 28 January 2024.

———. 2024e. Urgent Request for Additional Measures Under Article 75(1) of the Rules of the Court of the International Court of Justice, 12 February, https://www.icj-cij.org/sites/default/files/case-related/192/192-20240212-wri-01-00-en.pdf. Accessed 14 February 2024.

———. 2024f. Decision of the Court on South Africa's Request for Additional Provisional Measures, 16 February, https://www.icj-cij.org/sites/default/files/case-related/192/192-20240216-pre-01-00-en.pdf.   Accessed   22 February 2024.

———. 2024g. *The Republic of Nicaragua Institutes Proceedings Against the Federal Republic of Germany and Requests the Court to Indicate Provisional Measures.* International Court of Justice, 1 March, https://www.icj-cij.org/sites/default/files/case-related/193/193-20240301-pre-01-00-en.pdf. Accessed 4 March 2024.

———. 2024h. *Urgent Request and Application for the Indication of Additional Provisional Measures and the Modification of the Court's Prior Provisional Measures Decisions Pursuant to Article 41 of the Statute of the International Court of Justice and Articles 75 and 76 of the Rules of the Court of the International Court of Justice.* International Court of Justice, 6 March, https://www.icj-cij.org/sites/default/files/case-related/192/192-20240306-wri-01-00-en.pdf. Accessed 7 March 2024.

Iraq Coordination and Follow-Up Committee. 2003. Iraqi Opposition Conference: Final Statement of the Meeting of the Coordination and Follow-Up Committee. *Relief Web,* 3 March, https://reliefweb.int/report/

iraq/iraqi-opposition-conference-final-statement-meeting-coordination-and-follow-committee. Accessed 20 June 2023.

Islamic Republic News Agency. 2024a. Yemen's Ansarullah Warns Regional States Against US Deception, 11 January, https://en.irna.ir/news/85361444/Yemen-s-Ansarullah-warns-regional-states-against-US-deception. Accessed 21 January 2024.

———. 2024b. Russia's Adherence to Iran's Sovereignty to Be Included in Bilateral Deal: DM. *Islamic Republic News Agency (IRNA)*, 15 January, https://en.irna.ir/news/85355443/Russia-s-adherence-to-Iran-s-overeignty-included-in-bilateral. Accessed 21 January 2024.

Ismael, Tareq. 2019. Legacy, Legitimacy and Compromise: Baghdad's Visionary Yusuf Al-Ani and Postcolonial Iraq. *Journal of Contemporary Iraq & the Arab World* 13(1), 21–39. https://intellectdiscover.com/content/journals/10.1386/jciaw.13.1.21_1. Accessed 4 February 2024.

Ismael, Tareq Y., and Jacqueline S. Ismael, eds. 1991. *The Gulf War and the New World Order: International Relations of the Middle East.* University Press of Florida.

———. 2004. *The Iraqi Predicament.* London: Pluto Press.

———. 2011. *Government and Politics of the Contemporary Middle East.* Routledge.

———. 2015. *Iraq in the Twenty-First Century: Regime Change and the Making of a Failed State.* Routledge.

———. 2020. Pax Americana and the Dissolution of Arab States: The Humanitarian Consequences (1990–2019). *Arab Studies Quarterly* 42 (1–2): 25–45. https://doi.org/10.13169/arabstudquar.42.1-2.0025. Accessed 2 July 2023.

———. 2021. *Iraq in the Twenty-First Century: Regime Change and the Making of a Failed State.* Routledge.

Jackson, Ashley. 2018. *Persian Gulf Command: A History of the Second World War in Iran and Iraq.* Yale University Press.

Jacobsen, Eric. 2015. A Coincidence of Interests: Kennedy, U.S. Assistance, and the 1963 Iraqi Ba'th Regime. *Diplomatic History* 37 (5, Nov.), 1029–1059. https://www.jstor.org/stable/44254343. Accessed 21 May 2023.

Jawad, Saad Naji, and Sawsan Ismail Al-Assaf. 2024. The Iraqi Youth October 2019 Uprising (Tishreen Intifada): Reality and Prospects. *Journal of Contemporary Iraq & the Arab World 18* (2–3), pp. 147–165.

Jenkins, Simon. 2007. In Iraq's Four-Year Looting Frenzy, the Allies Have Become the Vandals. *Guardian*, 8 June, http://www. guardian.co.uk/Iraq/Story/0,2098273,00.html. Accessed December 2008.

Johnson, Jake. 2024. Western Officials Warn of War-Crimes Complicity. *Consortium News*, 2 February, https://consortiumnews.com/2024/02/02/western-officials-warn-of-war-crimes-complicity/. Accessed 3 February 2024.

Johnson, Larry, and Andrew Napolitano. 2024. Larry Johnson: Ukraine War Viewed from MOSCOW! (vid.). *Judging Freedom*, 26 February, https://www.youtube.com/watch?v=Acwrv4KIblc. Accessed 27 February 2024.

Johnston, Charles. 2000. *Blowback: The Costs and Consequences of American Empire*. Metropolitan Books.

Johnston, Chalmers. 2004. *The Sorrows of Empire: Militarism, Secrecy, and the End of the Republic*. Metropolitan Books.

———. 2007. *Nemesis: The Last Days of the American Republic*. Metropolitan Books.

Johnstone, Caitlin. 2024. How the Imperial Media Report on an Israeli Massacre. *Consortium News*, 1 March, https://consortiumnews.com/2024/03/01/caitlin-johnstone-how-the-imperial-media-report-on-an-israeli-massacre/. Accessed 6 March 2024.

Kadri, Ali. 2015. *Arab Development Denied: Dynamics of Accumulation by Wars of Encroachment*. Anthem Press.

———. 2016. *The Unmaking of Arab Socialism*. Anthem Press.

Kaleck, Wolfgang. 2016. *The Iraq Invasion Is a Crime*. European Centre for Constitutional and Human Rights. https://www.ecchr.eu/en/publication/the-iraq-invasion-is-a-crime/. Accessed 24 March 2023.

Kamrava, Mehran. 2018. *Inside the Arab State*. Hurst.

Kathem, Mehiyar, Eleanor Robson, Lina G. Tahan. 2022. Cultural Heritage Predation in Iraq. *Chatham House*, 24 March, https://www.chathamhouse.org/2022/03/cultural-heritage-predation-iraq/02-historical-context-conflict-and-destabilization. Accessed 2 March 2024.

Kennedy, John F. 1963. World Peace, 10 June, John F. Kennedy Presidential Library and Museum. https://www.jfklibrary.org/asset-viewer/archives/usg-01-07. Accessed 29 January 2024.

Kensaku, Yuree. 2015. When Two Elephants Fight, the Grass Gets Trampled. Hong Kong, https://www.artbasel.com/catalog/artwork/14402/yuree-kensaku-when-two-elephants-fight-the-grass-gets-trampled. Accessed 16 April 2023.

Kerry, John. 2016. Leaked Audio of John Kerry's Meeting with Syrian Revolutionaries/UN (Improved Audio), 4 October, https://www.youtube.com/watch?v=e4phB-_pXDM&t=1552s. Accessed 9 March 2023.

Khouri, Rami. 2019. Why We Should Worry About the Arab Region, *Agence Global*, 10 February, https://www.belfercenter.org/publication/why-we-should-worry-about-arab-region. Accessed 9 May 2023.

Kinzer, Stephen. 2007. *Overthrow: America's Century of Regime Change from Hawaii to Iraq*. Times Books.

———. 2017. *The True Flag: Theodore Roosevelt, Mark Twain, and the Birth of American Empire*. Henry Holt and Co.

Kirk, Michael. 2003. The War Behind Closed Doors: Excerpts from 1992 Draft "Defense Planning Guidance". *PBS: Frontline*, https://www.pbs.org/wgbh/pages/frontline/shows/iraq/etc/script.html. Accessed 3 April 2023.

Klein, Naomi. 2007. *The Shock Doctrine*. Alfred A. Knopf Canada.

Klippenstein, Ken. 2024. U.S. Military Personnel in Iraq Put on Standby to Support Ground Involvement in Israel's War on Gaza. *The Intercept*, 30 January, https://theintercept.com/2024/01/30/us-military-ground-israel-hamas-gaza/#:~:text=Black/U.S. Army-,U.S. Military Personnel in Iraq Put on Standby to Support,Has Prepared for the Possibility. Accessed 31 January 2024.

Kramer, Andrew E. 2008. Deals With Iraq Are Set to Bring Oil Giants Back. *New York Times*, 19 June, https://www.nytimes.com/2008/06/19/world/middleeast/19iraq.html. Accessed 29 April 2023.

Krieger, David. 2002. Farewell to the ABM Treaty, 13 June, Nuclear Age for Peace Foundation, https://www.wagingpeace.org/farewell-to-the-abm-treaty/. Accessed 19 January 2024.

Krishnan, Nandini, and Sergio Olivieri. 2016. Losing the Gains of the Past: The Welfare and Distributional Impacts of the Twin Crises in Iraq 2014. Policy Research Working Paper; No. WPS 7567. Washington, DC: World Bank Group. https://documents1.worldbank.org/curated/en/217401467995379476/pdf/WPS7567.pdf. Accessed 29 March 2023.

Kuperman, Alan. 2013. A Model Humanitarian Intervention? Reassessing NATO's Libya Campaign. *International Security* 38 (1, Summer): 105–136.

Kurtz-Phelan, Daniel. 2018. *The China Mission: George Marshall's Unfinished War, 1945–1947*. W. W. Norton & Company.

Lackner, Helen. 2019. *Yemen in Crisis: Road to War*. Verso.

Lanard, Noah. 2023. How Joe Biden Became America's Top Israel Hawk. *Mother Jones*, 22 December, https://www.motherjones.com/politics/2023/12/how-joe-biden-became-americas-top-israel-hawk/. Accessed 9 January 2024.

Landler, Mark, Helene Cooper, and Eric Schmitt. 2018. Trump to Withdraw U.S. Forces From Syria, Declaring "We Have Won Against ISIS". *New York Times*, 19 December, https://www.nytimes.com/2018/12/19/us/politics/trump-syria-turkey-troop-withdrawal.html. Accessed 23 June 2024.

Lascaris, Dimitri. 2024. What Now, Genocide Justin? 26 January, https://dimitrilascaris.org/2024/01/26/what-now-genocide-justin/#respond. Accessed 27 January 2024.

Lauria, Joe. 2022. Why Putin Went to War. *Consortium News*, 24 February, https://consortiumnews.com/2024/02/24/why-putin-went-to-war/. Accessed 25 February 2024.

———. 2023. Covering the "Vial Display". *Consortium News*, 19 March, https://consortiumnews.com/2023/03/19/iraq-20-years-joe-lauria-one-resignation-may-have-stopped-the-disastrous-invasion/. Accessed 22 March 2023.

———. 2024. Why Putin Went to War. *Consortium News*, 24 February, https://consortiumnews.com/2024/02/24/why-putin-went-to-war/. Accessed 25 February 2024.

Lavrov, Sergey. 2024a. Russia Now Knows West Cannot Be Trusted, Says Lavrov. *Tass*, 18 January, https://tass.com/politics/1734063. Accessed 18 January 2024.

———. 2024b. *Foreign Minister Sergey Lavrov's Remarks and Answers to Media Questions Following a UN Security Council meeting on Ukraine and an Open Debate on "The Situation in the Middle East, Including the Palestinian Question.* Ministry of Foreign Affairs of the Russian Federation, New York, January 24, 2024, https://mid.ru/en/press_service/photos/meropriyatiya_s_uchastiem_ministra/1927568/?TSPD_101_R0=08765fb817ab2000d728a27cbc3df5c6ddbaea464004396d27e2085e70894fab3b130986b8375c1908566a0b73143000042a4d9e368c49c6b2378d8a490c0160ce736eb6ef-d1922ad0cd95daf79fb772fb05e4aee76430326ab52be6300b081f

Lawrence, Patrick. 2023. Europe's Fate. *Consortium News*, 3 May, https://consortiumnews.com/2023/05/03/patrick-lawrence-europes-fate/. Accessed 5 May 2023.

Lerner, Adam B. 2015. Hillary Clinton Says Her Iraq War Vote Was a "Mistake". *Politico*, 19 May, https://www.politico.com/story/2015/05/hillary-clinton-iraq-war-vote-mistake-iowa-118109. Accessed 23 June 2023.

Livni, Ephrat. 2024. Brazil's President Angers Israel After Comparing War in Gaza to the Holocaust. *New York Times*, 18 February, https://www.nytimes.com/2024/02/18/world/middleeast/brazil-lula-israel-gaza-holocaust.html. Accessed 18 February 2024.

Livshitz, Felix. 2023. Goodbye Empire? US Sanctions Are Failing in the Face of Multipolarity Washington's Go-to methods Can't Prevent the Rise of Other Powers, an Influential Establishment Journal Admits. RT, 25 January, https://www.rt.com/news/569926-us-sanctions-not-work/. Accessed 2 May 2023.

Lloyd, Richard, and Theodore A. Postol. 2014. Possible Implications of Faulty US Technical Intelligence in the Damascus Nerve Agent Attack of August 21, 2013. MIT, Science, Technology, and Global Security Working Group, 14 January, https://s3.amazonaws.com/s3.documentcloud.org/documents/1006045/possible-implications-of-bad-intelligence.pdf. Accessed 18 March 2023.

Longley, Alex and Quinn, Áine. 2024. Chinese Ships Get Insurance Edge Navigating Red Sea, GCaptain, Bloomberg, 6 February, https://gcaptain.com/chinese-ships-get-insurance-edge-navigating-red-sea/

Loughlin, Sean. 2003. Rumsfeldw on Looting in Iraq: "Stuff Happens". *CNN*, 12 April, https://www.cnn.com/2003/US/04/11/sprj.irq.pentagon/. Accessed 4 April 2023.

Loyd, Anthony. 2016. 'Iraqi General Offers Isis an Escape Route in Battle for Mosul. *The Times*, 17 October, https://www.thetimes.co.uk/article/iraqi-general-offers-isis-an-escape-route-in-battle-for-mosul-s9cj39jt8. Accessed 15 March 2023.

Luft, Gal. 2003. How Much Oil Does Iraq Have? Global Politics Iraq Memo 16, 12 May, The Brookings Institution, www.brookings.edu/views/op-ed/fellows/luft20030512.htm. Accessed 10 October 2007.

Lukin, Alexander. 2016. Russia in a Post-Bipolar World. *Survival: Global Politics and Strategy* 58 (1, Feb.): 91–112.

Maass, Pater. 2005. The Way of the Commandos. *New York Times*, 1 May. https://www.nytimes.com/2005/05/01/magazine/the-way-of-the-commandos.html. Accessed 29 April 2023.

MacArthur, John R. 1994. *Second Front: Censorship and Propaganda in the 1991 Gulf War*. University of California Press.

MacAskill, Ewin, and Julian Borger. 2004. Iraq War Was Illegal and Breached UN Charter, Says Annan. *The Guardian*, 16 September, https://www.theguardian.com/world/2004/sep/16/iraq.iraq. Accessed 16 February 2024.

Macgregor, Douglas, and Andrew Napolitano. 2024a. Wrongheaded US Military Priorities (vid.), *Judging Freedom*, 3 January, https://www.youtube.com/watch?v=GqNWKJENDLY. Accessed 6 January 2024.

———. 2024b. NATO's Misguided Actions Towards Russia. *Judging Freedom*, 4 March, https://www.youtube.com/watch?v=Gpi5sJHpOkY. Accessed 7 March 2024.

Magnier, Eliajah. 2022. François Hollande Confirms Minsk Agreements Were a Western Ploy. *Voltaire Network*, 31 December, https://www.voltairenet.org/article218584.html. Accessed 20 January 2024.

Mansoor, Peter R. 2013. *Surge: My Journey with General David Petraeus and the Remaking of the Iraq War*. Yale University Press.

Maté, Aaron. 2019. Top Scientist Slams OPCW Leadership for Repressing Dissenting Report on Syria Gas Attack. *The Greyzone*, 18 June, https://thegrayzone.com/2019/06/18/theodore-postol-opcw-syria-gas-attack-douma/. Accessed 18 March 2023.

Maté, Aaron, and Andrew Napolitano. 2024. Aaron Maté—(The GrayZone): Nuland and the Leaked German Plot (vid.). *Judging Freedom*, 13 March, https://www.youtube.com/watch?v=rOul7N0H6UA. Accessed 13 March 2024.

Matthews, W.C. 2011. The Kennedy Administration, Counterinsurgency, and Iraq's First Ba'thist Regime. *International Journal of Middle East Studies 43* (4): 635–653.

Mazzetti, Mark, and Matt Apuzzo. 2016. U.S. Relies Heavily on Saudi Money to Support Syrian Rebels. *New York Times*, 23 January, https://www.nytimes.

com/2016/01/24/world/middleeast/us-relies-heavily-on-saudi-money-to-support-syrian-rebels.html. Accessed 19 May 2023.

McCoy, Alfred W. 2009. *Policing America's Empire: The United States, the Philippines, and the Rise of the Surveillance State*. University of Wisconsin Press.

———. 2017. *In the Shadows of the American Century: The Rise and Decline of US Global Power*. Haymarket Books.

McDowell, David. 1985. The Kurds: The Minority Rights Group Report No. 23.

———. 1996. *The Kurds*. The Minority Rights Group, 1 December, https://minorityrights.org/publications/the-kurds-december-1996/. Accessed 11 June 2023.

McGovern, Ray. 2023a. Iraq 20 Years: The Uses and Abuses of National Intelligence Estimates. *Consortium News*, 19 March, https://consortiumnews.com/2023/03/19/iraq-20-years-ray-mcgovern-the-uses-and-abuses-of-national-intelligence-estimates/. Accessed 20 March 2023.

———. 2023b. The Missiles at the Heart of the Ukraine War. *Consortium News*, 8 May, https://consortiumnews.com/2023/05/08/watch-the-missiles-at-the-heart-of-the-ukraine-war/. Accessed 9 May 2023.

———. 2024. Nuland's Game Is Up as Russia Smashed Ukraine's Army—History Matters! (vid.). *Dialogue Works*, https://www.youtube.com/watch?v=uw_wap0sqDk. Accessed 11 March 2024.

McGovern, Ray, and Andrew Napolitano. 2024a. Ray McGovern: Will CIA help BiBi? (vid.). *Judging Freedom*, https://www.youtube.com/watch?v=kRkUx4Kbv6E. Accessed 11 January, 2024.

———. 2024b. Ray McGovern: Neocons and Wider Middle East War (vid.). *Judging Freedom*, 22 January, https://www.youtube.com/watch?v=fgQTsTX6r7g&list=TLPQMjMwMTIwMjSLKFcfFWfDag&index=3. Accessed 22 January 2024.

———. 2024c. Ray McGovern: Germany Caught Off-guard by Leak of Secret Ukraine War Talks. *Judging Freedom*, 4 March, https://www.youtube.com/watch?v=M-jWZQ72qFo&t=11s. Accessed 5 March 2024.

McGovern, Ray, Larry Johnson, and Andrew Napolitano. 2024a. INTEL Roundtable: Johnson/McGovern: Are British Troops In Gaza? (vid.). *Judging Freedom*, 11 January, https://www.youtube.com/watch?v=iIcPC62rdvg. Accessed 11 January 2024.

———. 2024b. INTEL Roundtable: Johnson & McGovern: CIA and Neocon Intransigence. (vid.). *Judging Freedom*, 19 January, https://www.youtube.com/watch?v=jRGkoBSFLRA. Accessed 20 January 2024.

———. 2024c. INTEL Roundtable: Johnson & McGovern: Ukraine's Last Gasp; ICJ Analysis. (vid.). *Judging Freedom*, 26 January, https://www.youtube.com/watch?v=T_IH3y_Q0-Y. Accessed 26 January 2024.

———. 2024d. INTEL Roundtable: Johnson & McGovern: (vid.), 2 February, https://www.youtube.com/watch?v=LarCz-UCYnU. Accessed 2 February 2024.

McNerney, Michael J., Gabrielle Tarini, Nate Rosenblatt, Karen M. Sudkamp, Pauline Moore, Benjamin J. Sacks Grise, and Larry Lewis. 2022. *Understanding Civilian Harm in Raqqa and Its Implications for Future Conflicts.* Rand Corporation. https://www.rand.org/content/dam/rand/pubs/research_reports/RRA700/RRA753-1/RAND_RRA753-1.pdf. Accessed 16 March 2023.

Mearsheimer, John J. 2001. *The Tragedy of Great Power Politics.* W. W. Norton & Company.

Mearsheimer, John J. 2014. Why the Ukraine Crisis Is the West's Fault: The Liberal Delusions That Provoked Putin. *Foreign Affairs* 93: 77–84, September/October, https://www.foreignaffairs.com/articles/russia-fsu/2014-08-18/why-ukraine-crisis-west-s-fault. Accessed 11 January 2024.

Mearsheimer, John J. 2015. UnCommon Core: The Causes and Consequences of the Ukraine Crisis (vid.). University of Chicago, 25 September, https://www.youtube.com/watch?v=JrMiSQAGOS4. Accessed 11 January 2024.

———. 2018. *The Great Delusion: Liberal Dreams and International Realities.* Yale University Press.

———. 2023a. Is China the Real Winner of Ukraine War? (vid.). *Endgame*, 28 April, https://www.youtube.com/watch?v=Yl7goPRw_eE. Accessed 14 May 2023.

———. 2023b. *Death and Destruction in Gaza.* John's Substack, 11 December, https://mearsheimer.substack.com/p/death-and-destruction-in-gaza. Accessed 12 December 2023.

———. 2024a. *Genocide in Gaza.* John's Substack, 4 January, https://mearsheimer.substack.com/p/genocide-in-gaza. Accessed 9 January 2024.

———. 2024b. *The Death of Ideology* (vid.). Institute of Art and Ideas, 24 January, https://www.youtube.com/watch?v=ClitqYW8HVk. Accessed 18 February 2024.

Mearsheimer, John J., and John Anderson. 2023. Ukraine, Taiwan and The True Cause of War (vid.), 7 December, https://www.youtube.com/watch?v=huDriv7IAa0. Accessed 10 January 2024.

Mearsheimer, John J., and Glenn Greenwald. 2024. Prof. John Mearsheimer: Yes, Israel Is Committing Genocide (vid.). System Update, 7 January, https://www.youtube.com/watch?v=vnNDEhqIlvE. Accessed 9 January 2024.

Mearsheimer, John J., and Andrew Napolitano. 2024a. Prof John Mearsheimer: Accusations of Genocide Against Israel: A Historical and Legal Analysis (vid.). *Judging Freedom*, 5 January, https://www.youtube.com/watch?v=3wjLKakAvPM. Accessed 6 January 2024.

———. 2024b. Prof. John Mearsheimer: Not a War Crime, But GENOCIDE (vid.). *Judging Freedom*, 11 January, https://www.youtube.com/watch?v=n3GmgMa-4ac. Accessed 11 January 2024.

———. 2024c. Prof. Mearsheimer: Israel's Unsuccessful Legal Assertions at the International Court of Justice (vid.). *Judging Freedom*, 15 January, https://www.youtube.com/watch?v=F-4UDLU03E4. Accessed 16 January 2024.

———. 2024d. Is Armageddon Coming in the Middle East? (vid.). *Judging Freedom*, 15 February, https://www.youtube.com/watch?v=HAOB8g63tDc. Accessed 15 February 2024.

———. 2024e. US and the Unipolar Moment (vid.). *Judging Freedom*, 22 February 2024, https://www.youtube.com/watch?v=P0zLXaO48eY. Accessed 22 February 2024.

———. 2024f. Prof. John Mearsheimer: When Will Middle East and Ukraine Explode (vid.). *Judging Freedom*, 29 February, https://www.youtube.com/watch?v=nqxgnrR20gs&t=1286s. Accessed 1 March 2024.

Mearsheimer, John J., and Jeffrey Sachs. 2023. A Missed Opportunity for Peace (vid.). *Jeffrey Sachs of Fans*, 16 November, https://www.youtube.com/watch?v=sWmWWxsrBAY. Accessed 16 November 2023.

Mearsheimer, John J. and Stephen M. Walt. 2006. The Israel Lobby. *London Review of Books*, 23 March, https://www.lrb.co.uk/the-paper/v28/n06/john-mearsheimer/the-israel-lobby. Accessed 17 January 2024.

Mearsheimer, John J., and Stephen M. Walt. 2009a. An Unnecessary War. *Foreign Policy*, 3 November, https://foreignpolicy.com/2009/11/03/an-unnecessary-war-2/. Accessed 1 April 2023.

———. 2009b. *The Israel Lobby and U.S. Foreign Policy*. Macmillan.

Mearsheimer, John J., Bassam Haddad, and Lisa Wedeen. 2024a. *JJM Teach-In on Gaza Catastrophe* (vid.). John's Substack, 10 January, https://mearsheimer.substack.com/p/jjm-teach-in-on-gaza-catastrophe. Accessed 12 January 2024.

Mearsheimer, John, Alexander Mercouris, and Glenn Diesen. 2024b. The West in Decline (vid.). *The Duran*, 16 March, https://www.youtube.com/watch?v=UNoUHzd1LcM. Accessed 16 March 2024.

Menmy, Dana Taib. 2024. US Court Summons Iraqi Kurdistan PM Masrour Barzani Over Multiple Charges. *The New Arab*, 19 February, https://www.newarab.com/news/us-court-summons-kurdish-pm-barzani-over-multiple-charges. Accessed 22 February 2024.

Mercouris, Alexander. 2024a. Crisis Ukraine: Avdeyevka Collapse, Reports Zaluzhny Sacked Budanov Taking Over; Al-Asad Base Attack (vid.). *Alexander Mercouris*, 21 January, https://rumble.com/v48dn6w-crisis-ukraine-avdeyevka-collapse-reports-zaluzhny-sacked-budanov-taking-ov.html. Accessed 21 January 2024.

———. 2024b. Ukraine Terrible Day: Missiles Rock Kiev, South Avdeyevka Lost, 18 Tanks Lost; NYT US-Iran War Coming (vid.). *Alexander Mercouris*, 23

January, https://rumble.com/v48sza9-ukraine-terrible-day-missiles-rock-kiev-south-avdeyevka-lost18-tanks-lost-n.html. Accessed 24 January 2024.

———. 2024c. Rus Defeats Ukr Avdeyevka Attack, Ukr Troops Surrender, Zelensky Evasive IL76: US Iraq Syria Pullout (vid.). *Alexander Mercouris*, 25 January, https://rumble.com/v499qyl-rus-defeats-ukr-avdeyevka-attack-ukr-troops-surrender-zelensky-evasive-il76.html. Accessed 25 January 2024.

———. 2024d. ICJ Rules Against Israel; Shock Decision; Texas Defies Biden, Prospect of US Funds For Ukraine Fade (vid.), 26 January, https://rumble.com/v49hthk-icj-rules-against-israel-shock-decision-texas-defies-biden-prospect-of-us-f.html. Accessed 26 January 2024.

———. 2024e. Rus Advance Quickens Patriots' Destroyed; 8 Year Anti Rus CIA Ukr Operation; G7 Asset Seize Backs Off (vid.), 26 February, https://rumble.com/v4fullk-rus-advance-quickens-patriots-destroyed-8-year-anti-rus-cia-ukr-operation-g.html. Accessed 26 February 2024.

———. 2024f. EU Leaders Isolate Macron, Scrounge MidEast/Africa for Shells; Ukr May Coup Rumours; Rus Orlovka, 28 February, https://rumble.com/v4g88x3-eu-leaders-isolate-macron-scrounge-mideastafrica-for-shells-ukr-may-coup-ru.html. Accessed 28 February 2024.

———. 2024g. More EU Panic, Quarrels, Germans Talk Kerch Bridge, Krasnodar Strikes, Putin Warns Counter Strikes, 2 March, https://rumble.com/v4gtdxi-more-eu-panic-quarrels-germans-talk-kerch-bridge-krasnodar-strikes-putin-wa.html. Accessed 2 March 2024.

Messina, Piero. 2024. *Planning the Aftermath, Rand Corporation Evokes a Nuclear Clash between Russia, China and the United States.* South Front, 18 February, https://southfront.press/planning-the-aftermath-rand-corporation-evokes-a-nuclear-clash-between-russia-china-and-the-united-states/. Accessed 18 February 2024.

Meyssan, Thierry. 2022. The EU Brought to Its Knees By the Straussians. *VoltaireNet*, 13 September, https://www.voltairenet.org/article217976.html. Accessed 4 May 2023.

———. 2023. The War in Ukraine to Maintain the European Union under Tutelage. *VoltaireNet*, 24 January, https://www.voltairenet.org/article218706.html. Accessed 24 January 2023.

Middle East Eye. 2024a. 'It's a Genocide': Brazil's Lula Compares War on Gaza to Holocaust, Sparking Controversy. *Middle East Eye*, https://www.middleeasteye.net/news/its-genocide-brazils-lula-compares-war-gaza-holocaust. Accessed 19 February 2024.

———. 2024b. Palestinians' Use of Force to Resist Foreign Oppression 'Well Founded' in International Law: China', Middle East Eye, 22 February, https://www.middleeastmonitor.com/20240222-palestinians-use-of-force-to-resist-foreign-oppression-well-founded-in-international-law-china/. Accessed 29 February 2024.

Miller, Judith, and Michael R. Gordon. 2002. Threats and Responses: The Iraqis; U.S. Says Hussein Intensifies Quest For A-Bomb Parts. *New York Times*, 8 September, https://www.nytimes.com/2002/09/08/world/threats-responses-iraqis-us-says-hussein-intensifies-quest-for-bomb-parts.html. Accessed 5 April 2023.

Mitchell, Timothy. 2013. *Carbon Democracy: Political Power in the Age of Oil.* Verso.

Mokhiber, Craig, and Chris Hedges. 2024. Gaza: ICJ Ruling, UN Failures, and US Complicity (vid). *The Chris Hedges Report, The Real News Network*, 26 January, https://www.youtube.com/watch?v=aQUopbLHOtg. Accessed 27 January 2024.

Moon of Alabama. 2012a. "Al Qaida in Syria" As Propaganda for Intervention, 12 July, https://www.moonofalabama.org/2012/07/index.html. Accessed 15 March 2023.

———. 2012b. Could The War On Syria Create Regime Change in Ankara? 8 August, https://www.moonofalabama.org/2012/08/index.html. Accessed 13 March 2023.

———. 2012c. Obama to Assad—Do Whatever You Need to Do, 24 August, https://www.moonofalabama.org/2012/08/index.html. Accessed 12 March 2023.

———. 2012d. Syria: Destruction Is Their Aim, 30 September, https://www.moonofalabama.org/2012/09/index.html. Accessed 11 March 2023.

———. 2012e. Obama to Erdogan: Don't Trick Us, 28 October, https://www.moonofalabama.org/2012/10/index.html. Accessed 11 March 2023.

———. 2012f. A Black-Hole Prison in Benghazi, and Syria: The New Coalition for Further Destruction, 12 November, https://www.moonofalabama.org/2012/12/index.html. Accessed 10 March 2023.

———. 2013a. More Disarray in the Syrian Opposition, 24 March, https://www.moonofalabama.org/2013/03/index.html. Accessed 10 March 2023.

———. 2013b. Syria: NYT Starts Telling the Truth About Syria, 28 April, https://www.moonofalabama.org/2013/04/index.html. Accessed 10 March 2023.

———. 2013c. Syria: News Roundup, 17 May, https://www.moonofalabama.org/2013/05/index.html. Accessed 10 March 2023.

———. 2013d. What We DO Know About Chemical Weapons in Syria, 14 June, https://www.moonofalabama.org/2013/06/index.html. Accessed 9 March 2023.

———. 2013e. Syria: Another False Flag "Chemical Weapon" Attack, 21 August, https://www.moonofalabama.org/2013/08/index.html. Accessed 9 March 2023.

———. 2013f. A Short History of the War on Syria—2006–2014, 14 September, https://www.moonofalabama.org/2013/09/index.html. Accessed 9 March 2023.

———. 2013g. Syria: NYT, HRW Wrong to Claim Chemical Attack Origin, 22 September, https://www.moonofalabama.org/2013/09/index.html. Accessed 9 March 2023.

———. 2013h. The "de-Americanized" World' and 'NYT's OPCW "He Said, She Said" Reporting Misses Major Judgement, 15 October, https://www.moonofalabama.org/2013/11/index.html. Accessed 9 March 2023.

———. 2014a. U.S., Fearing Terrorists, Provides Them with Weapons, 10 January, https://www.moonofalabama.org/2014/01/index.html. Accessed 9 March 2023.

———. 2014b. Libya, Syria and Now Ukraine—Color Revolution by Force, and Kerry, al-Zawahri United In Call for Rebel Unity, 14 January, https://www.moonofalabama.org/2014/01/index.html. Accessed 9 March 2023.

———. 2014c. Syria: U.S. Resumes Arms Delivery to Al-Qaeda, Furthers Destruction, 28 January, https://www.moonofalabama.org/2014/01/index.html. Accessed 9 March 2023.

———. 2014d. McCain on Syria: "We Were Winning ...," January 25, https://www.moonofalabama.org/2014/01/index.html. Accessed 9 March 2023.

———. 2017a. The End of Mingling—"Moderate Rebels" Join Al-Qaeda in Syria, 28 January, https://www.moonofalabama.org/2017/01/index.html. Accessed 9 March 2023.

———. 2017b. Al-Qaeda Consolidates Its Front Groups in Syria, 26 January, https://www.moonofalabama.org/2017/01/index.html. Accessed 9 March 2023.

———. 2017c. How The U.S. Enabled ISIS to Take Deir Ezzor, 17 January, https://www.moonofalabama.org/2017/01/index.html. Accessed 9 March 2023.

———. 2017d. ISIS, Al-Qaeda and the U.S. Airforce Wage War on Syria's Public Utilities, 9 January, https://www.moonofalabama.org/2017/01/index.html. Accessed 9 March 2023.

———. 2023. Mediated by China Iran and Saudi Arabia Restore Ties—There Are Winners and Losers, 10 March, https://www.moonofalabama.org/2023/03/mediated-by-china-iran-and-saudi-arabia-restore-ties-there-are-winners-and-losers.html#more. Accessed 10 March 2023.

———. 2024a. Mainstream Media Lies About U.S. Wars in Iraq Wear On, 18 January, https://www.moonofalabama.org/2024/01/mainstream-media-lies-about-us-wars-in-iraq-wear-on.html. Accessed 19 January 2024.

———. 2024b. U.S. Claims No Alternative to Larger Middle East War, 22 January, https://www.moonofalabama.org/2024/01/us-claims-no-alternative-to-larger-middle-east-war.html#more. Accessed 22 January 2024.

———. 2024c. To Hope That China Will Help with Yemen is Delusional Bullshit, https://www.moonofalabama.org/2024/01/hoping-that-china-will-help-with-yemen-is-delusional-bullshit.html#more. Accessed 23 January 2024.

———. 2024d. The ICJ Could Not Order a General Ceasefire. It Ordered Israel to Cease Fire, 26 January, https://www.moonofalabama.org/2024/01/the-icj-could-not-order-a-general-ceasefire-it-ordered-israel-to-cease-fire.html#more. Accessed 27 January 2024.

———. 2024e. Ending The U.S. Presence in Middle East, 3 February, https://www.moonofalabama.org/2024/02/ending-us-presence-in-middle-east.html. Accessed 3 February 2024.

Morris, Roger. 2003. A Tyrant 40 Years in the Making. *New York Times*, 14 March, https://www.nytimes.com/2003/03/14/opinion/a-tyrant-40-years-in-the-making.html. Accessed 19 May 2023.

Morris, Loveday. 2017. How the Kurdish Independence Referendum Backfired Spectacularly. *Washington Post*, 17 October, https://www.washingtonpost.com/world/how-the-kurdish-independence-referendum-backfired-/2017/10/20/3010c820-b371-11e7-9b93-b97043e57a22_story.html. Accessed 9 June 2023.

Mortada, Radwan. 2023. Iraq's ex-PM Adil Abdul-Mahdi: "The US Doesn't Defeat Terror, It Only Tries to Balance It". *The Cradle*, 9 June, https://thecradle.co/article-view/25706/iraqs-ex-pm-adil-abdul-mahdi-the-us-doesnt-defeat-terror-it-only-tries-to-balance-it. Accessed 11 June 2023.

Murray, Craig. 2023. Activating the Genocide Convention. *Craig Murray*, 13 November, https://www.craigmurray.org.uk/archives/2023/11/activating-the-genocide-convention/. Accessed 11 January 2024.

———. 2024. Murray: UN Court Spurned Israel's Key Argument. *Consortium News*, 29 January, https://consortiumnews.com/2024/01/29/craig-murray-un-court-spurned-israels-key-argument/. Accessed 29 January 2024.

Muttitt, Greg. 2012. *Fuel on the Fire: Oil and Politics in Occupied Iraq.* The New Press.

Nahigyan, Pierce. 2014. Seymour Hersh Links Turkey to Benghazi, Syria and Sarin. *Foreign Policy*, 6 May, https://www.foreignpolicyjournal.com/2014/05/06/seymour-hersh-links-turkey-to-benghazi-syria-and-sarin/. Accessed 18 March 2023.

Nasrallah, Hassan. 2023a. Hezbollah's Hassan Nasrallah Speech on Israel-Hamas War: Key Takeaways. *Al-Jazeera*, 3 November, https://www.aljazeera.com/news/2023/11/3/hezbollahs-hassan-nasrallah-speech-on-israel-hamas-war-key-takeaways. Accessed 22 January 2024.

———. 2023b. Hezbollah Leader Nasrallah: October 7 Proves Israel Is as "Fragile as a Spider's Web," Why Else Would U.S. Send Aircraft Carrier? *Real Clear Politics*, https://www.realclearpolitics.com/video/2023/11/03/hezbollah_leader_hassan_nasrallah_to_prevent_a_regional_war_israel_must_stop_attack_on_gaza.html. Accessed 28 January 2024.

National Security Archive. 2001. The Iraq War—Part I: The U.S. Prepares for Conflict, 2001, 21 September, https://nsarchive2.gwu.edu/NSAEBB/NSAEBB326/print.htm. Accessed 22 March 2023.

———. 2020. Inside the Gorbachev-Bush "Partnership" on the First Gulf War 1990, 9 September, https://nsarchive.gwu.edu/briefing-book/russia-programs/2020-09-09/inside-gorbachev-bush-partnership-first-gulf-war-1990. Accessed 20 May 2023.

Nebenzia, Vassily. 2023. Statement by Permanent Representative Vassily Nebenzia at UNSC Briefing Dedicated to the Anniversary of Resolution 2202 That Endorsed the Minsk Package of Measures. Permanent Mission of the Russian Federation to the United Nations, 17 February, https://russiaun.ru/en/news/170223_n. Accessed 20 January 2024.

Nehamas, Nicholas, and Reid J. Epstein. 2024. "Uncommitted" Draws Strong Support Against Biden in Minnesota. *New York Times*, 5 March, https://www.nytimes.com/2024/03/05/us/politics/biden-uncommitted-protest-vote-minnesota.html. Accessed 6 March 2024.

Nereim, Vivian. 2024. Honed at Home in Yemen, Houthi Propaganda Is Going Global. *New York Times*, 24 January, https://www.nytimes.com/2024/01/24/world/middleeast/yemen-houthis-propaganda.html?campaign_id=9&emc=edit_nn_20240124&instance_id=113315&nl=the-morning&regi_id=7062190&segment_id=156155&te=1&user_id=e1ddf1d17d81e96d432c42ea2c1367b5. Accessed 24 January 2024.

New York Times. 2004. From The Editors; *The Times* and Iraq, 26 May, https://www.nytimes.com/2004/05/26/world/from-the-editors-the-times-and-iraq.html?searchResultPosition=1. Accessed 22 March 2023.

———. 2018. Update: Kurdistan and the Battle over Oil, 8 October, https://www.nytimes.com/2018/10/08/business/update-kurdistan-and-the-battle-over-oil.html. Accessed 10 June 2023.

Nye, Joseph S., Jr. 2022. What New World Order? *Foreign Affairs*, Spring 1992. https://www.foreignaffairs.com/united-states/what-new-world-order. Accessed 15 December 2022.

Oasis International Foundation. 2013. The Crisis of Moral Decline in Iraqi Society, 17 October, https://www.oasiscenter.eu/en/the-crisis-of-moral-decline-in-iraqi-society. Accessed 14 August 2023.

Obama, Barack. 2012. Remarks by the President to the White House Press Corps. *The White House*, 20 August, https://obamawhitehouse.archives.gov/the-press-office/2012/08/20/remarks-president-white-house-press-corps. Accessed 30 April 2023.

———. 2014. Remarks by the President in Address to European Youth. *The White House*, 26 March, https://obamawhitehouse.archives.gov/the-press-office/2014/03/26/remarks-president-addresseuropean-youth#:~:text=But even in Iraq, America,decisions about its own future. Accessed 21 June 2024.

OPCW. 2017. Press Release on Allegations of Chemical Weapons Use in Southern Idlib, Syria, 4 April, https://www.opcw.org/media-centre/news/2017/04/opcw-press-release-allegations-chemical-weapons-use-southern-idlib-syria. Accessed 15 March 2023.

Oren, Amir. 2009. British Author: Rabin Asked Jordan to Arrange Secret Visit with Saddam. *Haaretz*, 27 February, https://www.haaretz.com/2009-02-27/ty-article/british-author-rabin-asked-jordan-to-arrange-secret-visit-with-saddam/0000017f-e127-d568-ad7f-f36f67b60000. Accessed 29 April 2023.

Ose, Hoshnag. 2008. A Secret Relationship. *Niqash*, 8 September, http://www.niqash.org/content.php?contentTypeID=75&id=2285&lang=0. Accessed March 2009.

Parry, Robert. 2015. Saddam's "Green Light". *Consortium News*, 11 May, https://consortiumnews.com/2015/05/11/saddams-green-light/. Accessed 3 April 2023.

Parsi, Trita. 2024. Will Israel Drag the US Into Another Ruinous War President Biden Refuses to Pursue the Most Obvious Way of De-escalating Tensions and Avoid American Deaths: A Cease-fire in Gaza. *The Nation*, 3 January, https://www.thenation.com/article/world/israel-hamas-hezbollah-iran/. Accessed 5 January 2024.

Patterson, Graham. 2007. Alan Greenspan Claims Iraq War Was Really for Oil. *The Sunday Times.* https://www.thetimes.co.uk/article/alan-greenspan-claims-iraq-war-was-really-for-oil-5vr9rqdvbgp. Accessed 27 June 2023.

PBS. 1991. PBS Frontline: The War We Left Behind. https://www.youtube.com/watch?v=HcOzpkxT3Z4. Accessed 20 May 2023.

———. 2006. The Lost Year in Iraq, 17 October, http://www.pbs.org/wgbh/pages/frontline/yeariniraq/documents/bremermemo.pdf. Accessed 1 March 2023.

Pearls and Irritations. 2024. South Africa Urgently Appeals to ICJ on Gaza Famine. *Consortium News*, 7 March, https://consortiumnews.com/2024/03/07/south-africa-urgently-appeals-to-icj-on-gaza-famine/. Accessed 7 March 2024.

Peries, Sharmini. 2019. New Evidence Suggests 2018 Chemical Attack in Douma, Syria Was Staged. *The Real News Network*, 10 June, https://therealnews.com/new-evidence-suggests-2018-syria-chemical-attack-in-douma-was-staged. Accessed 19 May 2023.

Perle, Richard, James Colbert, Charles Fairbanks, Jr., Douglas Feith, Robert Loewenberg, David Wurmser, and Meyrav Wurmser. 1996. A Clean Break: A New Strategy for Securing the Realm, the Institute for Advanced Strategic and Political Studies, Study Group on a New Israeli Strategy Toward 2000. https://web.archive.org/web/20140125123844/, http://www.iasps.org/strat1.htm. Accessed 3 April 2023.

Nederveen Pieterse, Jan. 2024. Iraq, Afghanistan, Pakistan: Patterns Old and New. *Journal of Contemporary Iraq & the Arab World 18* (2–3), pp. 117–133.

Pilger, John. 2002. John Pilger Reveals the American Plan. *The New Statesman*, 16 December, https://www.web.archive.org/web/20110224030050/http://www.newstatesman.com/200212160005. Accessed 2 April 2023.

———. 2022. The War You Don't See: Why Propaganda Hides the True Face of War (Documentary), https://www.youtube.com/watch?v=rCKCksmJpBg. Accessed 14 August 2023.

Pleming, Sue. 2009. US Plans "Substantial" Pledge at Gaza Meeting. *Reuters*, 24 February, https://www.reuters.com/article/us-palestinians-clinton-idUSN2350280520090224. Accessed 29 April 2023.

Pope, Hugh. 1992. National Agenda: Exiled Opponents of Hussein Start to Harmonize Their Voices: Salahuddin Conference Is a Watershed for the Splintered Forces Opposed to the Iraqi Dictator. *Los Angeles Times*, 33 November, https://www.latimes.com/archives/la-xpm-1992-11-03-wr-1337-story.html. Accessed 21 June 2023.

Porter, Gareth. 2016. US Strikes on Syrian Troops: Report Data Contradicts "Mistake" Claims: Moscow and Damascus Cited the Attacks as the Reason for Declaring an End to the Ceasefire in Syria. *Antiwar.com*, 8 December, https://original.antiwar.com/porter/2016/12/07/us-strikes-syrian-troops-report-data-contradicts-mistake-claims/. Accessed March 14, 2023.

Postol, Theodore. 2017. With Error Fixed, Evidence Against "Sarin Attack" Remains Convincing. *Truthdig*, 22 April, https://www.truthdig.com/articles/with-error-fixed-evidence-against-sarin-attack-remains-convincing-2/. Accessed 18 March 2023.

Powell, Jerome. 2003. *U.S. Secretary of State Colin Powell Addresses the U.N. Security Council.* National Security Archive, 5 February, https://georgewbush-whitehouse.archives.gov/news/releases/2003/02/20030205-1.html. Accessed 21 March 2023.

———. 2005. Colin Powell on Iraq, Race, and Hurricane Relief. *ABC News*, 8 September, https://abcnews.go.com/2020/Politics/story?id=1105979&page=1. Accessed 21 March 2023.

Prashad, Vijay. 2012. *Arab Spring, Libyan Winter.* AK Press.

PressTV. 2023. China to US: Stop Plundering Syrian Resources, Pull Troops Out, 10 March, https://www.presstv.ir/Detail/2023/03/10/699630/China-US-Syria-Chinese-Foreign-Ministry-spokesperson-Mao-Ning. Accessed 10 March 2023.

Priebe, Miranda, and Samuel Charap. 2024. *The Day After: Postwar U.S. Strategy Toward Russia.* Rand Corporation, 9 February, https://www.rand.org/pubs/research_briefs/RBA2510-1.html. Accessed 18 February 2024.

PUKMedia. 2023. Court Handed over the Kurdistan Region's Oil Sales to Baghdad, 11 April, https://pukmedia.com/EN/Details/75642. Accessed 21 June 2023.

Putin, Vladimir. 2007. *Speech and the Following Discussion at the Munich Conference on Security Policy.* President of Russia, 10 February, http://en.kremlin.ru/events/president/transcripts/24034. Accessed 15 January 2024.

———. 2018. *Presidential Address to the Federal Assembly.* President of Russia, 1 March, http://en.kremlin.ru/events/president/transcripts/messages/56957. Accessed 20 January 2024.

———. 2022a. Address by the President of the Russian Federation, 24 February 2022, President of Russia, http://en.kremlin.ru/events/president/news/67843. Accessed 20 February 2024.

Putin, Vladimar. 2022b. Western "Empire of Lies" Has Resources, But It Cannot Defeat Truth and Justice—Putin. *TASS,* 16 March 2022, https://tass.com/world/1423145. Accessed 4 February 2023.

Putin, Vladimir. 2024. West Flirting with Nuclear War—Putin. *RT,* 29 February, https://www.rt.com/russia/593443-putin-west-flirting-nuclear-war/. Accessed 2 March 2024.

Razoux, Pierre. 2015. *The Iran-Iraq War.* Translated by Nicholas Elliott. Belknap Press.

Republic of South Africa. 2024. Statement by South Africa Welcoming the Provisional Measures Ordered by the International Court of Justice against Israel, 26 January, https://dirco.gov.za/statement-by-south-africa-welcoming-the-provisional-measures-ordered-by-the-international-court-of-justice-against-israel/. Accessed 27 January 2024.

Rideau Institute. 2024a. The NDP and the Green Party of Canada call for Canada to support ICJ Decisions in the Israeli Genocide Case, 13 January, https://www.ceasefire.ca/the-ndp-and-the-green-party-of-canada-call-for-canada-to-support-icj-decisions-in-the-israeli-genocide-case/. Accessed 22 January 2024.

———. 2024b. US Allies Must Demand Decisive Action to Stop the Gaza Carnage, 21 January, https://www.ceasefire.ca/us-allies-must-demand-decisive-action-to-stop-the-gaza-carnage/. Accessed 23 January 2024.

Riedel, Bruce. 2019. Order from Chaos: What Iran's Revolution Meant for Iraq. Brookings, 24 January, https://www.brookings.edu/blog/order-from-chaos/2019/01/24/what-irans-revolution-meant-for-iraq/. Accessed 14 April 2023.

———. 2021. *9/11 and Iraq: The Making of a Tragedy.* Brookings, September 17, https://www.brookings.edu/blog/order-from-chaos/2021/09/17/9-11-and-iraq-the-making-of-a-tragedy/. Accessed 3 April 2023.

Ritter, Scott. 2002. *Scott Ritter Opposing Iraq Invasion,* August 2002 (vid.). Consortium Research, 21 March 2023, https://consortiumnews.

com/2023/03/21/watch-scott-ritter-opposing-iraq-invasion-august-2002/. Accessed 21 March 2023.

———. 2017. Ex-Weapons Inspector: Trump's Sarin Claims Built on "Lie". *The American Conservative*, June 29, https://www.theamericanconservative.com/ex-weapons-inspector-trumps-sarin-claims-built-on-lie/. Accessed 15 March 2023.

———. 2023a. *Scott Ritter Opposing Iraq Invasion*, August 2002 (vid.). Consortium Research, March 21, 2023, https://consortiumnews.com/2023/03/21/watch-scott-ritter-opposing-iraq-invasion-august-2002/. Accessed 21 March 2023.

———. 2023b. Iraq 20 Years: Disarmament, the Fundamental Lie. *Consortium News*, 19 March, https://consortiumnews.com/2023/03/19/iraq-20-years-scott-ritter-disarmament-the-fundamental-lie/. Accessed 20 March 2023.

———. 2023c. The End of US Nuclear Superiority. *Consortium News*, 28 November, https://consortiumnews.com/2023/11/28/scott-ritter-the-end-of-us-nuclear-superiority/. Accessed 1 December 2023.

Ritter, Scott, and Andrew Napolitano. 2024. Scott Ritter: How Close Is US to War? (vid.). *Judging Freedom*, 11 March, https://www.youtube.com/watch?v=w3C8ihfeQ_w. Accessed 13 March 2024.

Rittich, Kerry. 2018. Occupied Iraq: Imperial Convergences. *Leiden Journal of International Law* 31: 479–508.

Roberts, Hugh. 2011. Who Said Gaddafi Had to Go? *London Review of Books* 33 (22, Nov.): 8–18.

Robertson, Nick. 2024. Half of Biden Voters Say Israel Committing Genocide in Gaza: Poll. *The Hill*, 25 January, https://thehill.com/policy/defense/4429906-half-biden-voters-israel-committing-genocide-in-gaza-poll/. Accessed 13 March 2024.

Robinson, Piers. 2002. *The CNN Effect: The Myth of News Media, Foreign Policy and Intervention*. Routledge.

Rodgers, Winthrop. 2022. The "Full Barzani": How Diplomatic Meetings with the Barzani Family are Shaping Iraqi Kurdish Politics, 8 April, https://www.washingtoninstitute.org/policy-analysis/full-barzani-how-diplomatic-meetings-barzani-family-are-shaping-iraqi-kurdish. Accessed 7 June 2023.

Roelofs, Joan. 2023. *The Trillion Dollars Silencer: Why There Is So Little Anti-war Protest in the US*. Clarity Press, Inc.

Rose, David. 2008. The Gaza Bombshell. *Vanity Fair*, April 2008, http://www.vanityfair.com/politics/features/2008/04/gaza200804. Accessed 29 April 2023.

Rosen, Nir. 2008. The Myth of the Surge. *Rolling Stone*, 6 May, https://www.academia.edu/969403/The_Myth_of_the_Surge. Accessed 29 April 2023.

Ross, Carne. 2016. Iraq: The Story of My Evidence. *Personal Blog*, 13 June, https://www.carneross.com/index.php/2016/06/13/iraq-the-story-of-my-evidence/. Accessed 19 May 2023.

———. 2017. *Independent Diplomat: Despatches from an Unaccountable Elite*. C Hurst & Co Publishers.

Rossi, Lorenza, Rochelle Davis, Grace Benton, Sinan Zeyneloglu, and Salma Al-Shami. 2018. Iraqi IDPs Access to Durable Solutions: Results of Two Rounds of a Longitudinal Study. *International Migration* 57 (2, Apr.): 48–64.

Rumsfeld, Donald. 2003. Defense Department Briefing. *C-SPAN*, 11 April, https://www.c-span.org/video/?176134-1/defense-department-briefing. Accessed 4 April 2023.

Sachs, Jeffrey. 2013. *To Move the World: JFK's Quest for Peace*. New York: Random House.

———. 2019. Exclusive Interview with American Economist Jeffrey Sachs (vid.), 3 November, https://www.youtube.com/watch?v=ZMTZHaEmBek. Accessed 8 April 2023.

———. 2023a. The Geopolitics of Peace (vid.), 2 March, https://oxpakprogramme.org/the-new-geopolitics/. Accessed 8 April 2023.

———. 2023b. *On the Path to Peace in Ukraine* (vid.). Canadian Foreign Policy Institute, 4 May, https://www.youtube.com/watch?v=k_uyfb6OyZ8. Accessed 15 May 2023.

Sachs, Jeffrey S. 2023a. NATO Chief Admits NATO Expansion Was Key to Russian Invasion of Ukraine (vid.). Common Dreams, 20 September, https://www.commondreams.org/opinion/nato-chief-admitsexpansion-behind-russian-invasion and https://www.jeffsachs.org/newspaper-articles/nato-chief-admits-expansion-behind-russian-invasion. Accessed 15 January 2024.

Sachs, David. 2024. A War of Lies. *X*, 17 February, https://twitter.com/DavidSacks/status/1758976951744897179?lang=en. Accessed 28 February 2024.

Sachs, Jeffrey S. 2024a. Israel Cannot Hide From the UN Court. *Consortium News*, 31 January, https://consortiumnews.com/2024/01/31/israel-cannot-hide-from-the-un-court/. Accessed 31 January 2024.

———. 2024b. How the CIA Destabilizes the World. *Consortium News*, 15 February, https://consortiumnews.com/2024/02/15/how-the-cia-destabilizes-the-world/. Common Dreams, 12 February, https://www.commondreams.org/opinion/cia-destablizes-the-world. Accessed 17 February 2024.

Sachs, Jeffrey, and Chris Hedges. 2023. What JFK Tried to Do Before His Assassination (vid.). *The Chris Hedges Report, The Real News Network*, 29 September, https://www.youtube.com/watch?v=Wqm9Yl1gGEY. Accessed 29 January 2024.

Sachs, Jeffrey, and Andrew Napolitano. 2024a. Prof. Jeffery Sachs: A Deep Dive into the ICJ Ruling and Diplomacy (vid.). *Judging Freedom*, 26 January, https://www.youtube.com/watch?v=iUNrUclBnsA. Accessed 26 January 2024.

———. 2024b. Prof. Jeffrey Sachs: US Misunderstands Russia (vid.). *Judging Freedom*, 29 February, https://www.youtube.com/watch?v=p8L1Y2APY9E. Accessed 7 March 2024.

———. 2024c. Prof. Jeffrey Sachs: US/Russia/China: Worst Tensions in 30 Years (vid.). *Judging Freedom*, 14 March, https://www.youtube.com/watch?v=2EZg8mPatv4. Accessed 14 March 2024.

———. 2024d. Prof. Jeffrey Sachs: The Israeli Government is Criminal. *Judging Freedom*, 19 March, https://www.youtube.com/watch?v=7RYSUsbQfrE. Accessed 19 March 2024.

Sachs, Jeffrey, and Robert Wright. 2023. The Epic Failures of US Foreign Policy, (vid.). *Nonzero*, https://www.youtube.com/watch?v=3z_EUtLZVz0. Accessed 18 May 2023.

Saeed, Yerevan. 2023. In Iraq, the Kurds Are Their Own Worst Enemy. *Fikra Forum*, 17 June, https://www.washingtoninstitute.org/policy-analysis/iraq-kurds-are-their-own-worst-enemy. Accessed 18 June 2023.

Sahiounie, Steven. 2023. *Saudi Crown Prince Defies the U.S. Policy Against Syria*. Strategic Culture Foundation, 23 January, https://strategic-culture.org/news/2023/01/23/saudi-crown-prince-defies-us-policy-against-syria/. Accessed 19 May 2023.

Salem, Amr. 2024. Iraq Discusses Security Cooperation with NATO. *Iraqi News*, 17 January, https://www.iraqinews.com/iraq/iraq-discusses-security-cooperation-with-nato/. Accessed 19 January 2024.

Sanders, Richard. 2002. Regime Change: How the CIA put Saddam's Party in Power, 24 October 2002, *Blog*, http://www.hartford-hwp.com/archives/51/217.html. Accessed 20 May 2023.

Sanger, David E., & Julian E. Barnes. 2024. Intelligence Officials Warn of Losses for Ukraine Without More U.S. Aid. *New York Times*, 11 March, https://www.nytimes.com/2024/03/11/us/politics/intelligence-officials-ukraine-aid.html. Accessed 13 March 2024.

Sargent, Daniel J. 2014. *A Superpower Transformed: The Remaking of American Foreign Relations in the 1970s*. Oxford University Press.

Sassoon, Joseph. 2011. *Saddam Hussein's Ba'th Party: Inside an Authoritarian Regime*. Cambridge University Press.

Schenker, David. 2024. Leaving Iraq May Be Washington's Best Choice. *Foreign Policy*, 26 February, https://foreignpolicy.com/2024/02/26/us-iraq-iran-military-militia-attacks-sudani/. Accessed 27 February 2024.

Schmitt, Eric. 2024. Mix-Up Preceded Deadly Drone Strike in Jordan, U.S. Officials Say. *New York Times*, 29 January, https://www.nytimes.

com/2024/01/29/world/middleeast/jordan-drone-strike-us-soldiers.html. Accessed 30 January 2024.

Schwarz, Jon. 2023. The Architects Of The Iraq War: Where Are They Now? They're All Doing Great, Thanks for Asking. *The Intercept*, 15 March, https://theintercept.com/2023/03/15/iraq-war-where-are-they-now/. Accessed 10 April 2023.

Schwenniger, Sherle. 2003. Revamping American Grand Strategy. *World Policy Journal* 20 (3): 25–44.

Sciolino, Elaine, and Micheal R. Gordon. 1990. Confrontation in the Gulf: US Gave Iraq Little Reason Not to Mount Iraq Assault. *New York Times*, 23 September, https://www.nytimes.com/1990/09/23/world/confrontation-in-the-gulf-us-gave-iraq-little-reason-not-to-mount-kuwait-assault.html. Accessed 15 February 2024.

Shaibani, Senan. 2024. *Indictment of the U.S. Federal Government*. Urbana, IL: AuthorHouse.

Sharahra. 2023. The Sponsorship of International Powers Competing with the United States for Reconciliations and Rapprochement Processes in the Region Pushes the Latter to Adopt Policies of Sabotage and Arson (vid, Arabic). Al-Akhbar, 31 March, https://www.youtube.com/watch?v=itI_zy9Cnm4. Accessed 29 January 2024.

Shoigu, Sergei. 2024. Ukrainian Army Loses 444,000 Troops during Military Operation—Shoigu. *Tass*, 26 February, https://tass.com/politics/1752183. Accessed 28 February 2024.

Simon, Steven. 2023. *Grand Delusion*. Penguin Random House.

Simon, Steven, and Jonathan Stevensonm. 2015. The End of Pax Americana: Why Washington's Middle East Pullback Makes Sense. *Foreign Affairs*, November–December, https://www.foreignaffairs.com/articles/middle-east/end-pax-americana. Accessed 19 May 2023.

SIPRI. 2019. Global Arms Trade: USA Increases Dominance; Arms Flows to the Middle East Surge. Stockholm International Peace Research Institute, 11 March, https://www.sipri.org/media/press-release/2019/global-arms-trade-usa-increases-dominance-arms-flows-middle-east-surge-says-sipri. Accessed 19 May 2023.

Sjursen, Danny. 2015. *Ghost Riders of Baghdad: Soldiers, Civilians, and the Myth of the Surge*. ForeEdge / University Press of New England.

Sky, Emma. 2016. *The Unraveling: High Hopes and Missed Opportunities in Iraq*. Public Affairs.

Farouk–Sluglett, Marion, and Peter Sluglett. 2001. *Iraq Since 1958: From Revolution to Dictatorship*. I.B. Tauris.

Smith, Michael E. 2003. This Is Not the "Antiques Roadshow". 23 April, http://www.public.asu.edu/~mesmith9/Antiquities.html. Accessed 29 April 2023.

Smith, Stephen. 2006. "Furious Envy": Baudrillard and the Looting of Baghdad. *International Journal of* Baudrillard *Studies* 3 (2), July, https://baudrillard-studies.ubishops.ca/furious-envy-baudrillard-and-the-looting-of-baghdad/. Accessed 1 March 2023.

Smith, Yves. 2024. International Court of Justice Rules Forcefully Against Israel in Landmark Genocide Ruling, Including Restricting Military Action. *Naked Capitalism*, 26 January, https://www.nakedcapitalism.com/2024/01/international-court-of-justice-rules-forcefully-against-israel-in-landmark-genocide-ruling-including-restricting-military-action.html. Accessed 27 January 2024.

Smith, Michael. n.d. The Downing Street Memos. https://www.michaelsmith-author.com/the-downing-street-memos.html. Accessed 6 April 2023.

Snow, Andrew. 2018. *Kurdistan Region's Debt Crisis Threatens Iraq's Economy.* United States Institute of Peace, 9 May, https://www.usip.org/publications/2018/05/kurdistan-regions-debt-crisis-threatens-iraqs-economy. Accessed 10 June 2023.

Sökmen, Müge Gürsoy. 2005. Testimony from War Tribunal on Iraq, 28 February, https://www.iraqtribunal.org/muge_sokmen. Accessed 1 April 2023.

———. 2015. Roy, Arundhati, Falk, Richard, 'World Tribunal on Iraq: Making the Case Against War, https://www.jstor.org/stable/j.ctt1rfzxf9. Accessed 10 April 2023.

Sommerville, Quentin, and Riam Dalati. 2017. Raqqa's Dirty Secret. *BBC*, 13 November, https://www.bbc.co.uk/news/resources/idt-sh/raqqas_dirty_secret. Accessed 16 March 2023.

Sosnowski, Piotr. 2019. Rentier Economy of the Kurdish Region in Iraq as a Source of Barriers for the Regional Security Sector Reform. *Security & Defense Quarterly* 23 (1, Jan.). https://securityanddefence.pl/Rentier-economy-of-the-Kurdish-region-in-Iraq-as-a-source-of-barriers-for-the-regional,105429,0,2.html. Accessed 10 June 2023.

Spectacles. 2024. This Will Change How You Think about the Iraq War, 4 November, https://www.youtube.com/watch?v=-cjriLK-y14. Accessed 5 February 2024.

Stein, Jonathan, and Tim Dickinson. 2006. Lie by Lie: A Timeline of How We Got Into Iraq, Mushroom Clouds, Duct Tape, Judy Miller, Curveball. Recalling How Americans Were Sold a Bogus Case for Invasion. *Mother Jones*, September–October, https://www.motherjones.com/politics/2011/12/leadup-iraq-war-timeline/. Accessed 4 April 2023.

Stephen, Linda. 2016. Iraq—Comprehensive Food Security and Vulnerability Analysis (CFSVA). World Food Program, 1 May, https://www.wfp.org/. Accessed 1 May 2023.

Stockman, David. 2024. To Hell With Fighting the Houthis! *Anti-War.com*, 15 January, https://original.antiwar.com/david_stockman/2024/01/14/to-hell-with-fighting-the-houthis/. Accessed 16 January 2024.

Sullivan, Andrew ('the Daily Dish'). 2009. We're an Empire Now, and When We Act, We Create Our Own Reality, *The Atlantic*, 23 April, https://www.theatlantic.com/daily-dish/archive/2009/04/were-an-empire-now-and-when-we-act-we-create-our-own-reality/202751/. Accessed 3 April 2023.

Suskind, Ron. 2004a. *The Price of Loyalty: George W. Bush, the White House, and the Education of Paul O'Neill*. Simon & Schuster.

———. 2004b. Faith, Certainty and the Presidency of George W. Bush. *New York Times Magazine*, 17 October, https://www.nytimes.com/2004/10/17/magazine/faith-certainty-and-the-presidency-of-george-w-bush.html. Accessed 3 April 2023.

Susman, Tina. 2007 Poll: Civilian Toll in Iraq May Top 1M. *Los Angeles Times*, 14 September, https://www.latimes.com/world/la-fg-iraq14sep14-story.html. Accessed 30 April 2023.

Switzer, Tom. 2013. Foreign Policy Begins at Home, by Richard N. Haass—Review. *The Spectator*, 6 July, https://www.spectator.co.uk/article/foreign-policy-begins-at-home-by-richard-n-haass-review/.

Syria Propaganda Media. 2019. Engineering Assessment of Two Cylinders Observed at the Douma Incident, 21 February, http://syriapropagandamedia.org/wp-content/uploads/2019/05/Engineering-assessment-of-two-cylinders-observed-at-the-Douma-incident-27-February-2019-1.pdf. Accessed 19 May 2023.

Tacitus. n.d. *Agricola*, 29–32, The Latin Library. https://www.thelatinlibrary.com/imperialism/readings/agricola.html. Accessed 18 February 2024.

Talabani, Ala, and Mohammed Sayyed Muhsin. 2024. Unresolved Issues (vid., Arabic), 20 March, https://www.youtube.com/watch?v=3qcz2xx-mik. Accessed 20 March 2024.

Taylor, Adam. 2014. Behind Biden's Gaffe Lie Real Concerns about Allies' Role in Rise of the Islamic State. *Washington Post*, 10 October, https://www.washingtonpost.com/news/worldviews/wp/2014/10/06/behind-bidens-gaffe-some-legitimate-concerns-about-americas-middle-east-allies/.   Accessed 20 May 2023.

The Cradle. 2023. Exclusive Interview with Hezbollah Commander in Iraq: 'The Americans Did Not Fight ISIS'. *The Cradle*, 4 January, https://thecradle.co/article-view/19989/exclusive-interview-with-hezbollah-commander-in-iraq-the-americans-did-not-fight-isis. Accessed 11 June 2023.

———. 2024. Palestinian Factions Strive for 'National Unity' in Moscow. *The Cradle*, 1 March, https://thecradle.co/articles-id/23699. Accessed 9 March 2024.

The New Arab. 2024. Key Differences in Algeria, US's UN Resolution Text on Gaza Ceasefire, 20 February, https://www.newarab.com/news/gaza-key-differences-algeria-us-un-resolution-text. Accessed 22 February 2024.

Thompson, Mark. 2008. Shinseki, a Prescient General, Re-Enlists as VA Chief. *Time*, 8 December, https://content.time.com/time/politics/article/0,8599,1864915,00.html. Accessed 19 May 2023.

———. 2015. How Disbanding the Iraqi Army Fueled ISIS. *Time*, 28 May, https://time.com/3900753/isis-iraq-syria-army-united-states-military/. Accessed 5 February 2024.

Times of Israel. 2015. The Kennedy Speech that Obama Hopes to Echo. *Times of Israel*, 5 August, https://www.timesofisrael.com/liveblog_entry/the-kennedy-speech-that-obama-hopes-to-echo/. Accessed 29 January 2024.

Todd, Emmanuel. 2003. *After the Empire: The Breakdown of the American Order*. Translated by C. Jon Delogu. Columbia University Press.

Tripp, Charles. 2007. *A History of Iraq*. 3rd ed. Cambridge University Press.

U.S. Department of State, Office of International Religious Freedom. 2019. 2019 Report on International Religious Freedom: Iraq. https://www.state.gov/reports/2019-report-on-international-religious-freedom/iraq/#:~:text=Restrictions%20on%20freedom%20of%20religion,of%20non-governmental%20organizations%20(NGOs). Accessed 28 January 2024.

Uddin, Rayhan. 2024. Iraq: PM Says Government to Start Process of Removing US-led Forces. *Middle East Eye*, 5 January, https://www.middleeasteye.net/news/iraq-prepares-end-us-coalition-after-drone-strike-kills-commander. Accessed 19 January 2024.

UN News. 2024. US Vetoes Algerian Resolution Demanding Immediate Ceasefire in Gaza, 20 February, https://news.un.org/en/story/2024/02/1146697. Accessed 15 March 2024.

UN Office for the Coordination of Humanitarian Affairs. 2015. Iraq: Humanitarian Needs Overview—2016 (November 2015), November, https://reliefweb.int/report/iraq/iraq-humanitarian-needs-overview-2016-november-2015. Accessed 3 May 2023.

UNICEF. 2015. Education Under Fire: How Conflict in the Middle East Is Depriving Children of Their Schooling. UNICEF, 3 September, https://reliefweb.int/report/syrian-arab-republic/education-under-fire-how-conflict-middle-east-depriving-children-their. Accessed 3 May 2023.

———. 2019. *Iraq Multiple Indicator Cluster Survey*. UNICEF, 2018, https://mics.unicef.org/files?job=W1siZiIsIjIwMTkvMDMvMDEvMTkvMjMvMTgvNTg5L0VuZ2xpc2gucGRmIl1d&sha=aea1de7cc6f6ec09.Accessed 7 April 2023.

———. n.d. Iran, (Islamic Republic of), Demographic Indicators. UNICEF. https://data.unicef.org/country/irn/. Accessed 2 May 2023.

United Kingdom. 2016. The Iraq Inquiry (Chilcot Report). The National Archives, 6 July, http://blogs.bbk.ac.uk/bbkcomments/2016/07/06/chilcot-report-the-consequences-for-international-law/. Accessed 24 March 2023.

United Nations Assistance Mission for Iraq (UNAMI) and the Office of the United Nations High Commissioner for Human Rights (OHCHR). 2015. *Report on the Protection of Civilians in the Armed Conflict in Iraq, 1 May–31 October,* https://www.ohchr.org/en/documents/country-reports/report-protection-civilians-armed-conflict-iraq-1-may-31-october-2015. Accessed 4 May 2023.

United Nations Security Council. 2015. Resolution 2202 (2015), Adopted by the Security Council at its 7384th Meeting, on 17 February 2015, https://www.securitycouncilreport.org/atf/cf/{65BFCF9B-6D27-4E9C-8CD3-CF6E4FF96FF9}/s_res_2202.pdf. Accessed 20 January 2024.

United States 107th Congress. 2002. H.J.Res.114—Authorization for Use of Military Force Against Iraq Resolution of 2002. https://www.congress.gov/bill/107th-congress/house-joint-resolution/114. Accessed 5 April 2023.

United States Department of State. 2003. Oil and Energy Working Group. Future of Iraq Project, https://nsarchive2.gwu.edu/NSAEBB/NSAEBB198/FOI Oil.pdf. Accessed 28 February 2023.

US Army. 2019a. *The U.S. Army in the Iraq War Volume 1: Invasion Insurgency Civil War 2003–2006.* United States Government.

———. 2019b. *The U.S. Army in the Iraq War Volume 2: Surge and Withdrawal 2007–2011.* United States Government.

Vinograd, Cassandra. 2024. Iran Denies Ordering Drone Strike as Biden Weighs a Response. *New York Times,* 29 January, https://www.nytimes.com/2024/01/29/world/middleeast/iran-us-troops-jordan.html?campaign_id=9&emc=edit_nn_20240130&instance_id=113843&nl=the-morning&regi_id=7062190&segment_id=156791&smid=url-share&te=1&user_id=e1ddf1d17d81e96d432c42ea2c1367b5. Accessed 30 January 2024.

Visser, R. 2010. The Kurdish Issue in Iraq: A View from Baghdad at the Close of the Maliki Premiership. *World Affairs* 43 (1): 77–93.

Vogler, Gary. 2017. *Iraq and the Politics of Oil: An Insider's Perspective.* University Press of Kansas.

Wahab, Bilal. 2023. *The Rise and Fall of Kurdish Power in Iraq.* Spring., https://www.washingtoninstitute.org/policy-analysis/rise-and-fall-kurdish-power-iraq. Accessed 13 June 2023.

Walt, Stephen M. 2019. *The Hell of Good Intentions: America's Foreign Policy Elite and the Decline of U.S. Primacy.* Picador.

———. 2021. It's Time to End the 'Special Relationship' With Israel: The benefits of U.S. support no longer outweigh the costs. *Foreign Policy,* 27 May, https://

foreignpolicy.com/2021/05/27/its-time-to-end-the-special-relationship-with-israel/. Accessed 1 January 2024.

Walt, Stephen M., and John J. Mearsheimer. 2008. *The Israel Lobby and U.S. Foreign Policy*. Farrar, Strauss and Geroux.

Watkins, Simon. 2023. Iraq Takes First Step Towards Becoming the World's Biggest Oil Producer. *OilPrice.com*, 11 July, https://oilprice.com/Energy/Crude-Oil/Iraq-Takes-First-Step-Towards-Becoming-The-Worlds-Biggest-Oil-Producer.html. Accessed 16 July 2023.

Webb, Gary. 1999. *Dark Alliance: The CIA, the Contras, and the Crack Cocaine Explosion*. Seven Stories Press.

Webster, Paul C. 2013. Roots of Iraq's Maternal and Child Health Crisis Run Deep. *Lancet* 381 (9870): 891–894, 16 March, https://www.thelancet.com/journals/lancet/article/PIIS0140-6736(13)60658-3/fulltext. Accessed 2 May 2023.

West, Cornell. 2024. We Want Equality (vid). https://www.youtube.com/watch?v=Q2A6puTbfsU. Accessed 14 January 2024.

Weston, J. Kael. 2016. *The Mirror Test: America at War in Iraq and Afghanistan*. Vintage.

Wheeler, Nicolas J. 2002. A Solidarist Moment in International Society? The Case of Safe Havens and No-Fly Zones in Iraq Get Access. In N.J. Wheeler, ed., *Saving Strangers: Humanitarian Intervention in International Society*: 139–171, Oxford. https://doi.org/10.1093/0199253102.003.0006. Accessed 11 June 2023.

Whitesell, Sarah E. 1993. The Kurdish Crisis: An International Incident Study. *Denver Journal of International Law & Policy* 21 (2): 455. https://digitalcommons.du.edu/djilp/vol21/iss2/10/. Accessed 20 July 2023.

Wilhelmsen, Julie, and Geir Flikke. 2005. *"Copy That...": A Russian "Bush Doctrine in the CIS?"*. Norwegian Institute of International Affairs. https://nupi.brage.unit.no/nupi-xmlui/bitstream/handle/11250/2393750/Rapport_nr285_05_Flikke_Wilhelmsen.pdf?sequence=3. Accessed 16 March 2023.

Williams, Daniel. 2003. Summit of Iraq's Splintered Opposition Ends in Confusion. *Washington Post*, 1 March, https://www.washingtonpost.com/archive/politics/2003/03/01/summit-of-iraqs-splintered-opposition-ends-in-confusion/5d42a255-9ff6-4f51-90c5-fa765ea424de/. Accessed 20 June 2023.

Winstanley, Asa. 2024. Israeli HQ Ordered Troops to Shoot Israeli Captives on 7 October. Electronic Intifada, 20 January, https://electronicintifada.net/blogs/asa-winstanley/israeli-hq-ordered-troops-shoot-israeli-captives-7-october. Accessed 21 January 2024.

Wintour, Patrick. 2023. Long Shadow of US Invasion of Iraq Still Looms Over International Order. *The Guardian*, 13 March, https://www.theguardian.

com/world/2023/mar/13/long-shadow-of-us-invasion-of-iraq-still-looms-over-international-order. Accessed 30 March 2023.

Wolfowitz, Paul. 1992. Defense Planning Guidance, 13 May, https://www.archives.gov/files/declassification/iscap/pdf/2008-003-docs1-12.pdf. Accessed 4 April 2023.

———. 2001. *Interview with BBC*. Press Release, US Department of Defence, 6 November, https://www.scoop.co.nz/stories/WO0111/S00044/deputy-secretary-wolfowitz-interview-with-bbc.htm?from-mobile=bottom-link-01. Accessed 16 March 2023.

Wong, Edward, and Matina Stevis-Gridneff. 2024. Over 800 Officials in U.S. and Europe Sign Letter Protesting Israel Policies. *New York Times*, 2 February, https://www.nytimes.com/2024/02/02/us/politics/protest-letter-israel-gaza.html. Accessed 3 February 2024.

World Bank. 2019. *Child Labour in Iraq*. World Bank. https://www.dol.gov/agencies/ilab/resources/reports/child-labor/iraq. Accessed 2 May 2023.

———. n.d. Mortality Rate, Under-5 (per 1000 Live Births)—Middle East & North Africa. https://data.worldbank.org/indicator/SH.DYN.MORT?end=2021&locations=ZQ-KW&start=2016. Accessed 2 May 2023.

World Food Program. 2016. Iraq—Comprehensive Food Security and Vulnerability Analysis (CFSVA). https://www.wfp.org/publications/iraq-comprehensive-food-security-vulnerability-analysis-2016. Accessed 29 March 2023.

World Health Organization. 2022. Child Mortality (Under 5 Years). 28 January, https://www.who.int/news-room/fact-sheets/detail/levels-and-trends-in-child-under-5-mortality-in-2020. Accessed 2 May 2023.

Xinmin, Ma. 2024. China's Legal Representative at ICJ Emphasises Rights to Palestinian Self-determination (vid). *Middle East Eye*, 22 February, https://www.youtube.com/watch?v=wmJUkWfIzTM. Accessed 25 February 2024.

Yahoo News. 2013. U.S. to Russia: Turn over Snowden or Risk "Long-term Problems", 16 July, https://news.yahoo.com/u-s%2D%2Dto-russia%2D%2Dturn-over-snowden-or-risk%2D%2Dlong-term-problems%2D%2D185119239.html. Accessed 9 March 2023.

Yergin, Daniel. 2006. Ensuring Energy Security. *Foreign Affairs*, 1 March, https://www.foreignaffairs.com/world/ensuring-energy-security. Accessed 25 June.

Zadeh, Yoosef Abbas, and Sherko Kirmanj. 2017. The Para-Diplomacy of the Kurdistan Region in Iraq and the Kurdish Statehood Enterprise. *The Middle East Journal* 71 (4, Autumn): 587–606.

Zakir-Hussain, Maryam. 2023. Twenty Years On: The Shocking Numbers Behind the Iraq War Trillion-dollar War. *The Independent*. https://www.independent.co.uk/news/world/middle-east/iraq-war-bush-twentieth-anniversary-b2302031.html. Accessed 24 March 2023.

Zerouky, Hassane. 2006. *Hamas Is a Creation of Mossad*. Global Research. http://globalresearch.ca/articles/ZER403A.html. Accessed 28 February 2023.

Zhang Zhouxiang. 2022. The "Empire of lies" Is the US. *China Daily*, March 13, http://global.chinadaily.com.cn/a/202203/13/WS622d4de9a310cdd39bc8c3a6.html. Accessed 9 May 2023.

Zizek, Slavoj. 2004. Iraq's False Promises. *Lacanian Ink*, Jan–Feb., https://www.lacan.com/zizek-iraq2.htm. Accessed 2 May 2023.

INDEX

228   INDEX

Law of Administration for the State of
Iraq for the Transitional Period
(TAL), 133, 134
League of Nations, 122, 136
Lebanon, 9, 32, 70, 75, 76, 110,
136, 149
Lebanonization, 136
Lemay, Curtis, 160
Levin, Carl, 63
Libby, Lewis 'Scooter,' 39, 40
Libya, x, 8, 12, 17, 18, 24, 32, 70, 71,
75, 110, 121, 123, 125, 141
Louisiana territory, 108
Luft, Gal, 48
Luftwaffe, 145
Lugansk, 140
Lugansk People's Republic, 141
Lula da Silva, Luiz Inacio, 157

M
Macbeth, 118, 122
MAD, *see* Mutually assured destruction
Maliki, 72
Marfleet, Philip, 62, 69
Marjaeya, 134, 135
McCain, John, 124
McPherson, Peter, 65
Mearsheimer, John, 2, 7, 9, 10, 52,
110, 111, 113, 137, 139,
140, 144–146
Merkel, Angela, 140
Mesopotamia, 56, 59, 60
Meyer, Christopher, 116
Michigan, 153
Middle East, vii, ix–xii, 1, 3, 4, 6–12,
20–25, 32, 38–42, 46, 47, 50,
55, 56, 61, 66, 67, 69, 70, 75,
90, 96, 100, 102, 107, 109, 110,
116, 121, 123, 125, 133,
136–138, 143, 146, 147,
152–154, 156–159

Militarism, 6, 11, 20
Military-industrial complex, 7, 21,
145, 146
Miller, Judith, 115
Minnesota, 153
Minsk I, 140
Minsk II, 140
MI6, 115
Mortality rate, 76, 121
Mossad, 35, 53, 54, 149
Mossadegh, Mohammad, ix, 3, 110
Mosul, 73
Multiple Indicator Cluster Survey
(MICS), 121
Mutually assured destruction
(MAD), 114

N
al-Naqib, Falah, 44
Nasrallah, Hassan, 157
Nasser, Gamal Abdul, 3, 125
National Energy Policy, 47
National Energy Policy Development
Group, 47
Nationalism, 41, 43, 52–54, 60,
90, 92, 101
National Library, 56
National Museum, 56
National Security Council, 32
NATO-Russia war, 142
Nazi, 108
Nemesis, 52, 147
Neoconservative, 25, 38–42, 47, 67,
69–71, 102, 112, 113, 117–119
Netanyahu, Benjamin, 147, 148
New World Order, 12, 112
New York City, 114
New York Times, 34, 49, 91, 115,
145, 150
Nicaragua, 156
1948 Genocide Convention, 137, 147